ONCE A
GRAND DUKE

by

ALEXANDER
GRAND DUKE OF RUSSIA

British Library Cataloguing-in-Publication Data
A catalogue record for this book is available from
the British Library

ONCE A GRAND DUKE

GRAND DUKE ALEXANDER DURING THE WAR WHEN COMMANDER-
IN-CHIEF OF THE RUSSIAN AIR FORCES.

FOREWORD

THE history of the last fifty turbulent years of the Russian Empire provides only a background, but is not the subject of this book.

In compiling this record of a grand duke's progress I relied on memory only, all my letters, diaries and other documents having been partly burned by me and partly confiscated by the revolutionaries during the years of 1917 and 1918 in the Crimea.

Naturally enough, I am dealing at greater length with those who played an important part in my personal life: Emperor Alexander II, Emperor Alexander III, the last Czar Nicholas II, my mother-in-law Dowager-Empress Marie of Russia, my wife Grand Duchess Xenia, and my parents and brothers. The others—generals, ministers and statesmen—appear to have been generously taken care of both in their own memoirs and in the numerous volumes dedicated to the Russian Revolution.

I have no desire for post-mortems and I have done my utmost to keep bias and prejudice from influencing my judgment. In fact, there is no bitterness left in my heart.

ALEXANDER, GRAND DUKE OF RUSSIA.

Paris, Autumn, 1931.

CONTENTS

✤✤

ILLUSTRATIONS

ILLUSTRATIONS

Someone has proposed the toast, "Our Memories." Goethe knocked on the table and said: "I do not like these words. The toast seems to imply that we have forgotten and that some outer event recalls our memories to us. Those things which are great and beautiful never leave us; they become part of ourselves. It is not the past but the eternally new which our desires would have us seek. . . . The new is itself the creation of ever-growing elements of the past. True longing must always be productive and fashion a new and better self."

ROMAIN ROLLAND: *Goethe and Beethoven.*

ONCE A GRAND DUKE

CHAPTER ONE

OUR FRIENDS OF DECEMBER THE FOURTEENTH

A TALL man of military bearing crossed the rain-drenched courtyard of the Imperial Palace in Taganrog and rapidly made for the street.

The sentinel jumped to attention, but the stranger ignored the salute. The next moment he disappeared in the dark November night that had wrapped this small southern seaport in a thick blanket of yellowish fog.

"Who was it?" asked the sleepy corporal of the guard, returning from his tour around the block.

"I think," answered the sentinel hesitatingly, "that it was His Imperial Majesty going for an early stroll."

"Are you mad, man? Don't you know that His Imperial Majesty is gravely ill? The doctors gave up hope last evening and expect the end will come before dawn."

"It may be so," said the sentinel, "but no other man has those stooping shoulders. I guess I ought to know, having seen him daily for the last three months."

A few hours later a heavy knell filled the air for miles around, announcing that His Imperial Majesty, the Czar of all the Russias and the conqueror of Napoleon—Alexander I —had passed away in peace.

Several special couriers were dispatched immediately to notify the Government in St. Petersburg and the Heir Apparent, the brother of the late Czar, Grand Duke Constantin in Warsaw. Then a trusted officer was called in and ordered to accompany the imperial remains to the capital.

For the following ten days the entire nation breathlessly watched a pale, worn-out man crouching behind a sealed coffin and driving in a funeral coach at a speed suggestive of

3

a raid by the French cavalry. The veterans of Austerlitz, Leipzig and Paris, stationed along the long route, shook their heads dubiously and said that it was a strange climax indeed for a reign of unsurpassed glamour and glory.

"The late sovereign is not to be laid in state," said the laconic statement issued by the Government on receipt of the dispatches from Taganrog.

In vain did the foreign ambassadors and powerful courtiers try to find a plausible explanation for this mystery. Everybody pleaded ignorance and expressed bewilderment.

In the meantime something else happened which caused all eyes to be turned from the imperial mausoleum in the direction of the Plaza of the Senate. Grand Duke Constantin had abdicated in favor of his brother Nicholas. Happily married to a Polish commoner, he felt reluctant to exchange his carefree existence in Warsaw for the vicissitudes of the throne. He asked to be excused, and hoped his decision would be respected.

His letter had been read by the puzzled Senate in an atmosphere of gloomy silence.

Grand Duke Nicholas—his name sounded but vaguely familiar. Of course there were four sons in the family of Czar Paul I, but who could have expected that the handsome Alexander would die without issue, and that the robust Constantin would spring such a surprise on his beloved Russia? Several years younger than his brothers, the Grand Duke Nicholas followed until December, 1825, the well-established routine of a man following a military career, and the Minister of War seemed the only official in St. Petersburg to have formed an idea of the new Czar's habits and talents.

An excellent officer, a dependable executor of orders, a patient solicitor who had spent many hours of his youth waiting in the antechambers of high commanders. A likable chap of sterling qualities, but a poor boy who knew nothing of the complicated affairs of state, for he had never been invited by his brother to participate in the deliberations

4

of the Imperial Council. Fortunately for the future of the empire, he would have to rely upon the judgment of statesmen, experienced and patriotic. This last thought brought a certain comfort into the hearts of the ministers as they went to meet the youthful ruler of Russia.

A certain coolness marked their encounter. First of all, declared the new Czar, he wanted to see with his own eyes the letter of Grand Duke Constantin. One had to be prepared for all sorts of intrigues when dealing with persons who did not belong to the army. He read it carefully and examined the signature. It still seemed unbelievable to him that an heir apparent to the Russian throne should disobey the command of the Almighty. In any event, brother Constantin should have advised the late Czar of his plans in due time, so that he, Nicholas, could have been afforded a possibility of learning *le métier d'un Empereur* (the profession of an Emperor).

He clenched his fists and got up. Tall, handsome and athletically built, he looked a perfect specimen of manhood.

"We shall carry out the orders of our late brother and the wishes of Grand Duke Constantin," he concluded curtly, and his usage of the plural did not escape the ministers. This young man talked like a czar. It remained to be proved whether he was capable of acting as one. The occasion presented itself sooner than expected.

Next day—December 14, 1825—having been set for the army to take its oath of allegiance to the new Czar, a secret political society headed by young men of noble birth decided to seize this opportunity for an open revolt against the dynasty.

It is very difficult, even after the passing of a century, to form a definite opinion of the program of those who were to be known as "the Men of December" (Dekabristy). Officers of the Guard, gentlemen-philosophers and writers, they decided to work together not because of the similarity of their ambitions, but because of that feeling of self-identification with the oppressed which had been released by the French Revolution and was common to all of them. No semblance of an agreement ever entered their discussions as to what should be done on the day after the fall of the existing régime. Colonel Pestel, Prince Troubetzkoi, Prince Volkonsky and other moderate leaders of the St. Petersburg branch of the society dreamed of building the state along the lines of the constitutional monarchy adopted by England. Mouravieff and the theoreticians of the provincial branches clamored for a Robespierrian republic. With a possible exception of Pestel, a sad man of mathematical mind who undertook the trouble of working out a detailed project of the Russian constitution, the rank and file of the organization preferred to center their imaginations on the spectacular side of their attempt. The poet Rylyeff saw himself in the part of Camille Desmoulins, haranguing the crowds and proclaiming freedom. A poor unbalanced youth by the name of Kakhovsky preached the necessity of imitating "the noble example of Brutus."

Among the numerous young followers attracted by the names of the scions of Russia's best families were Kukhelbecker and Pouschchin, two school chums of the famous poet Poushkin. The latter, advised of the approaching events, left his country place and started for St. Petersburg, when a frightened hare crossed the road in front of his carriage. The superstitious poet stopped the driver and turned back.

In any event, such was the story told by him to his friends the conspirators, but he did write a beautiful poem dedicated to their daring undertaking.

Although the secret society was formed as far back as 1821, its activities had never gone beyond the heated meetings that took place in the apartments of Pestel, Rylyeff and Bestujeff-Rumin. Considering the well-known Russian ability to engage in endless debates, chances are they would have talked themselves out of the whole idea of doing anything at all, had it not been for the powerful impetus provided by the mysterious death of Alexander I and the abdication of Grand Duke Constantin.

"Now or never," said Kakhovsky, waving his enormous pistol. Colonel Pestel hesitated, but the majority seconded the fiery tribune.

On the evening of December 13, having failed to reach a unanimous decision, they left for the military barracks and spent the night in conversations with the soldiers of the St. Petersburg garrison.

The plan, if any, consisted in leading out several regiments to the Plaza of the Senate and forcing the Emperor to agree to certain amendments to the constitution. Long before dawn it became clear that the attempt had failed. Notwithstanding the fine eloquence of the aristocratic orators and the lengthy quotations from Jean-Jacques Rousseau, the soldiers remained noncommittal. The only question asked by them had to do with the meaning of the word "constitution." Could it be the wife of Grand Duke Constantin the gentlemen were referring to?

"It is time yet," suggested Pestel, "to call everything off."

"Too late," answered his associates. "The Government is already notified of what is going on. We are bound to be arrested and tried. Let us die fighting."

Finally a few battalions commanded by the popular officers belonging to the secret society agreed to march. Their progress through the streets toward the Plaza of the Senate encountered no resistance. The military governor of St. Petersburg, General Miloradovich, one of the surviving heroes of 1812, who bowed to no one in his passion for the dramatization of historical events, placed a regiment of loyal cavalry and a battery of artillery at the foot of the Senate Building, but permitted the plotters to reach their destination without interference.

All morning long a heavy fog had been creeping up from the banks of the Neva. When it lifted toward noon, the shivering crowds of curious spectators beheld the two opposing armies standing in front of each other, divided by some three hundred feet of no man's land.

Minutes, hours, went by. The soldiers commenced to complain of hunger. The leaders of the secret society felt helpless and miserable. They were willing to sacrifice their lives, but the Government did not seem inclined to start hostilities, and it would have been sheer madness on their part to attempt sending the infantry against the combined forces of cavalry and artillery.

"It's a standing revolution," said a voice from behind, and an outburst of laughter greeted this historical phrase.

Suddenly a hush fell over the crowds.

"The young Czar, the young Czar! Look at him riding next to Miloradovich."

Disregarding all advisers, who pointed out that he had no right to risk his life, Emperor Nicholas I decided to assume personal charge of the situation. At the head of a group of officers, mounted on a tall horse, he presented an easy target for the revolutionaries. Even a mediocre shot could hardly have missed him.

"Your Imperial Majesty," pleaded the frightened Miloradovich, "I beg of you to return to the palace."

"I will stay right here," came the firm answer. "Someone must save the lives of these poor misguided people."

Miloradovich spurred his famous white mount and galloped toward the opposite end of the Plaza. Not unlike his master, he had no fear of the Russian soldiers. They would never dare fire at a man who had led them against the Old Guard of Napoleon.

Stopping in front of the revolutionaries, Miloradovich made one of those colorful speeches that had inspired many a regiment during the battles of 1812. Every word went home. They smiled at his jokes. They brightened up at the familiar allusions. One minute more, and they would have followed his "brotherly advice of an old soldier" and started back for the barracks.

8

FRIENDS OF DECEMBER FOURTEENTH

Just then a dark figure appeared between them and Milora-dovich.

Pale, disheveled, smelling of brandy, and having never parted with his pistol since early morning, Kakhovsky fired point-blank: the resplendent general sank back in the saddle.

A riot of indignant vociferations broke loose on both sides.

The Emperor bit his lip and glanced in the direction of the battery. The echo repeated the bark of the guns all over the city.

The standing revolution had come to an end. Several score of soldiers were killed, and every one of the leaders was arrested by midnight.

"I shall never forget my friends of December the fourteenth," said the Emperor weeks later, and signed the sentences condemning Pestel, Kakhovsky, Bestujeff-Rumin, Rylyeff and Mouravieff to the gallows, and the rest of their associates to penal servitude in Siberia.

He never did. During one of his journeys through Siberia he inquired into the minutest details of the lives of the exiled aristocrats who had unwittingly become the predecessors of a movement which was to achieve its goal ninety-two years later.

He had likewise expressed the desire to talk to a hermit known as Feodor Kousmich, and had made a long detour in order to visit his humble log cabin in the wilderness. There was no witness to their meeting, but the Emperor remained closeted with the saintly man for over three hours. He came out in a pensive mood. The aides-de-camp thought they had noticed tears in his eyes. "After all," wrote one of them, "there may be something to the legend which tells us that a simple soldier had been buried in the imperial mausoleum in St. Petersburg, and that Emperor Alexander I is hiding in the guise of this strange man."

My late brother, Grand Duke Nicholas Michailovich, spent several years working in the archives of our family, trying to find a corroboration of this astounding legend. He believed

9

in its emotional plausibility, but the diaries of our grandfather Emperor Nicholas I, strangely enough, failed to mention even the fact of his visit to Feodor Kousmich.

The sentinel of the imperial palace in Taganrog may have conceived his story under the influence of the rumors which had gripped the popular imagination in the early thirties of the nineteenth century. The fact remains, however, that the mystic mentality developed by Emperor Alexander in the latter years of his reign could be used as a powerful argument by the historians inclined to uphold the imperial identity of the silent Siberian hermit.

Worn out by the continuous wars with Napoleon, thoroughly disillusioned by the insincerity of his German, Austrian and English allies, my imperial granduncle liked for months to stay in the provincial retirement of his Taganrog palace, reading the Bible to his sad and beautiful consort, who had never ceased to grieve over their childlessness. Suffering with insomnia, he would get up at all hours of the night and try in vain to relieve his mind, filled with the images of a stormy past.

Two particular scenes used to haunt his memory: Count Pahlen entering his room on the morning of March 11, 1801, announcing the assassination of his father, Emperor Paul I; Napoleon at Tilsit embracing him and promising to maintain eternal peace in Europe. These two people robbed him of his youth ad covered his hands with blood.

Over and over again he read the words of the Preacher, heavily outlined by him in pencil: "I have seen all the works that are done under the sun; and behold, all is vanity and vexation of spirit."

CHAPTER TWO

A GRAND DUKE IS BORN

"A boy has just been born in the family of His Imperial Highness," announced an aide-de-camp of Grand Duke Michael, then Viceroy of the Caucasus, bursting into the office occupied by the commandant of the Tiflis fortress on the morning of April 1, 1866. "Have the imperial salute of one hundred and one guns fired immediately."

"It ceases to be funny," answered the old general, looking gloomily at the calendar hanging over his head. "I have been pestered all morning long. Try your April first jokes on someone else, or I shall report you to His Imperial Highness."

"You don't seem to understand, Excellency," said the aide-de-camp impatiently. "This is no joke. I come straight from the palace and would advise you to carry out the orders."

The commandant shrugged his shoulders, glanced once more at the calendar and started for the palace to verify the news.

Half an hour later the guns commenced to boom, and a special proclamation informed the excited Georgians, Armenians, Tartars and Highlanders promenading along the main thoroughfare of the Caucasian capital that the newly-born grand duke was to be christened Alexander, in honor of his imperial uncle, Emperor Alexander II.

On April 2, 1866, at the tender age of twenty-four hours, I became the honorary colonel of the 73rd Krimsky Infantry Regiment, an officer of the fourth rifle battalion of the Imperial Guard, an officer of the Guard Hussars, an officer of the Guard Artillery Brigade and an officer of the Caucasian

Grenadier Division. A beautiful wet-nurse had to exercise all her ingenuity to pacify the holder of all these exalted positions. . . .

Following in the steps of his uncompromising father Emperor Nicholas I, my father thought it only natural that his sons should be raised in an atmosphere of militarism, strict discipline and exacting duties. Inspector-general of the Russian artillery and viceroy of an enormously rich, half-Asiatic province incorporating some twenty-odd nationalities and fighting tribes, he had but small regard for the niceties of modern education.

My mother, Princess Cecilia of Baden before her marriage, came of age in the days when Bismarck kept all Germany spellbound by his sermon of iron and blood.

Small wonder that the joys of my care-free childhood came to an abrupt end on my seventh birthday. Among the many gifts presented to me on that occasion I found the uniform of the colonel of the Seventy-third Krimsky Infantry Regiment and a sword. I shrieked with delight, imagining that it meant a possibility of getting rid of my usual costume, which up to then had consisted of a shirt of pink silk, broad trousers and high red-leather boots.

My father smiled and shook his head negatively. Of course, I would occasionally be permitted to don the glittering uniform if I were a good boy, but first of all I had to deserve the honor of wearing this noble sword. I had to study hard for many years.

My face became rather long, but the worst was yet to come.

"Beginning with tomorrow," explained my father, "you are to live in the same quarters with your brothers Michael and George. You will take your orders from their tutors."

Good-by, my kind nurses. Good-by, fairy tales. Good-by, peaceful dreams. My head sank into the pillows; I cried all night long, refusing to listen to the comforting words of the big-hearted Cossack Shevtchenko. Finally, seeing that his promises to visit with me each and every Sunday failed to produce the necessary effect, he whispered to me in a frightened tone: "Think what shame it would mean for you if His Imperial Majesty should mention it in an army order that his nephew, Grand Duke Alexander, does not deserve to command the Seventy-third Krimsky Infantry Regiment because he likes to cry like a girl."

I jumped up from the bed and rushed to wash my face. To think that I very nearly disgraced my entire family in the eyes of the imperial court!

An event of still greater importance coincided with this seventh birthday of mine. I suppose it amounted to a veritable spiritual dawn, so strong was the shock caused to my young soul.

The custom of the Greek Orthodox Church required every boy to be taken to his first confession before venturing upon the road of worldly knowledge. The kind Father Titoff did his best to soften the ordeal, but he had to obey the relentless regulations.

For the first time in my life I learned of the existence of various sins accurately classified and described at length by this holy man. A child of seven was called upon to confess his intercourse with the Devil. The God who talked to me in murmurs of red, white and blue flowers growing in our garden had suddenly given way to a menacing and unforgiving Being.

Trying to avoid my horrified look, Father Titoff spoke of the damnations and tortures of hell guaranteed for anyone who would attempt to hide his sinfulness. He raised his voice, and I glanced tremblingly at the Cross on his breast, lighted by the rays of the hot Caucasian sun. Could it be that I had committed some frightful crime, unconsciously and unwittingly?

"Very often little boys steal small things from their parents. They mean no harm, but their deed constitutes a sin!"

No, I felt quite certain of never having stolen even a piece of candy out of the big silver bowl that stood on the mantelpiece in the dining-room, although more than once I had been tempted to do so. My mind traveled back to the previous summer spent in Italy. While in Naples, admiring a group of fruit trees behind our villa, I did pick a luscious red apple, which had a sharp flavor that made me feel homesick for the Caucasus.

"Father Titoff, am I to be thrown into Hell for picking an apple in Naples?"

Well, he could see a way to square this sin of mine if I would promise never to repeat the grave misdeed.

His willingness to compromise prompted my courage. Stuttering, stammering and swallowing the words, I expressed my bewilderment at the existence of Hell.

"You always said, Father Titoff, when you came to lunch to the palace, that God loved all men, women, children, animals and flowers. Then how could He permit these awful tortures to be practiced in Hell? How could He love and hate us at the same time?"

It was the turn of Father Titoff to become terrified.

"Never say it again! It is a sacrilege! Of course, God loves us all; there is no such thing as hatred in His Kingdom."

"But, Father Titoff, you just told me yourself of those awful tortures awaiting all sinners. Then you mean to say that God loves only the virtuous people and does not love the sinners?"

He sighed deeply and put his soft white hand on my head.

"My dear boy, you will understand all this in due time. Some day when you have become a great commander, you will thank me for developing a spirit of true Christianity in your soul. Now, just follow my advice and do not ask me any more questions."

I left the church with a firm conviction of having lost something exceedingly precious which nothing could replace, even if I should become the Emperor of Russia.

"Did you say your adieus to the nurses?" asked my father when I climbed on his chair to kiss him good night.

Nothing mattered for me any more. What good could the nurses do if we were all doomed to Hell?

And from then to the age of fifteen my education resembled the training in a regiment. My brothers Nicholas, Michael, Sergei, George and myself lived as in barracks. We slept on narrow iron beds, only the thinnest possible mattress being allowed over the wooden planks. I remember that even in later years, after my marriage, I could not become accustomed to the luxury of a large bed with double mattresses and linen sheets, and ordered my old hard bunk to be put next to it.

We were called every morning at six o'clock. We had to jump out of our beds immediately, for a severe punishment swiftly followed an attempt to sleep "just five minutes more."

Kneeling in a row in front of the three ikons, we said our prayers, then took a cold bath. Our breakfast consisted of tea, bread and butter. Any other ingredients had been strictly forbidden, lest we should develop a taste for a luxurious life.

A lesson in gymnastics and practice with firearms filled another hour, particular attention being paid to the handling of a mountain gun placed in the garden. Very often our father would pay us an unexpected visit and watch with a critical eye our progress in the study of artillery. At the age of ten I would have been able to take part in the bombardment of a large city.

From eight to eleven, and from two to six, we had to study and do our homework. According to the etiquette of the imperial court, no grand duke was allowed to enter a private or a public school, in consequence of which we were always surrounded by an army of special tutors. Our educational program planned for eight years consisted of lessons in religion (Old and New Testament, Divine Service, history of the Greek Orthodox Church, comparative history of other

15

churches, Russian grammar and literature, foreign literature, history of Russia, history of Europe, history of America, history of Asiatic countries, geography, mathematics (which covered arithmetic, algebra, geometry, trigonometry), natural history, French, German, English, calligraphy and music. On top of that we were taught the handling of all sorts of firearms, riding, fencing, and bayonet fighting. My eldest brothers Nicholas and Michael had to learn Latin and Greek as well, but we, the youngest three, were fortunately relieved of that nonsensical torture.

Learning presented no difficulties either for me or for my brothers; but the unnecessary severity of our tutors created considerable bitterness. No doubt a mammoth meeting of protest would be staged by the fond American parents were their children to be treated in the manner approved of by the imperial family of Russia.

The smallest mistake in spelling of a German word deprived us of dessert; the miscalculation of the meeting-place of those two fatal trains, which seem to exert a strange fascination on the teachers of arithmetic all over the world, meant that the guilty party had to kneel for a full hour, with his nose turned toward the wall; a shy repartee never failed to bring the heavy ruler on our heads or wrists, and the very thought of disobeying the orders of this or that teacher was accompanied by a resounding slap.

Once in a while, feeling the formation of a lump in our throats, we would attempt to come out with a declaration of independence; then a grave report would be presented to our father just before lunch-time, mentioning the names of the ringleaders, as it was his exclusive prerogative to attend to the thrashing.

It shall always remain a mystery to me how such an inane system did not succeed in dulling our wits and fostering a hatred for all subjects we had to study in our childhood.

I must add, however, that all the sovereigns of Europe seemed to have agreed that their sons should be beaten into the realization of their future responsibilities. Many years afterward, while exchanging reminiscences with Kaiser Wilhelm, I appreciated the comparative mildness of my Tiflis teachers; his heir, the crown prince of Germany, who had married one of my nieces by that time, dryly added that the amount of punishment dealt to an imperial father invariably fails to soften the path of his son.

Lunches and dinners, so enjoyable in most families, brought no relief to the hard routine of our upbringing.

The viceroy of the Caucasus had to represent the Emperor in his relations with the millions of people inhabiting the southeast of Russia, and we could never sit at the table with less than thirty or forty guests. Government officials who came from St. Petersburg; Oriental potentates on their way to see the Czar; commandants of the outlying military districts; socially prominent persons accompanied by their wives; aides-de-camp and ladies-in-waiting; officers of the bodyguard and a score of tutors—all used this opportunity of expressing their political views and soliciting special favors.

We children had to watch our p's and q's, and not speak until spoken to. How many times, nearly bursting with a desire to tell our father of the marvelous fortress built by us on the top of the mountain back of the palace, or of the new Japanese flowers planted by our gardener, we had to keep silent and listen to a pompous general commenting on the folly of Disraeli's latest undertaking!

Whenever addressed by the guests, which was done of course solely as a matter of politeness toward the powerful viceroy, we had to confine our answers to the expressions prescribed by a rigorous etiquette.

A lady inquiring with an unnaturally sweet smile on her lips as to my ambitions for the future, knew in advance that Grand Duke Alexander would be severely reprimanded by his parents should he express an intention to become a fireman or an engineer. My choice of a career lay between the cavalry commanded by my uncle Nicholas, the artillery supervised by my father, and the imperial fleet headed by my uncle Constantin.

"Nothing could be so splendid for a boy in your position," usually said the lady, "as to follow in the steps of your illustrious father."

What sensible reply could have been made to this supposition, considering that twelve pairs of eyes of my teachers were glaring straight into my face and were putting the dignified words in my mouth?

My brother George once chanced to confess his inclination for portrait painting. He was greeted with the ominous silence of all parties assembled at the table, and understood his mistake shortly afterward, when the majestic tower of cherry and vanilla ice-cream glided past his place without a stop.

The seating order of the table precluded any possibility of giggling at the peculiarities of the guests or whispering among ourselves: we were never permitted to sit next to each other, but were sandwiched between the grown-up persons. It was pointed out to us in no uncertain terms that we had to behave toward our neighbors just as the viceroy would have done himself. Laughing at poor jokes and simulating a vivid interest in the political developments abroad entered into our obligations of hospitality, and developed in us a sense of self-relying resourcefulness.

Every minute of our time we had to bear in mind that some day we would be taken to that Russia which lay hidden behind the chain of mountains. There while visiting in the palace of our reigning uncle, we would be grateful to those who had made us acquire all these excellent manners! Otherwise our cousins would point fingers at us and call us "the savage Caucasians."

Then for an hour after lunch and twenty minutes after dinner we were allowed to play in our father's study, an enormous room laid with gorgeous Persian rugs and decorated with Caucasian swords, rifles and pistols. Its windows overlooking the Golovinsky Prospect (the main thoroughfare of Tiflis) provided an unforgettable view of Oriental pageantry. We never tired watching the tall swarthy mountaineers in their gray, brown and red *cherkeskas,* mounted on splendid spirited horses, with their hands resting on the hilts of gold and silver daggers covered with glittering precious stones. Accustomed to the different nationalities who came to see the viceroy, we recognized the lackadaisical Persians wearing silken robes that stood out vividly against the background of the sober black costumes of the Georgians and the conventional uniforms of our guards. Armenian vendors of fruit, gloomy Tartars astride their mules, and yellow-skinned Bucharans yelling at their overburdened camels provided the rest of this ever-moving picture.

The enormous bulk of Kasbek mountain—its snow-covered peak piercing skies of the richest blue—dominated the narrow winding streets which ran toward the market-places sizzling with restless humanity, and the melodious sound of the rapid river Kura brought an element of peaceful harmony into the atmosphere of this shrieking capital.

Too much beauty in one's early surroundings may tend to develop a sad character, but we were supremely happy during those short intermissions between drills and the educational grind. We wanted to stay forever in Tiflis. We had no use for European Russia. Our local Caucasian patriotism made us consider the gold-braided envoys of St. Petersburg with a mixture of mistrust and contempt. The Emperor of Russia would have been painfully surprised to learn that every day, from one to two and from eight to eight-thirty in the evening, his five nephews in the far-away south were plotting a near-secession. Fortunately for the empire, our tutors kept their vigilant guard, and just at the moment when we were about to distribute most important posts among the five of us, an unpleasant voice would be certain to remind us that the French irregular verbs awaited their victims in the classroom.

At the stroke of nine we had to retire to our bedroom, put on long white shirts (pajamas had not reached Russia as yet) and fall asleep at once. Even then we continued to be under close observation. Not less than five times during the night a tutor would enter our quarters and cast a suspicious look at the five human bundles hidden under the blankets.

Shortly before midnight we would be aw ned by the sound of clinking spurs which signified the arrival of our father. Disregarding the remonstrances of our mother, he believed that future soldiers should sleep despite the most terrific noises.

"What are they going to do later on," he used to remark, "when they will have to steal a few hours' rest to the accompaniment of a heavy cannonade?"

I can still see his tall figure and serious handsome face bending over our beds, while he blessed us with the broad movement of his strong hand. Before leaving, he would mutter a short prayer asking the Almighty to help him make good Christians and faithful subjects of Russia out of his five sons. No religious doubt ever entered his clear-cut convictions. He believed in every word written in the Scriptures, and his accounts with the Divine Forces were being kept in perfect order: as a powerful administrator, he supervised rendering unto God that which was God's, expecting that everything which was Cæsar's would in turn be rendered unto Cæsar.

From the point of view of our parents and tutors we grew to be a nice bunch of healthy children, but the modern scientists would have detected in our natures the unmistakable traces of love-starvation. We ourselves did suffer from extreme loneliness. We had nobody to talk with. Our position kept us away from other children of our age, and each one of us was too proud to complain of his sufferings to his brothers.

The very thought of interrupting our father's busy occupations with a vague conversation on no particular subject would have struck us as something little short of madness.

GRAND DUKE ALEXANDER
AT THE AGE OF FOUR

THE FUTURE
EMPRESS
MARIE OF
RUSSIA, IN
1876, HOLD-
ING HER
DAUGHTER
XENIA

GRAND DUKE ALEXANDER IN ITALY
AT THE AGE OF FIVE

AN IMPERIAL PICNIC PARTY IN THE EARLY 80's, WITH CZAR ALEXANDER III STANDING
IN THE CENTER AND GRAND DUCHESS XENIA ON THE EXTREME LEFT

Our mother dedicated all her efforts to the ungrateful task of suppressing even the slightest exterior signs of tenderness or affection; in her early youth she fell a victim to the far-fetched ideas of Spartan education advocated in her native Germany.

While thoroughly democratic in our dealings with the servants, we had to remember that a grand duke should never show the tiniest weakness in the presence of his inferiors. He must always keep a satisfied appearance, hiding his sorrows beneath a bright Russian shirt of blue silk.

There remained our sister Anastasia. We worshiped that tall dark-haired girl who was the exclusive favorite of our father; but when talking to her, we liked to pose as the faithful knights ready and willing to execute the orders of their "dame sans merci." We put at her feet all the love stored during months and years of dull military drills. We were extremely jealous of her and felt a terrific heartache when the young Grand Duke of Mecklenburg-Schwerin came to Tiflis to make the acquaintance of his fiancée. Our instinctive dislike for his elegant German manner of clicking his heels and kissing hands reached the proportions of hatred when our brother Nicholas discovered the real purpose of his visit. The arrival of our future brother-in-law deprived us of the only outlet for our affection, and we turned toward Nature—that had always been kind and spoke in terms of hope.

Allowed to remain outside during the winter but one hour, we counted impatiently the days separating us from the advent of spring. Our vacations lasted six weeks, and were spent either in Borjom, the enormous country estate of our father near Tiflis, or on the Black Sea, in the Crimean residence of the Emperor.

I shall always think kindly of scarlet fever, for this illness enabled me to experience the happiest summer of my life. I was eight. I fell ill and became unconscious on the way to Borjom, whence my parents intended to go to St. Petersburg to visit with the Czar. The doctors diagnosed scarlet fever at once, and I was left in Borjom in the care of a lady-in waiting, an aide-de-camp and two court physicians. For six joyful weeks I stayed in bed, being petted by them and feeling myself the center of attention.

Every afternoon a military band brought close to the house played my favorite songs. Scores of persons passing through the Caucasus journeyed to Borjom to pay their respects to the son of the viceroy, and the majority of them brought boxes of candy, toys and books by Fenimore Cooper. My two doctors readily consented to play Indians. Armed with the sword of the aide-de-camp, they would attempt to scalp the terror-stricken lady-in-waiting, who then in strict accord with her part would call for the help of the Fearless-White-Man-of-Two-Guns. The latter, leaning against the pillows, took an excellent aim at her torturers, and his pellets crashed straight against their foreheads.

The period of my convalescence brought about a series of picnics in the near-by woods and mountains. With every one of the tutors away in St. Petersburg, there were no lessons to attend, and we would leave early in the morning in a comfortable carriage drawn by four sturdy native horses. It took one's breath away to watch these little animals climb with utmost ease up the stiffest hills over a slippery road. Their calisthenics always reminded me of an episode which happened the year before during the visit of the Shah of Persia in Tiflis. This Oriental sovereign, a short man of generous plumpness, had become frightened while taken on a tour of inspection in the mountains, and jumping out of the vehicle, yelled at my mother: *"Mourez seule!"* ("You'll have to die alone!")

My happy days were filled with gathering blackberries, playing dominoes and listening to tales of the old Caucasus. I nearly cried with disappointment when the doctor pronounced me completely cured and a telegram arrived advising us of the approaching return of my family. I knew that for the first and last time in my childhood I had been given the chance of a friendly intercourse with grown-up people, who saw nothing unusual or offensive in showing a little affection for a lonely boy left in their care.

Back in Tiflis I listened with indifference to the excited conversation of my brothers. They never stopped admiring the splendors of the imperial palace in St. Petersburg, but I wouldn't have exchanged my summer in Borjom for all the diamonds of the Russian crown. I could have told them that while they had to behave at the table of our uncle, surrounded by smiling courtiers and tiptoeing butlers, I lay for hours in the tall grass watching the red, blue, yellow and mauve patches of flowers covering the slopes of the mountain, and following the flight of the larks that had a habit of rising all the way up and then coming down like a stone to protect their nests. I remained silent, however, for I feared my simple happiness would be ridiculed.

The year 1875 marks a significant date in my childhood: my brother Alexis was born shortly after Christmas, and I met two persons who were destined to become my lifelong friends.

My parents took all possible precautions to conceal from us the real circumstances accompanying the birth of a child. We were expected to combine a thorough knowledge of modern artillery with a sincere belief in the stork.

The booming of one hundred and one guns caused us considerable surprise.

"The Almighty deemed it necessary," explained our military tutor, "to send another son to Their Imperial Highnesses."

On the second day we were permitted to enter our mother's apartment and see our brother. For no good reason at all everybody smiled and thought we boys should be jealous. My brothers said nothing. I myself was filled with sympathy for the newcomer. I hoped for his sake that by the time he grew up, all our teachers would have passed out of existence. Looking at the wrinkled reddish face of the baby, I felt distinct pity.

The ceremony of baptism took place three weeks later and was preceded by a mammoth parade of the garrison. The music played and the crowds shouted, while the baby, carried in the arms of the eldest lady-in-waiting, was being escorted to the cathedral by numerous military and civil dignitaries.

Poor Alexis rested quietly on a silk cushion, in his long white-lace robe, with the blue ribbon of St. Andrew—the highest decoration in Russia—attached to his tiny breast. The touch of cold water made him shriek at the top of his voice. He had to be submerged three times while the archbishop read a special prayer. Then amidst the same pomp, music and excitement, he was taken back to his mother. Neither she nor our father could have been present at the ceremony, as the Greek Orthodox Church does not allow parents to witness the dedication of their child to God. This age-old rule happened to be extremely significant in the case of our little brother: Alexis remained on this earth for but a short time: he died from galloping consumption at the age of twenty. Although attached to him stronger than to any other member of my family, I never regretted his passing away. A brilliant boy of liberal heart and absolute sincerity, he suffered acutely in the atmosphere of the palace.

That spring we left Tiflis earlier than usual, to spend six weeks in the Crimean estate of our uncle. We were met at the port of Yalta by the Emperor himself, who said he was anxious to see the most savage of his Caucasian nephews, and proceeded to the beautiful palace of Livadia, famous for its exquisite gardens.

A long spectacular flight of stairs led straight down to the Black Sea. That same day, while jumping over its marble steps, in a great flurry of pleasant anticipations, I bumped into a smiling boy of my age walking beside a nurse with an infant in her arms. We sized each other up; then he extended his hand and said:

A GRAND DUKE IS BORN

"I guess you are my cousin Sandro. I didn't see you last summer in St. Petersburg. Your brothers said you were ill with scarlet fever. Don't you know me? I am your cousin Nicky, and this is my little sister Xenia."

His kind eyes and pleasant manner appealed to me at once. My distrust of all northerners suddenly gave way to a strong desire to be chummy with this particular one. He also must have taken a fancy for me, because our friendship, formed at that very moment, lasted forty-two years. The elder son of the then heir apparent, Alexander Alexandrovich, he was to inherit the throne in 1894, the last representative of the house of Romanoff to rule over the Russian Empire.

I frequently disagreed with his policies and wished he had shown better judgment in choosing his counselors and more determination in some of his decisions; but all this concerned Emperor Nicholas II and did not in the least affect my relations with "Cousin Nicky." Nothing could have altered in my mind the image of the cheerful boy in a little pink shirt, who stood on the marble steps of the long stairs in Livadia pointing at the sailing ships on the horizon and squinting his dreamy, curiously shaped eyes at the sunset. . . . I married his sister Xenia nineteen years later.

Now I was entering upon the tenth year of my life and the third year of my learning, which meant that a new set of studies and military exercises would be added to my duties.

Brought up amongst the grown-ups and hearing so much talk of the heavy responsibilities facing a grand duke, I was already pondering over problems which are usually reserved for a more mature age. Strange to say, my emotional, spiritual and intellectual development had preceded my sexual awakening by several years. Not until 1882, when my parents moved definitely to St. Petersburg, where I commenced to attend the ballet performances, did that troublesome restlessness make itself felt. Up to that time, possibly as a result of severe discipline, I had remained pure, both in desire and in thought. The study of the Old Testament, so likely to affect a child's imagination, impressed me from an entirely different angle. Utterly unconscious of its sexual significance, I worried over the legal aspects of the Adam and Eve episode. I thought it extremely unjust on the part of God to banish these two innocent people from Paradise. In the first place, God could have ordered Satan to let them alone; and in the second place, why did He create the perfidious fruit that caused humanity so much suffering?

Father Titoff, slightly suspicious of me since the day of my first confession, had tried in vain to plead the cause of the Old Testament. He let me go on for a while, praying for the salvation of my soul from the abyss of disbelief, but finally lost patience and threatened to report me to my father. This unanswerable argument killed my interest in his lessons, and I turned my battery of questions against the teachers of geography and natural history.

Like most Russian boys, I contemplated the possibility of running away to America, and learned the names of all the states, principal cities and rivers in the United States. I never gave a moment of peace to Admiral Vesselago, who was considered somewhat of an expert on American affairs, having participated in the Russian naval demonstration staged in American territorial waters in 1863 as a protest of Emperor Alexander II against British interference in the Civil War. I wanted to know whether it was safe for a boy to walk in the streets of New York without being properly armed.

Half a century later, swapping tales of childhood with my late friend Myron T. Herrick, I was deeply moved by his description of the effect produced in the Middle West by the arrival of the Russian squadron.

"I realize," Herrick related, "that it must have been the darkest moment in the history of the Union. I was too young to follow the events, but my mother walked around the farm with eyes swollen by constant crying. She had the greatest difficulty in finding laborers, as all the young men had joined the army. One morning, when I played in the back yard, I suddenly heard my mother scream:

" 'Myron, Myron, come here quick!' I rushed to her, thinking that something awful had happened. Standing in the center of the room, with a single sheet of newspaper in her hands, heavy tears of joy streaming down her cheeks, she repeated over and over again: 'Myron, we are saved.' The Russians had arrived. 'Myron, we are saved!' At that time I knew very little of the nations living outside the United States. There were the perfidious English whom we had to beware of, and there were the French who had written those naughty books so often discussed in the general store; but who were the Russians? 'Mother,' I asked, 'are they anything like the Indians? Do they scalp people?'

"Too bad," concluded Mr. Herrick, "that you did not run away to America. We would have had lots of things to tell to each other if you had reached Ohio in time to catch me on the farm."

Beginning with the fall of 1876 the conversation around our dinner-table centered on the imminence of a war with Turkey. All other topics were brushed aside, as everybody realized that our proximity to the Turkish border would force the Caucasian army to act with lightning speed. The visitors from St. Petersburg gave vivid pictures of the atrocities committed by the Turks in the Slavonic states, and several officers on father's staff had asked his permission to join the Bulgarian army as volunteers.

Our daily military exercises acquired a new significance. We discussed how we should act in case the Turks attempted to attack Tiflis and the palace. We envied the age of our elder brother Nicholas. At eighteen, he would certainly be entitled to join the army and cover himself with glory; we had been taught from infancy that war meant glory. Nobody told us of the casualties suffered by Russia during the Napoleonic and Crimean wars. We knew the names of the generals decorated with the Order of St. George, and we thrilled at the exploits of the heroes who had defended Sebastopol. Our teachers and our books neglected to mention the existence of hospitals, badly in need of bandages, and the heavy toll of human lives exacted by typhoid fever. Death itself was never discussed in our presence. Our reigning forebears never died: they "passed away in peace."

Around that time a bold murder took place in Tiflis. The two bandits had been promptly caught, court-martialed and condemned to the gallows. Their execution took place on an elevated platform not far from the palace.

Coming down to the classroom, we saw all our tutors gathered in front of the windows in a state of terrific excitement and glaring at something. Instead of ordering us back to our quarters, they made a motion for us to approach the windows. Not realizing what was really happening, we witnessed the gruesome spectacle.

Dense crowds were standing in front of the gallows, looking at the executioner, who was attending to the last preparations.

Then two pale figures appeared and were pushed toward him from behind. A moment later two pairs of stockinged feet swung in the air. I screamed and turned my head away.

"Grand Duke Alexander will never make a good soldier," said our military tutor sententiously.

I wanted to shriek at him, jump on him, strike him; but a nauseating feeling of sickness kept me paralyzed.

Several days passed before that awful sight left my mind. I walked around as in a dream, not daring to look through the windows lest I should see those two again. I did my lessons and answered the questions put to me, but could not gather my thoughts. It was as though a hurricane had passed over my soul, leaving in its wake the débris of all that had been planted there by three years of study.

CHAPTER THREE

MY FIRST WAR

I

THE month of January, 1877, brought the long awaited declaration of war by Russia on Turkey.

The events of 1877 and 1878 appear thoroughly incomprehensible when analyzed after the passing of fifty-three years: one does not know whether to marvel at the nearsightedness of Disraeli or to deplore the naïveté of the Russian Imperial Government. It may be true that we had no business interfering in Balkan affairs, but then, what mysterious considerations led Lord Beaconsfield to believe in the advisability of provoking the Russian ire? One word from London would have checked the series of massacres of Slavs organized by the Turkish Government, and the most perfunctory effort at reading the future would have disclosed to Downing Street the macabre consequences of fostering any Balkan disturbances whatsoever. As it was, Emperor Alexander II found himself actually in duty bound to accept the British challenge, although opposed to war with all the forces of his kind heart and clear mind.

For nearly two years, while slowly marching through the wild Balkan provinces toward Constantinople, the Russian Army was in reality engaged in a merciless fight with the British Empire. The Turkish soldiers were invariably armed with the newest British rifles; the generals of the Sultan were following the instructions of the British strategists; and the fleet of Her Britannic Majesty made its threatening appearance in the Near Eastern waters just at the moment when the capture of Constantinople by our army was but a question of a few weeks. The Russian diplomats once more lived up to their reputation of unsurpassed stupidity and advised Emperor Alexander II to accept the so-called "friendly services" of Bismarck and to settle the Russo-Turkish differences at a Congress in Berlin.

"Der alte Jude, das ist ein Mann," said Bismarck admiringly of Disraeli, when the latter succeeded in bluffing the Russian delegation into accepting the most grotesque terms of peace which traveled a long way toward making the future World War inevitable. In fact, "der alte Jude," in his perennial desire to assure the maintaining of the Turkish Empire in Europe, glorified Berlin in the eyes of Constantinople, thus laying the foundation for the deadly intrigues of Kaiser Wilhelm in the Balkans. Thousands of British soldiers were to meet their doom in Gallipoli thirty-seven years later because Disraeli was trying to make things uncomfortable for St. Petersburg in 1878. No excuse, however, could be advanced for the conduct of the Russian diplomats, who instead of countering Disraeli's move with an immediate proclamation of a Russo-German Alliance, commenced to promote a nonsensical and eventually fatal entente with France and Great Britain.

2

In the meanwhile, I was still eleven and experiencing the thrill of my first war.

My father having been appointed commander-in-chief of the Russian Army, the peaceful capital of the Caucasus had assumed overnight the stern appearance of General Headquarters.

The mobilized soldiers crossing afoot the mountains separating European Russia from the Southern Caucasus—at that time there was no direct railroad communication between Moscow and Tiflis—were fed daily in the spacious gardens of our palace, and an emergency hospital opened its activities in the halls of the ground floor.

MY FIRST WAR

Each morning, we kids escorted our father on his tours of inspection of the newly arrived troops, listening breathlessly to his simple soldierly speeches tending to explain the causes of the war and the urgent necessity for quick action.

Then the Great Day came: my own 73rd Krimsky Infantry Regiment passed through Tiflis on its way to the front, ready and waiting to make the acquaintance of its undersized colonel.

Six a.m. found me standing in front of the mirror and glaring in complete delight at my brilliant uniform, highly polished boots and impressive saber. Back of me I felt jealousy and animosity: my four brothers resented my triumph. They cursed the fate that had kept their regiments in the north. They anticipated that each and every victory scored by our army would be accredited by "that boisterous Sandro" to the prowess of his 73rd Krimsky Infantry Regiment.

"They seem to be pretty tired, those soldiers of yours," said brother Michael, looking through the window at the four thousand men placed in front of the palace and all along the Golovinsky Prospect.

I ignored this petty remark. They looked beautiful, as far as I was concerned.

I thought I should make an appropriate speech to this regiment of mine and was trying to recall some spectacular expressions contained in the history of the Napoleonic campaigns.

"My dear heroes!"

No, that would sound too much like a translation from the French.

"My glorious soldiers!"

Or better still, "My glorious brethren!"

"What in Heaven's name are you trying to do?" asked father, entering the room and noticing my calisthenics.

"He wants properly to inspire his regiment," answered Michael, and it took the strong right arm of father to stop the righteous indignation of the colonel of the 73rd Krimsky Infantry Regiment.

"Try to be serious, children. No necessity to tease Sandro. Nobody expects him to make speeches, anyway."

That sounded disappointing.

"But, I say, father, am I not supposed to address the soldiers?"

"Just wish them Godspeed. That's all. Now let us go. And remember: you have to look cheerful and pleased, no matter how tired you feel."

By midday I understood the meaning of my father's warning. It took us four hours to pass in review the sixteen companies of the regiment, all made of healthy bearded giants, pleasantly amused at the sight of their very young and exceedingly self-conscious colonel. Sixteen times in succession I had to repeat—"Hail the First Company, hail the Second Company" etc., and hear in reply an overwhelming chorus of two hundred fifty voices wishing me "good health." It was almost impossible for me to follow the gigantic stride of my father, who towered a full head over these warriors especially picked for their height. Never again in my life did I feel so exhausted, and yet so happy at the same time.

"I would advise your resting for a while," suggested mother, when we returned to the palace.

The very idea of resting while my four thousand soldiers were on their way to the battlefields! I went straight to the large relief map of the Caucasus attached to the wall and started to draw the line of march to be followed by the 73rd Krimsky Infantry Regiment.

"I never heard anyone doing so much spur-clicking," exclaimed brother Michael, and left the room in utter disgust. Although younger than he by three years I had outgrown him by an inch and a half that same winter, a thing that worried him considerably.

✛✛✛

3

A week later father left for the front. We envied him and could not sympathize with the sorrow of our sobbing mother. We were so proud to see him seated in an especially built large carriage, drawn by four horses, with six Cossacks galloping behind, and three Cossacks in front, one of them carrying the banner of the viceroy, bearing a Greek Orthodox cross on a white background in a frame of black and orange stripes, with an inscription "God Save and Protect" embroidered all over it and a massive bronze cross attached to the end of the pole. Innumerable carriages with generals and members of the staff followed right after, escorted by a squadron of Guard-Cossacks. The solemn bars of the Russian National Anthem and the frantic hurrahs of the population created a martial atmosphere. We could not think of returning to the routine of daily lessons. We wanted to talk war. We discussed the possibility of fighting continuing for several years, in which case we all would be given an opportunity to join our father.

Each morning brought something exceedingly exciting.

The Caucasian Army captured a Turkish fortress.

The Danube Army, commanded by our uncle Nicholas, crossed that great river and headed for Plevna, where the bitterest battles of the war were to be fought.

The Emperor visited Headquarters distributing decorations to numerous officers, all of them well known to us.

The first party of Turkish prisoners arrived in Tiflis.

The names of several of my father's assistants, principally that of General Loris-Melikoff, were being repeated every minute.

It was fascinating to realize that all these good friends of ours had suddenly become great national heroes. It was a joy to witness the departure of our military tutor, called to the colors shortly after the declaration of war, and the subsequent slackening of the relentless discipline dominating our education. Awful as this confession may sound, I did wish that a helpful Turkish bullet should spare us the necessity of ever seeing this ferocious man again. Fortunately for the future peace of my mind, he came back unscathed and highly decorated, although his place in the palace was by that time taken over by a tutor of milder disposition.

A regular service of special messengers established between the palace and the headquarters of our father in Alexandropol kept us in close touch with the latest events on the front, and the arrival of the daily army communiqué provided a signal for rushing toward the relief map and moving the flags indicating the positions of our army. The communiqué spared no colors in describing the achievements of our army; it usually mentioned the number of the Turks killed, wounded, and captured,—and these figures sounded like sweet music to our ears. Many years later, while in command of the Imperial Air Forces during the World War, I learned the curious mechanism directing the editing of the official communiqués and wished I could revive the gullibility of the eleven-year-old enthusiast, who watched with shining eyes the progress of the Russian Army through Turkey, not realizing the size of the human hecatombs it was leaving in its wake. In 1914-1917 I discovered that the "heavy losses" sustained by the "rapidly retreating enemy" were invariably accompanied by still heavier losses of our "glorious advancing troops." I suppose nothing will ever change the repertory of euphemisms used by the authors of military communiqués, nor their beastly habit of gloating over the gloomy sight of corpses found in the captured trenches. To the contrary, it has to be frankly admitted that the ethics of warfare have undergone a considerable change within the last forty years. Even that sufficiently thin veneer of chivalry which was still noticeable in 1877 and 1878 gave way to guerrilla-like methods by the time proud humanity had decided to bury 400,000 of its sons around the city of Verdun. Reading the reports describing the foul conditions prevailing in the prisoners' camps during the World War, I always thought of the refreshing sympathy and consideration with which the Turkish prisoners were treated by us in 1877. Emperor Alexander II thought it advisable to grant a personal audience to Osman-Pasha, the famous commander of the captured Turkish fortress Plevna; he returned him his sword and praised his courage and military genius in high terms. So much for the pre-the-Tribunal-of-The-Hague days. Thirty-seven years later, General Korniloff, when imprisoned by the Austrians in the Carpathians, was given a reception usually reserved for petty thieves and common criminals.

4

The comparative freedom enjoyed by the sons of the viceroy during his prolonged absence at the front, gave us now an opportunity to mingle with the different classes of the Tiflis population and to observe the real nature of the social structure.

During our visits to the hospitals and while walking in the streets, we were brought face to face with dire poverty. We noticed the misery, the sufferings, the hardships, that lay hidden in the neighborhood of the palace. We listened to life-stories that had the effect of upsetting all our previous plans and ambitions. My wearing a blue silk shirt and red-leather boots seemed shameful in the presence of boys of my own age whose shirts were torn and whose feet were stocking-less and swollen. Some of them complained of hunger; all of them cursed the war that had deprived them of their fathers. We mentioned it to our tutors; we asked to be provided with means to help those gray-faced youngsters. We received no answer, but shortly afterwards our walks were once more restricted to the palace grounds, this measure failing, however, to check the activity of our awakened minds.

The world had become quite a different place from what it had been up to that time.

"It's pretty soft for you, the sons of a grand duke," said one of our new acquaintances, "you have everything, you are living in luxury."

We remembered that strange phrase and we were wondering: what was luxury? Could it be true that while we had everything, these others had nothing?

There was a sentinel in front of our palace, a handsome cheerful lad, who welcomed us each morning with a wide smile which clashed somewhat with the strict procedure of presenting arms. We grew accustomed to him, and his sudden disappearance made us speculate whether he had been sent to the front. Then, during the luncheon, we overheard a conversation between the two aides-de-camp. The young sentinel had committed suicide, a letter from his home village found in his pockets and announcing the death of his wife providing the only explanation for his desperate action.

"You know how these village lads are," said the elder aide-de-camp, "they always want to attend the funeral of their relatives, and unless given leave to do it they grieve terribly."

That was all. Nothing else had been said about the smiling soldier who stood on his post in far-away Tiflis counting the days separating him from a reunion with his wife; but this single death impressed me more than the daily passing of thousands of Turks and Russians mentioned in the army communiqués. Again and again I went to inspect the spot where he had kept vigil each morning. His successor, a middle-aged veteran wearing several medals on his breast, looked at me curiously. He glanced at his boots and counted his buttons, thinking there must be something wrong in his appearance to attract such attention from the young grand duke. I wanted to talk to him and to ask him when he had seen his wife last. I knew, of course, that one was not supposed to engage a sentinel in conversation, so I just stood in front of him, both of us trying to read each other's thoughts:

GRAND DUKE MICHAEL NICHOLAEVICH, FATHER OF GRAND DUKE
ALEXANDER, IN 1865 WHEN VICE-ROY OF THE CAUCASUS.

GRAND DUCHESS OLGA FEODOROVNA, MOTHER OF GRAND DUKE
ALEXANDER.   FROM A PAINTING MADE IN THE EARLY 60'S.

I looking for sorrow, he trying to guess whether one of his buttons was missing. I am quite certain that were I to be transported to Tiflis this moment, I would have no difficulty in locating the spot where a Russian village youth grieved over the death of his wife in 1878.

5

Peace was signed in the summer of 1878. The following autumn we went to St. Petersburg to attend the wedding of my sister Anastasia to Friedrich, Grand Duke of Mecklenburg-Schwerin.

It being my first trip to European Russia, I was naturally the most excited member of our party. Glued to the window of the car I watched the endless panorama of the plains of Russia, so monotonous and distressing for a child raised in the vicinity of the snow-covered mountains and rapid rivers of the Caucasus. I did not like this strange country and refused to recognize it as my own. The subdued faces of the peasants, the shabbiness of the villages, the dusty towns—twenty-four hours after our train pulled out of Vladicavkas (where we arrived in carriages) I wished to be back in Tiflis. My disappointment did not escape father's attention.

"Do not judge Russia by the appearance of its provinces," he remarked rather apologetically, "wait till you see Moscow with its sixteen hundred churches and St. Petersburg with its palaces."

I sighed deeply. I had heard so much about the cathedrals of the Kremlin and the luxury of the imperial court that I knew in advance I was not going to like it.

We were supposed to remain in Moscow just long enough to worship at the shrine of the miraculous ikon of the Virgin Mary of Iveria and to visit the tombs of the saints buried in the Kremlin, it being almost the official duty of every member of the imperial family passing through the ancient capital of Russia.

The Iverskaya Chapel—a decrepit, small structure—was thronged with dense crowds of people anxious to see the powerful viceroy. The depressing smell of burning candles and the very squeaky voice of the priest reciting a short Te Deum robbed me of all feelings supposed to be inspired by the sight of the miraculous ikon. I did not believe that God would choose such surroundings to reveal Himself to his children. There was nothing Christian about the whole procedure. It rather suggested a sort of gloomy paganism. I had to pretend I was praying from fear of being punished but I knew that my God, the God of golden fields, prime forests and melodious waterfalls, would never visit Iverskaya Chapel.

Next we drove to the Kremlin and had to kiss the brownish foreheads of numerous saints lying in state in silver coffins and wrapped in luxurious silver-and-gold tissues. An elderly monk dressed in black escorted us from coffin to coffin, raising their lids and pointing to us the exact spot we were expected to kiss. My head started to ache. On moment more in that stuffy atmosphere and I would have fainted.

I do not want to appear sacrilegious, nor am I trying to offend the fanatical followers of the Greek Orthodox Church; I am merely relating this episode in order to show what an awful impression this medieval performance left on the soul of a boy thirsting for a religion of beauty and love. Since my first visit to Moscow and during the following forty years spent in Russia I must have kissed the skulls of those saints many hundreds of times. On each occasion I suffered acutely and never experienced even an inkling of religious ecstasy. Today, at the age of sixty-five, I am still fervent in my conviction that God should never be worshiped in the manner bequeathed to Christianity by the pagans.

The four hundred miles between Moscow and St. Petersburg were being closely guarded by soldiers. All along the route we saw bayonets and uniforms; at night thousands of camp-fires were lighting the way. At first we thought it had been done in father's honor, but then we learned that the Emperor expected to visit Moscow in the near future and that extraordinary measures had been taken to protect his train against the attempts of the revolutionaries. This revelation struck us all most painfully. Things were coming to a pretty bad pass if the Czar of all the Russias had to be guarded every inch of the distance between his two capitals. It was a far cry from the days of his father, Nicholas I, who traveled practically unescorted throughout the wildest provinces of the empire. Our father looked concerned and could not disguise his worry.

The morning of our arrival in St. Petersburg happened to coincide with the commencement of a period of dense pea-soup fogs, which are likely to make even a Londoner gasp in despair. Lamps and candles were burning all over our palace. At midday it became so dark that I was not able to see the ceiling of my room.

"Yours is a particularly attractive room," explained my tutor. "When the fog lifts you will see the Fortress of Peter and Paul, where all the Czars are buried, right across the way."

My heart sunk. It was bad enough to be obliged to spend several months in this dark city, but to live in the neighborhood of dead bodies! Tears appeared in my eyes. How I did hate St. Petersburg on that morning. For that matter, I hated it all my life. Whenever I feel homesick for Russia, I wish I could see once more the Caucasus and the Crimean Peninsula, but I sincerely hope I shall never again lay my eyes on the former capital of my ancestors.

I remember discussing this subject with my parents. Fond as they were of St. Petersburg, having spent there the first happy years of their married life, they could not blame me for remaining partial to the Caucasus. They recognized too that while the latter suggested harmony and content, the former reeked of imminent tragedy and continuous sorrow.

6

All large families suffer from the overlapping ambitions of its male members, and the Russian imperial family was no exception to this sour rule.

At the time of my first sojourn in St. Petersburg—the autumn of the year 1879—there were nearly two score young men in the family headed by Emperor Alexander II.

The Czar himself had five sons: Alexander (the future Emperor Alexander III), Vladimir, Alexis, Sergei and Paul.

His brother Michael (my father) had six sons: Nicholas (usually referred to as Nicholas Michailovich to distinguish him from his numerous namesakes in the family), Michael Michailovich, George Michailovich, myself, Sergei Michailovich, and my infant brother Alexis.

His other brother Nicholas Nicholaevich had two sons: "Nicholasha" (Nicholas Nicholaevich Jr. who became commander-in-chief of the Russian armies in 1914) and Peter.

Still another brother of the Czar, Constantin, had four sons: Constantin Constantinovich, Dimitry Constantinovich, Nicholas Constantinovich and Wiacheslav.

The eldest two sons of the Czar, Alexander (then the heir apparent) and Vladimir, having married at an early age, had in their turn three sons each: Nicky (the future Czar Nicholas II), George Alexandrovich ("Georgie"), and Michael Alexandrovich, being born from the marriage of the heir apparent to the Danish Princess Dagmar; and Cyril, Boris, and Andrew, the sons of Grand Duke Vladimir, constituting the youngest male trio of the imperial family.

With the natural exception of the heir apparent and his three sons whose future lay in the direction of the throne, all the other young male Romanoffs expected to make a career in the army and anticipated strenuous competition from their own cousins. Hence, there were several "parties" in the family, the close relationship existing between us fail-

40

ing to prevent certain animosities. To begin with, we, the Caucasians, were inclined to keep aloof from the majority of the northerners. They suspected us of enjoying special favors from our imperial uncle; we accused them of ridiculous haughtiness. We five had our favorites and our "bêtes noires." We all liked Nicky and Georgie. We all distrusted Nicholasha. The feud between my elder brother Nicholas Michailovich and the future commander-in-chief of the Russian Armies—dating far back to their first meeting, when both were still in their early teens—brought a sharp note of discord into the relations between the younger members of the imperial family: one had to decide whether one supported the tall Nicholasha or whether one's sympathies were with the learned Nicholas Michailovich.

Although a complete novice in St. Petersburg I had passed severe judgment on the "enemy" of my elder brother long in advance of our actual encounter in 1879; when I met him for the first time in my life at the Sunday family dinner in the Winter Palace I saw no reason to change my opinion.

There they sat, every one of my relatives, at the long table shining with baccara glasses and gold plate. The Emperor, the sweetness of his lovable character plainly marked in his soft large eyes; the heir apparent, stern, domineering, the bulk of his tremendous body making him look much older than his thirty-four years; Grand Duke Vladimir, esthetic, but rough; Grand Duke Alexis, the recognized Beau Brummell of the imperial family and the idol of the "belles of Washington" where he was in a habit of going at regular intervals; Grand Duke Sergei, snobbish, unapproachable, boredom and contempt written on his young face; Grand Duke Paul, the handsomest son of the Emperor and by far the most "democratic" one.

The four "Constantinovichi" were grouped around their father, Grand Duke Constantin, who was extremely unpopular among the "die-hards" of the family on account of his liberal political opinions.

And then our "enemy" Nicholasha! The tallest man in the Winter Palace, which was quite an achievement considering that six-feet-one represented at that time the average height in the imperial family. He must have stood six-feet-five in his stockinged feet, for even my father looked considerably smaller. All during the dinner Nicholasha kept such an erect position that I expected each moment to hear the bars of the National Anthem. Once in a while he shot a cold glance in the direction of the Caucasians and then quickly lowered his eyes, for he was met with a veritable salvo of chilling looks.

At the end of the dinner my policy was set: I decided to strengthen my friendship with Nicky and Georgie, whom I had met during our summer stays in the Crimea, and I was willing to take for playmates Grand Duke Paul and Grand Duke Dimitry Constantinovich. As for the rest of them, I wanted to keep as much room between us as would be permitted by the rules of etiquette and civility. Looking at the proud faces of my cousins I realized that the choice lay between becoming popular or keeping my personality intact. And so it happened that not only in the autumn of 1879 but in the course of all my life in Russia I had very little to do with the members of the imperial family outside of Nicky, his sisters and my own brothers. Poor Georgie died of galloping consumption in my house at Borjom in 1899. Grand Duke Paul (father of Grand Duchess Marie) contracted a morganatic marriage in 1902 and was obliged to leave Russia; as for Dimitry Constantinovich, he developed at an early age some very specific interests—limited to horses and military affairs—which did not favor the growth of our intimacy, although we always remained good friends.

Some day, a novelist possessing the qualifications of an Emile Zola and unafraid of spending long years in research and study, should choose the history of the modern Romanoffs as a subject deserving as many volumes as the epic of the Rougon-Macquards. Fathers and sons, cousins and brothers, uncles and nephews, we were all so different in our characters, inclinations and interests that it is almost impossible to believe that but forty short years and two reigns stood between the death of the Iron Ruler of Europe, Emperor Nicholas I, and the ascension to the throne of his hapless great-grandson, the last Czar of all the Russias: Nicholas II.

7

The marriage of my sister Anastasia signified in a certain measure the break-up of our family. My elder three brothers were about to commence their service in the Guards, and a decision had to be taken as to what should be done with me. In any event, it was plain that very soon we would have to be separated from each other. Anastasia was the first one to take up her own life. Tall, slim and dark-haired, she presented a really striking picture in her heavy silver dress—the traditional wedding gown of all grand duchesses—as the Emperor led her at the head of a solemn procession, including the representatives of all the reigning houses of Europe, through the long halls of the Winter Palace to the adjoining chapel. Immediately after the first wedding, performed according to the rites of the Greek Orthodox Church, a second one was conducted by the Protestant minister inside the palace. In such a way both the Emperor of Russia and the Emperor of Germany were given full satisfaction, and their relatives, Grand Duchess Anastasia of Russia and Grand Duke Friedrich of Mecklenburg-Schwerin, were united twice within forty minutes.

A family lunch served after the second religious ceremony and a state dinner at night filled the program of the day. Next morning was allotted to the reception of the foreign ambassadors and various court dignitaries. Then another family meal had to be attended. Only at the end of the second day were the newly-weds permitted to board their special train that was to take them to Germany.

The whistle blew, the guard of honor presented arms, and we lost our Anastasia. Mother cried; father pulled at his glove. The heartless law that forced the members of the Russian reigning house to marry foreigners of royal blood scored its first casualty in our family; it was to continue its tyranny up to the year 1894, when I broke its validity by marrying Grand Duchess Xenia, daughter of my cousin Emperor Alexander III.

The departure of Anastasia made my mother decide to go abroad in the spring. Officially she wanted her sons to meet her brother, the Grand Duke of Baden; unofficially she longed to see her favorite child. It meant that for four months we would have to be separated from the Caucasus by thousands of miles. I tried every conceivable ruse to be permitted to return to Tiflis but my parents were not in a habit of soliciting my advice. Thus, in the summer of 1880 I met for the first time the representatives of a nation which was destined to loom so large in my future life. There were two pretty American girls playing tennis in the park, not far from the ducal palace. I lost my heart to both of them, unable to decide which one of the two I liked better. This fact, however, had no influence on our relations, for I was strictly forbidden to talk to any and all Americans, an aide-de-camp of the Grand Duke of Baden watching my movements at close range. The girls noticed my admiring glances and unaware of the cruel edict of my mother decided that I must be either too shy or too stupid or both. Each time they would finish playing a hard-disputed set, they would come to rest on a bench next to the spot where I stood. Talking in a theatrical whisper they would pass remarks damaging to my manly self-respect.

"What is the matter with that boy?" the taller girl would ask. "Can it be that he is deaf and dumb? Do you think we should learn the language of the mutes?"

I wished to God the damnable aide-de-camp would leave me alone for a few minutes, so that I could show to those adorable creatures what kind of a mute I was, but the German officers are taught to obey orders implicitly: if necessary he would have stood by my side for forty-eight consecutive hours. Even my shy attempts at smiling became known at the palace and were seized upon as an occasion for merciless teasing by both my brothers and my German cousins led by the future Reich Chancellor Prince Max of Baden. I began to find short notes under my pillow written by Michael and George but signed—"your loving American girls." Tiny American flags would be stuck in the back of my overcoat, and my appearance in the drawing-room would be greeted by a few bars of a popular American march played on the piano by one of the torturers. After two weeks of silent struggle I gave in and kept away from the tennis court for the remainder of our stay in Baden-Baden.

In the beginning of that autumn we returned to Tiflis.

CHAPTER FOUR

AN EMPEROR IN LOVE

I

ON a foggy evening in the winter of 1880, a heavy explosion shook the Winter Palace in St. Petersburg, wrecking the quarters of the Guards situated on the ground floor and killing forty officers and soldiers. It occurred exactly at the moment when the grand master of ceremonies appeared on the threshold of the dining-room with his usual announcement—"His Majesty, the Emperor."

A slight mathematical error in the construction of the infernal machine which was placed in the basement saved the private apartments of the Czar from destruction. Just a few pieces of crockery were broken and several windows shattered.

A hurried investigation revealed the simultaneous disappearance of a recently hired janitor. The latter, no doubt, belonged to the same revolutionary party—nicknamed "nihilists" because of their determination to annihilate everything pertaining to the existing régime—which had commenced its terroristic activities in the early seventies and had gained additional momentum thanks to the system of criminal trials by jury introduced by the liberal Alexander II. Acquittal was almost assured for its members, and a young girl, Vera Zasoulich, who fired at the Governor-General of St. Petersburg in 1878 had the unique opportunity of hearing the presiding justice make an eloquent speech in her defense.

Writers, students, doctors, lawyers, bankers, merchants and high officials appeared equally anxious to see a republic established in the country that had witnessed the liberation of the serfs but nineteen years previously. Eighty per cent of the nation still remained illiterate but the impatient intelligentsia demanded the immediate granting of the universal franchise and the convocation of a parliament invested with extraordinary powers. The willingness to compromise displayed by the throne whetted the appetites of the would-be prime ministers, while the extreme weakness of the police encouraged the unperturbed development of the most daring revolutionary schemes.

The idea of regicide was in the air. Nobody felt it keener than Dostoievsky whose writings should be today considered a veritable prophecy of the Bolshevik upheaval. Shortly before his untimely death, in January, 1881, during a conversation with the famous Russian editor, Souvorin, he said in a tone of astounding sincerity:

"You seem to think that there was a great deal of clairvoyance in my last novel *Brothers Karamazoff*, but wait till you read its sequel. I am working on it now. I am taking Alesha Karamazoff out of his holy retreat in the monastery and am making him join the nihilists. My pure Alesha shall kill the Czar!"

2

The news of the tragic events in the Winter Palace made my father decide to go to St. Petersburg. He could not bear being separated by twelve hundred miles from his beloved imperial brother, and we were told to prepare to spend the coming winter in the north.

A dense cloud of gloom hung over the entire country. The official cheerfulness of the numerous generals who met us at the big stations along the route failed to disguise their anguish. Everybody understood that the Czar would not be able to escape much longer the continuous attempts on his life unless a firmer hand took the trembling wheel of state. The old-timers thought my father should be put in charge of the Government because his sterling soldierly qualities were favorably known throughout Russia.

Few people realized that even the most influential members of the imperial family had to reckon at that moment with the power of a woman, strange in their midst. We children learned of her existence on the eve of the arrival of our special train to the capital, when we were summoned to the salon car.

We saw at once that a heated conversation must have taken place between our parents. The face of our mother was covered with red spots while father puffed at a long black cigar, a thing he seldom risked doing in her presence.

"Listen, boys," said father, pulling at the Cross of St. George which he had received for conquering the Western Caucasus and which was always attached to the high collar of his coat, "there is something I want to tell you before we reach St. Petersburg. You have to be ready to meet the new Empress of Russia at your first dinner in the palace."

"She is not an Empress as yet," interrupted mother; "do not forget that the real Empress of Russia has died only ten months ago."

Father jumped up and stood erect, his six-feet-three towering over us.

"I wish you would let me finish," he said sharply, raising his deep voice, "we are, all of us, faithful subjects of the Emperor. We have no right whatsoever to criticize *his* decisions. A grand duke has to take his orders in the same spirit a simple soldier does. As I started to explain to you, boys, your imperial uncle deigned to marry Princess Dolgorouky. He has bestowed upon her the title of Princess Yourievskaya to be used until the period of state mourning for your late Aunt Marie has passed. Then Princess Yourievskaya shall be crowned Empress of Russia, but even now you are supposed to kiss her hand and follow all the other rules prescribed by etiquette. There are likewise three children by this second marriage of the Czar. A boy and two girls. They are naturally your cousins. Be friendly with them."

"Je pense que vous allez un peu fort quand même (I think you are going a little too strong)," remarked mother, trying to control her temper.

We five boys looked at each other. I remembered that during our previous stay in St. Petersburg we were not permitted to approach a large apartment in the Winter Palace occupied by a beautiful lady and several small children.

"How old are our new cousins?" suddenly asked my brother Sergei, who even at the age of eleven possessed an inclination for getting all available data.

Father did not like his question. He looked displeased.

"The boy is seven, the girls are six and four," he said dryly.

"How is it possible . . ." commenced Sergei, but father raised his hand:

"That will be all, boys. You may return to your car!"

We spent the balance of our journey discussing the mysterious goings-on in the Winter Palace. We decided that father must surely have made an error and that the Emperor was married to Princess Yourievskaya for much longer than ten months. But then it looked as though he possessed two wives at the same time. The real meaning of mother's distress became clear to me much later. She was horrified lest a bad example should confront her unspoiled children: the ominous word "mistress" had been rigorously kept out of our dictionary up to then.

3

Even the impassive grand master of ceremonies was visibly embarrassed next Sunday night, when the members of the imperial family gathered around the dinner-table in the Winter Palace ready to pass their pitiless judgment on "that awful woman." His voice expressed grave misgivings as he announced, tapping the floor three times with his ivory-handled staff:

"His Majesty, the Emperor, and Princess Yourievskaya."

My mother turned her head away in plain disgust. My future mother-in-law, then the wife of the heir apparent, Grand Duke Alexander Alexandrovich, lowered her eyes. She would not have minded it so much for herself but she was thinking of her sister Alexandra married to the Prince of Wales. What will old Queen Victoria say when she hears of this disgrace? . . .

The Emperor walked in briskly with a strikingly attractive woman on his arm. He gave a gay wink to my father and then sized up the massive figure of the heir apparent. He counted on the loyalty of the former but had no illusions as to the attitude of the latter. Princess Yourievskaya gracefully acknowledged the formal bows of the grand duchesses and sat down in Empress Marie Alexandrovna's chair! Prompted by curiosity, I never took my eyes off her. I liked the sad expression of her beautiful face and the radiance of her rich blond hair. Her nervousness was obvious. Frequently she turned to the Emperor, and he patted her hand gently. She would have succeeded in conquering the men had they not been watched by the women. Her efforts to join the general conversation were met with a polite silence. I felt sorry for her and could not comprehend why she should be ostracized for loving a handsome, kind and cheerful man who happened to be the Emperor of Russia.

A long association did not dampen their mutual adoration in the least. At sixty-four Alexander II acted as a boy of eighteen. He whispered words of encouragement into her small ear; he wanted to know whether she liked the wine; he agreed with everything she said; he looked at his relatives with a friendly smile inviting them to enjoy his idyllic happiness, and joked with me and my brothers, extremely satisfied that at least we youngsters had taken a fancy to the poor princess.

At the end of the dinner the governess brought in the three children.

"Ah, there is my Gogo," exclaimed the Emperor proudly, lifting the vivacious boy in the air and placing him on his shoulder. "Tell us, Gogo, what is your full name?"

"I am Prince George Alexandrovich Yourievsky," replied Gogo, and started to arrange the side-whiskers of the Emperor, brushing them with his two little hands.

"Well, we are all very glad to have made your acquaintance, Prince Yourievsky. By the way, prince, would you care to be a grand duke?"

"Please, Sasha, don't," nervously said the princess. This joking reference to the possibility of legitimizing their morganatic children made her blush. For the first time during the evening she forgot all about etiquette and addressed her husband by his little name.

Fortunately, Gogo was too much engulfed in playing barber to His Majesty to consider the advantages of a resplendent imperial title, and the Czar did not insist on an answer. It became clear, however, that in his quiet unobtrusive way Alexander II had decided to ignore the sulkiness of the shocked grand duchesses, for even at this first family reunion he was chiefly interested in providing a joyful Sunday for his little children. After dinner a show was given by an Italian prestidigitator, and then the younger guests were taken by Gogo into the adjoining salon, where he demonstrated his skill in riding a bicycle and sliding down the so-called Russian Mountains sitting on a rug. The little chap wanted to make friends with everybody, particularly with my cousin Nicky who seemed to enjoy immensely the idea of having acquired a seven-year-old uncle at the age of thirteen.

On the way back home from the Winter Palace we witnessed another hopeless dispute between our parents.

"No matter what you say or do," declared our mother, "I shall never recognize that scheming adventuress. I hate her. She is despicable. Imagine her daring to call your brother 'Sasha' in the presence of all the members of the imperial family."

Father sighed and shook his head in despair.

"You still refuse to realize, my dear," he retorted rather meekly, "that whether she is good, bad or indifferent, she is married to the Czar. Since when is a wife forbidden to use her husband's little name in public? Do you ever address me as 'Your Imperial Highness'?"

"How can you make such a silly comparison," said mother and tears appeared in her eyes. "I did not break up a family. I married you with the consent of your family and mine. I am not plotting to ruin the empire."

It was the turn of father to get mad.

"I positively forbid you"—he emphasized every word—"to repeat such disgraceful gossip. The future Empress of Russia will be treated with courtesy by you and every other member of the imperial family, including the heir apparent and his wife. The subject is closed once and forever."

4

But nobody could have closed that exciting subject in the winter of 1880-1881. The members of the imperial household and the venerable leaders of St. Petersburg society were openly accusing Princess Yourievskaya of planning to entrust her favorite, General Loris-Melikoff, with dictatorial powers and to bring about radical changes in the Constitution.

As is always the case, the women proved to be particularly merciless in their denunciations of Gogo's mother. Guided by hurt vanity and blinded by bitter jealousy, they rushed from house to house repeating the wildest possible rumors and spreading poisonous calumny. It mattered not that Princess Yourievskaya belonged to the old historical family of Dolgoroukys who traced their origin directly to Rurick, the Scandinavian conqueror of Russia. In fact, it made her situation more precarious, the insatiable gossipers dwelling with

THE IMPERIAL FAMILY OF RUSSIA IN 1888. ON THE BALCONY,
LEFT TO RIGHT: GRAND DUCHESS XENIA, EMPEROR ALEXAN-
DER III HOLDING GRAND DUCHESS OLGA ON HIS SHOULDER, HEIR
APPARENT AND THE FUTURE CZAR NICHOLAS II, EMPRESS MARIE.
BELOW, LEFT TO RIGHT: GRAND DUKE GEORGE ALEXANDROVICH
("GEORGIE") AND GRAND DUKE MICHAEL ALEXANDROVICH
("MISHA").

GRAND DUKE
SERGEI MICHAILOVICH

GRAND
DUKE
NICHOLAS
MICHAILOVICH

GRAND DUKE
GEORGE MICHAILOVICH

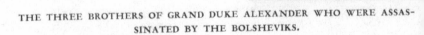

THE THREE BROTHERS OF GRAND DUKE ALEXANDER WHO WERE ASSAS-
SINATED BY THE BOLSHEVIKS.

relish upon the fantastic tales of the imaginary feud between the Romanoffs and the Dolgoroukys. They talked of a peasant prophet who had predicted two hundred years ago that swift death would befall any Romanoff marrying a Dolgorouky. They quoted the tragic end of Emperor Peter II to lend strength to this crazy theory. Did he not die on the day set for his wedding to the young Princess Nathaly Dolgorouky? Was it not significant that the best of physicians failed to save this only son of Peter the Great?

Our family doctor tried in vain to remind the superstitious scandalmongers that the medical science of the eighteenth century did not know how to fight smallpox, and that the young Emperor would have passed away in any event had he been engaged to the "luckiest" girl in the world. The gossipers appreciated his learned zeal but went ahead with their campaign. They thought it would require a greater eloquence than his to explain why the outburst of the present terroristic activities had coincided with the beginning of the romance of Alexander II.

"My dear doctor," said a titled lady of wide acquaintances, "with all due respect to the miracles of modern science, I really cannot see how the men of your profession could stop the nihilists from throwing bombs in the direction pointed out by our great Dictator . . ."

The last remark referred to General Loris-Melikoff whose conciliatory policies had aroused a storm of indignation in the ranks of the unemployed statesmen and the unrecognized saviors of the country. His spectacular career provided an inexhaustible topic for the fashionable tea parties. A brave commander of an army corps and an assistant of my father during the Russian-Turkish War in 1877-1878, he was described by the whisperers as the Man Friday of Princess Yourievskaya. Appointed to a post equivalent in importance to that of Prime Minister of England, he enjoyed the unlimited confidence of the Czar but his deep affection for the sovereign, no doubt, handicapped his actions: in a death-fight with the forces of anarchy he constantly kept in mind the pathetic vision of a pair of lovers in the Winter Palace begging him to prolong their short moments of happiness. The classical phrase about a man who knows the better way but prefers to follow the worst would have perfectly fitted the plight of this honest soldier. After a long period of hesitancy he decided to take the advice of a woman in love and to extend an olive branch to the nihilists. That in turn precipitated the tragic climax. The revolutionaries—a small fraction of the population of the larger cities—doubled their demands and threatened open revolt. The loyal supporters of the throne shrugged their shoulders in dismay and stepped aside. The people—one hundred twenty million peasants spread all over the empire—said that the landlords had hired an Armenian general to kill the Russian Czar because he had liberated the serfs!

A surprising conclusion but a logical one considering that outside of St. Petersburg, Moscow and a half dozen provincial towns where the daily papers were printed, the whole empire lived on rumors, and the grapevine telegraph provided the only channel for the spreading of political news. A well-known leader of the radical intelligentsia, Feodor Rodicheff, wrote in his memoirs that each time an important official was killed by the nihilists in the capital, the villagers reacted by burning the estate of a family suspected of revolutionary sympathies.

A cynical ruler could have easily used this singular mentality of the peasants for the purpose of upholding the principle of absolute monarchy, but the graduates of the Imperial Military Academy never were taught the fine art of governmental cynicism. On the eve of the New Year of 1881 General Loris-Melikoff placed on the desk of the Czar a project of radical reforms, which borrowed most of its ideas from the constitutions of England and France.

AN EMPEROR IN LOVE

+++

5

A series of festivities was planned for the month of January. The long illness of the late Empress and the uncertainty of Princess Yourievskaya's position had deprived the court of its pleasures for several years, so now the Emperor gave orders to arrange a magnificent state ball.

The enormous halls of the Winter Palace—so high that one could not see the ceilings—were decorated with orchids and other tropical flowers brought from the imperial hothouses; endless rows of palm trees were placed along the main stairway and in the mirrored corridors. Eight hundred attendants worked for two weeks putting everything in readiness, while the court caterers prepared to do their very best in the line of refreshments and various delicacies.

The end of the period of mourning gave a chance to the grand duchesses and the ladies of the court to display their priceless diamond diadems, pearl necklaces, emerald bracelets, sapphire brooches, and ruby rings, shining brightly in the light of the colossal chandeliers of the palace, against the impressive background of the glittering uniforms of the foreign ambassadors, courtiers, officers of the Guard regiments and visiting Oriental potentates.

I often speculate as to what happened to all this gorgeous jewelry. Is it being kept in the dark safes of the wholesale dealers in Amsterdam, London and Paris, or am I to see some day the famous sapphires of my mother decorating the arms of a gracious hostess in Park Avenue? I likewise wonder whether any of the two thousand odd men and women present on that January night in the Winter Palace in St. Petersburg could have foreseen that my cousin Nicky, pulling me by the sleeve to come and admire a real Persian Shah, would be shot in a cellar in Siberia thirty-seven years later?

Permitted to wear my uniform of colonel of the 73rd Krimsky Regiment, I strutted past the gigantic troopers of the Chevalier-Guards wearing helmets surmounted by the imperial double-headed eagle and stationed at the entrances to the halls. All during the evening I tried to keep away from my parents so that an inappropriate remark should not shatter my illusions of grandeur.

The arrival of the Emperor and Princess Yourievskaya accompanied by the elder grand dukes and the dignitaries of the court, gave the signal for the commencement of the ball. According to the etiquette it started with the polonaise, the Czar walking in the first pair with the wife of the heir apparent—a concession he had agreed to at the very last moment—and the grand dukes following in the order of priority. As there were not enough grand duchesses to be paired with the younger members of the imperial family, I had to dance with an elderly lady-in-waiting who remembered the childhood of my father.

Our procession—for the polonaise was really not a dance in the modern meaning of the word—had to pass through all the halls, with six chamberlains in front of us announcing our approach. We circled the palace three times, after which the dancing began in every hall, quadrille, waltz and mazurka being the only dances approved by etiquette.

As the clock struck midnight the dancing stopped and the Czar led the procession, in the same order as before, to the supper-tables. There was considerable speculation as to whether Princess Yourievskaya would actually sit down or follow the tradition of the sovereigns who always remained standing, walking from table to table and talking to the guests. To the utmost consternation of my dancing partner she did accompany the Emperor on his rounds of hospitality, but her face was twitching and her lips were tightly drawn.

Everybody noticed that General Loris-Melikoff left the room frequently. Each time on his return he approached the Czar and said a few words to him, no doubt reporting on the extraordinary measures of protection of the palace taken on the occasion of the ball. Their conversation was drowned by a chorus of the best artists of the imperial opera, who saddened the already tense atmosphere by a program made up of extremely mournful though beautiful songs. I never heard as yet of a Russian composer capable of writing gay music. Whatever the ultimate value of the French "chansons d'amour" or the American jazz may be, they could have certainly brought a desirable optimistic note into that gloomy ball. As it was, the ominous basses and the crying sopranos succeeded in chasing the cheerful smile from the Emperor's face. Working under a terrific strain, he tried to be pleasant with his guests but nobody could have been mistaken as to the attitude of his consort. She knew she was hated. She had no strength left to continue the struggle with the cruel world that would not forgive her success. She wanted to finish it all, at no matter what price. She would have consented to the declaration of a republic in order to be left alone with her Sasha and her children.

The imperial couple departed right after supper, thus suspending the rules of etiquette. Unrestricted dancing commenced, but my old lady-in-waiting fell asleep. I ran through the half-deserted halls to have a heart-to-heart talk with a former aide-de-camp of my father who had just arrived from Tiflis. I was anxious to hear the news of the dear old Caucasus where one slept quietly unafraid of the noises of the street: a two months' stay in St. Petersburg made me hear an explosion in every suspicious sound.

6

To say that we lived in a besieged fortress would be using a very poor simile. During the war one knows one's friends and enemies. We never did. The butler serving morning coffee might have been in the employ of the nihilists for all we knew. Ever since the November explosion a janitor coming to clean the fireplace was a potential bearer of an infernal machine.

The tremendous territory occupied by St. Petersburg made it impossible for the police to guarantee the safety of the members of the imperial family outside the walls of their palaces. The grand dukes begged the Emperor to transfer his residence to a much smaller palace situated in the well-protected suburban village of Gatchino, but the easy-going Alexander II had fully inherited the personal courage of his stern father, Nicholas I; he refused to leave the capital and he would not agree to change the itinerary of his daily drives. He insisted on following the usual routine, which included his walks in the public park and the Sunday review of the troops of the Guard. Nothing made our mother more nervous than the fact that our father was obliged to escort the Czar to this weekly parade. He laughed at her fears, pointing out that the loyalty of the army could not be questioned, but her unerring female instinct was stronger than logic.

"I am not afraid of the officers or the soldiers," she used to say, "but I have no faith in the local police, particularly on a Sunday. It is a long drive to the parade hall and every nihilist in town can see you passing through the streets. In any event, I will not permit you to risk the lives of the children. They shall stay at home from now on."

And so it happened that on Sunday, March 1, 1881, my father went to the parade at half past one as usual, while we boys decided to go skating in company with Nicky and his mother. We were to fetch them at the Winter Palace shortly after three.

At three o'clock sharp we heard the sound of a strong explosion.

"That was a bomb all right," said my brother George, "no mistake about that sound."

At this moment a still stronger explosion shattered the windows in our room. We made for the street but our military tutor held us back. Just then a servant rushed in, all out of breath.

"The Emperor has been killed," he screamed, "and your

father too. Their bodies are being taken to the Winter Palace."

Mother heard his words and ran out of her apartment. We took her to the waiting carriage and started a mad race toward the Winter Palace, passing on our way the Preobrajensky Regiment of the Guard quick-stepping in the same direction with fixed bayonets.

Thousands of people were already surrounding the palace. The women cried hysterically. We entered by the side door. There was no need to ask questions: large drops of black blood showed us the way up the marble steps of the stairs and then along a corridor into the study of the Emperor. Our father stood at the door giving orders to a group of officials. He had to lift mother in his arms. She had fainted on seeing him alive.

The Emperor lay on the couch near the desk. He was unconscious. Three doctors were fussing around but science was obviously helpless. It was a question of minutes. He presented a terrific sight, his right leg torn off, his left leg shattered, innumerable wounds all over his head and face. One eye was shut, the other expressionless.

Every instant members of the imperial family came in. The room was packed. I clung to the arm of Nicky, deathly pale in his blue sailor's suit. His mother, stunned by the catastrophe, was still holding a pair of skates in her trembling hands. I recognized the heir apparent by his broad shoulders; he was looking out of the window.

Princess Yourievskaya burst in half-dressed. Something or perhaps some overzealous guard had detained her. She fell flat on the couch over the body of the Czar, kissing his hands and screaming: "Sasha, Sasha!" It was unbearable. The grand duchesses began to sob aloud.

The agony lasted forty-five minutes. Not a detail of this scene could ever be forgotten by those who witnessed it. I am the only one left, all the others are dead, nine having been shot by the Bolsheviks thirty-seven years later.

The room was furnished in a rich Empire style, with different valuable little nothings ("bibelots") spread over the small tables and numerous pictures decorating the walls. Attached to the door was an enlarged photograph of my brothers, Nicholas, Michael, George, and myself drilling with the mountain gun in our Tiflis garden. The sight of it nearly broke my heart.

"Steady, my boy, steady," whispered the heir apparent, taking me by the shoulder.

The chief of police arrived with a complete report of the tragedy. The first bomb killed two passers-by and wounded a Cossack officer who was mistaken for my father on account of the similarity of their uniforms. The Emperor, unhurt, got out of the carriage. The coachman begged him to get off the sidewalk and proceed to the palace but he insisted on personally aiding the wounded. Then a man standing on the corner threw the second and fatal bomb, less than a minute before my father reached this spot. The fact that he had been detained by a visit to Grand Duchess Catherine saved his life.

"Silence, please," said a hoarse voice, "the end is near."

We came closer to the couch. That expressionless eye was still staring fixedly. The chief court surgeon, who was feeling the Czar's pulse, nodded and let the blood-covered hand drop.

"The Emperor is dead," he announced loudly. Princess Yourievskaya gave one shriek and dropped on the floor like a felled tree. Her pink-and-white negligee was soaked in blood.

We all knelt and prayed. Looking to my right I saw the new ruler of all the Russias. A strange change had already come over him. I could not believe it was the same Grand Duke Alexander Alexandrovich who liked to astound the little friends of his son Nicky by tearing a pack of cards or tying an iron poker into knots. In less than five minutes he had acquired a new personality. Something much bigger than a mere realization of imperial responsibilities had transformed his massive frame. A sort of sacred determination had suddenly appeared in his cold sharp eyes. He rose, and his relatives stood at attention.

"Have you any orders to give, Your Majesty?" asked the chief of police, who in the meanwhile had grown several inches smaller.

"Orders?" replied Alexander III. "Yes, of course. The police have apparently lost their heads. The army will take charge of the situation. I shall confer with my ministers at once in the Anichkoff Palace."

He motioned to his wife, and they walked out together, her tiny figure accentuating his bulk.

The crowds gathered outside the palace raised a tremendous cheer. No other Romanoff ever came so near to the popular conception of a Czar as this bearded giant with the shoulders of a Hercules.

Clinging to the windows we watched him march with long strides toward the carriage, his wife running after him. He stood for a while on the curb saluting the people, and then drove away, accompanied by a whole regiment of Don Cossacks galloping in attack formation, their red lances shining brightly in the last rays of a crimson March sunset.

Two guardsmen carried Princess Yourievskaya to her apartment, and the doctors proceeded to dress the body of the late Emperor.

Gogo was crying in tormented bewilderment.

CHAPTER FIVE

THE WINDLESS AFTERNOONS

Only as I gaze upon those windless afternoons, I find myself
always saying to myself involuntarily: "The evening will be a
wet one." The storm is always brooding through the massy
splendor of the trees, above those sun-dried glades or lawns,
where delicate children may be trusted thinly clad; and the
secular trees themselves will hardly outlast another generation.—
WALTER PATER, *A Prince of Court Painters.*

I

SHADOWS of tall candles. Chanting priests. Beautiful singing of a mammoth choir. Bald heads of kneeling generals.
Tear-stained faces of grand duchesses. Whisperings of worried courtiers. And all eyes centered upon the two Emperors: one lying in the coffin, peace and resignation written
on his face marred by the dark blots of wounds; another
standing by his side, forceful, majestic, subduing sorrow and
immune to fear.

Twice a day, seven days in succession, we attended the
divine services in the Winter Palace. The transportation of
the body to the Fortress of Peter and Paul took place on the
morning of the eighth day. The people wanted to see once
more the Czar-Liberator, so the longest route had to be
chosen enabling the procession to pass through the principal
streets of the capital.

We felt exhausted. Our nerves were strained. Physical
fatigue combined with anxiety brought us all to the verge of
hysteria. At night we sat in our beds, brooding over the
catastrophe of the previous Sunday and asking ourselves what
was going to happen next. The image of the man bending

over the body of a wounded Cossack and braving more bombs would not leave our minds. We knew that something immeasurably greater than a loving uncle and a courageous emperor had receded with him into the past. Idyllic Russia, the country of the ruling father and obedient sons ceased to exist on March 1, 1881. Never again would a Russian Czar be able to think of his subjects in terms of boundless confidence; never again would he be allowed to give his undisturbed attention to the cares of the state. The romantic traditions of the past and the sentimental conceptions of sovereignty followed Alexander II to his tomb in the Fortress of Peter and Paul. They too were mortally wounded by the explosion of that tragic Sunday, and nobody could have denied that the future of the empire, possibly of the entire world, depended upon the issue of the coming contest between the new Czar of Russia and the fast increasing forces of destruction.

2

Fortunately enough, Alexander III possessed all the qualities of a great administrator. A confirmed believer in the policies dictated by healthy national egotism, a thorough disciplinarian and a thinker of pronounced skepticism, he brought to the throne a complete freedom from all illusions. He had watched the passing show of the imperial court sufficiently long to acquire contempt for his father's collaborators, while his knowledge of the rulers of contemporary Europe gave birth to his well-motivated distrust of their intentions. He blamed the majority of Russia's ills on the irresponsible liberalism governing our domestic affairs and on an asinine tendency toward catering to the foreign powers, a tendency which influenced the actions of our diplomats.

Twenty-four hours after the funeral of his father, he announced a long series of swift reforms. Everything and everybody were to be changed: ministers, ambassadors, methods, mentality. He commenced by getting rid of General

Loris-Melikoff and all other members of the cabinet. Their successors were found outside the ranks of the courtiers, which created immediate jealousies among the idle chatterers of St. Petersburg.

"The days of the darkest reaction are here," said the disconsolate leaders of a would-be republic, but the biographies of the new ministers gave the lie to this biased opinion. Prince Khilkoff, entrusted with the administration of railroads and highways, spent his adventurous youth in the United States working as a hired laborer in the mines of Pennsylvania. Professor Vyshnegradsky enjoyed international recognition for the originality of his economic theories; his cleverness restored Russian finances to a flourishing state and contributed largely to the industrialization of our rural empire. General Vannovsky, the famous hero of the Russo-Turkish War, took charge of the army. Admiral Shestakoff, exiled by Alexander II because of his bitter criticism of the organization of our fleet, was recalled from Paris and made Minister of the Navy. Count Tolstoi, the new Minister of the Interior, was the first Russian administrator to realize that the prosperity of the peasant class should be considered the main care of the Imperial Government. Sergei Witte, a former modest employee of the South-Western railways and the future Prime Minister of Russia, likewise owed his meteoric rise to the farsightedness of Alexander III, who nominated him Under-Secretary of State, recognizing the unquestionable genius of this awkward gaunt provincial.

The appointment of Count de Giers, a soft-spoken gentleman known for his lack of initiative, to the post of Minister of Foreign Affairs caused a certain amazement both at home and abroad. The Emperor chuckled. He would have preferred to be his own Minister of Foreign Affairs but as he had to have a "dummy" in the foreign office, he decided to choose a faithful clerk who would be sure to follow the ideas of his master and who would be able to clothe the sometimes abrupt language of the Czar in the niceties of the high-mannered chancelleries. The record of the following thirteen years proved his wisdom. No "brilliant international mind" and no "favorite of all the capitals of Europe" could have outdone timorous De Giers in the religious execution of the Emperor's orders. For the first time in centuries Russia acquired a clear-cut international policy.

His cabinet formed and a plan of action worked out, Alexander III next turned toward the turbulent problem of the safety of the imperial family. He solved it in the only logical way by moving his residence to the Palace of Gatchino. His pride was hurt: "To think that after having faced the guns of the Turks I must retreat now before those skunks," he exclaimed in a fury. He realized, however, that Russia could ill afford to lose two Czars within one year. In so far as his work was concerned, he benefited greatly by the distance separating Gatchino from St. Petersburg. It provided him with an alibi for curtailing his innumerable social duties and it kept his relatives from calling on him too frequently. The family reunions bored him. He thought it extremely silly to waste so much valuable time in meaningless conversations with his brothers, uncles and cousins. He did not mind the youngsters—myself and Sergei paying almost daily visits to Nicky and Georgie—but he had no patience for the eternal demands of the grown-ups. During his reign the imperial palace became just what it should be: a place housing the busiest man in Russia.

3

Thanks to the British Government, Alexander III was given an early opportunity of demonstrating the firmness of his international policy. Less than a year after his ascension to the throne a grave incident took place on the Russo-Afghan border: prompted by the British, who viewed our progress in Turkestan with alarm, the Afghans invaded our territory in the neighborhood of the fortress Koushka. General Komaroff, the commander of that military district, wired to the Emperor and asked for instructions. "Drive them back and give them a sound thrashing," came the answer from Gatchino. The Afghans were routed and pursued several miles beyond the border, our Cossacks being anxious to catch the group of British instructors who were able, however, to escape owing to the superiority of their mounts.

The Government of Her Britannic Majesty registered a "most strenuous protest" and demanded "apologies." "We will do nothing of the kind," said Alexander III, "and what is more, I shall bestow a decoration upon General Komaroff. Nobody is permitted to invade our territory."

De Giers was trembling.

"Do you realize, Your Majesty, that it may mean war with England?"

"Even so."

Another threatening note arrived from London. This time the Czar ordered the mobilization of our Baltic fleet. A gesture of supreme courage, considering that the British Navy outnumbered our sea forces by at least five to one. Several weeks passed. London became strangely silent and finally suggested appointing a special commission to settle the Russo-Afghan question.

Europe began to look with different eyes in the direction of Gatchino. The young Russian Czar was obviously a person to be reckoned with.

Provocation number two came from Austria. The Vienna Government objected to our "continuous interference in the zone of influence of the Dual Monarchy," and the Austrian ambassador in St. Petersburg endeavored to give Alexander III a war scare. At a state dinner in the palace, while seated across the table from the Czar, he began discussing the troublesome Balkan question. The host ignored his remarks. The ambassador grew hotter. He said something about the possibility of Austria mobilizing two or three army corps. Never changing his habitual half-mocking facial expression, Alexander III picked up a silver fork, bent it into a knot, and threw it in the direction of the Austrian ambassador.

"That is what I am going to do to your two or three army corps," he added quietly.

"We have just two allies in this world," he used to repeat to his ministers, "our army and our navy. Everybody else will turn on us on a second's notice."

He expressed this cynical belief of his in a rather demonstrative form at a dinner given in the honor of the visiting Prince Nicholas of Montenegro and attended by all the foreign ambassadors. Raising his glass to drink the health of the guest, he deemed it advisable to explain his toast in the following words: "I am drinking the health of my friend, Nicholas of Montenegro, who is the only sincere and loyal friend possessed by Russia outside our borders."

De Giers opened his mouth; the ambassadors turned pale. The London *Times* next morning spoke of the "most amazing speech made by the Emperor of Russia upsetting all traditions of intercourse between friendly countries."

While Europe was still debating the consequences of the Koushka incident, the Czar came out with another declaration which made the Government of Her Britannic Majesty question the authenticity of its St. Petersburg ambassador's dispatch. Ignoring the provisions of the ignominious Peace Treaty of 1855, which forbade Russia's keeping a battle fleet in the Black Sea, Alexander III decided to launch several modern cruisers right in the same harbor of Sebastopol where the victorious allies had humiliated our country during the Crimean War. He had chosen an extremely opportune moment for his action as with the possible exception of England no European power felt inclined to threaten the Russian Empire. France was bitter against England for the latter's noncommittal attitude in the war of 1870-1871; Turkey remembered the lesson she received from us in 1877-1878; Austria was being kept in check by Bismarck who dreamed of concluding a Russo-German Alliance. The Iron Chancellor's project would have, no doubt, become a reality had it not been for the extreme dislike felt by Alexander III for the hysterical young Kaiser. Both the German sovereign and his illustrious Svengali failed to understand the character of the Russian Czar. In the course of their visit to St. Petersburg they behaved in a thoroughly disgusting manner. Kaiser Wilhelm made too many blatant speeches, while Bismarck dared to lecture Alexander III on the art of governing. It ended badly. Bismarck received a terrific calling down. The young Kaiser was simply laughed at. The interview between the two sovereigns had presented to its witnesses an instructive study in contrasts. The Kaiser pacing the floor, gesticulating, raising his voice, and quoting all the stock expressions of the international manipulators; the Czar, cool, reserved, externally amused by Wilhelm's excitability but internally offended by the cheapness of his methods.

Those of us who lived to see the cataclysm of 1914 are naturally inclined to reproach Alexander III for letting his personal feelings get the better of his richly developed sense of practical politics: how did it happen that this stalwart champion of common sense rejected the propositions of Germany and approved of the perilous pact with France? The explanation is simple. Not counting on the mistakes of his successor and not anticipating to see his empire bled white by the Japanese War and the abortive revolution of 1905, he overestimated our military strength. He believed that the cause of a perpetual peace in Europe would be better served through our extending moral support to the Republic of France and thus warning Germany against any attempts at repeating the adventure of 1870. The possibility of France getting involved in the bitter Anglo-German struggle for commercial supremacy of the world never entered his mind. Had he lived longer he would have rejected indignantly the rôle of a Franco-British steam-roller which was allotted to Russia in 1914.

He wanted peace, a century of uninterrupted peace. Nothing short of an open attack against Russia would have

TWO VIEWS OF THE AY-TODOR ESTATE OF GRAND DUKE
ALEXANDER.

CZAR
NICHOLAS II
WITH
GRAND DUKE
ALEXANDER IN
1914. GRAND
DUCHESS XENIA
IS SEATED IN
BACK OF
GRAND DUKE
ALEXANDER

CZAR
NICHOLAS II
PAYING A
VISIT TO
GRAND DUKE
MICHAEL
NICHOLAEVICH
(GRAND DUKE
ALEXANDER'S
FATHER)
SHORTLY
BEFORE THE
LATTER'S DEATH
IN 1909

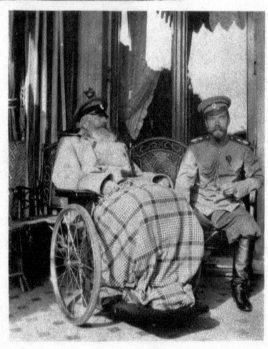

forced him to participate in a war, for the experience of the nineteenth century had taught him that each time we joined this or that party of professional European cock-fighters we shed bitter tears of regret later on. His granduncle Alexander I saved Europe from Napoleon, with the result that we helped to create the powerful states of Germany and Austria right across our border. His grandfather Nicholas I sent our army to Hungary in 1848 to protect the throne of the Hapsburgs against the attacks of the revolutionaries, and was rewarded by seeing the "grateful" Emperor Franz-Joseph standing back of the Allies besieging Sebastopol in 1854. His father Alexander II remained neutral in 1870, keeping good the word given by him to Emperor Wilhelm I, and eight years later Bismarck despoiled us of the fruits of our victory over the Turks.

The French, the British, the Germans, the Austrians—they were all alike in their perennial efforts to turn Russia into a weapon for their egotistical combats. Alexander III loathed the whole of Europe. Ever ready to accept its challenges, he made it unmistakably clear, however, that Russia was interested only in that which actually affected the welfare of 150,000,000 Russians.

4

The twenty-six months that elapsed between the assassination of Alexander II and the coronation of Alexander III, were marked by a magic improvement in the internal situation of Russia. The magnificent autocrat of Gatchino had dealt the revolution a severe blow. The majority of the nihilists were caught and punished; the minority went into hiding and exile. "A new deal for the peasants," proclaimed from the steps of the throne, signified that the Czar understood the necessity of bridging the gap between palace and people. The institute of the "Rural Magistrates" ("Zemsky Nachalnyk") created in 1882 filled the gap left wide open by the Manifesto of the Liberator of the Serfs. Acting in their capacity of official representatives of the Government, these magistrates assumed an important place in the life of the villages. They provided agricultural advice, they acted as lawyers, they supplied information about the free lands distributed by the Government to willing emigrants in Siberia and Turkestan, they helped the peasants secure loans and market farm products; but most important of all, they became instrumental in exterminating that subconscious anarchism of the Russian village which was molded by the centuries of Tartar oppressors and Moscow head-tax collectors. In order to appreciate the shrewdness of this particular reform of Alexander III, one has to realize that the Russian peasants liked the Czar but hated the state. Unaware of the vital functions fulfilled by the state, they viewed it as a monster that grabbed everything, giving nothing in return. The state demanded its recruits, it extracted its dues, it recited the endless list of its "don'ts," but it never gave the least bit of encouragement. As long as they remained serfs they felt that the landlord—bad as he was—protected them against the onslaught of the state; having obtained freedom in 1861 they lost the privilege of enlisting the assistance of their master and became an easy prey to the garrulous agitators who were promising the advent of a golden stateless era. Naturally enough, the appearance of the rural magistrate was met at first by hostile whispers and suspicious glances. The consensus of opinion had it that the state was sending "spies." The task of the new officials proved to be extremely hard; it called for tact and diplomacy. The confidence of the peasants had to be gained inch by inch.

Alexander III took a vivid interest in the progress made by his "ambassadors to Their Majesties the Villagers," intending to follow up the trial period of their activities with another reform, which was to help the peasants increase their meager land-holdings. It was unfortunate that his premature death interfered with the realization of his favorite idea of creating a strong class of prosperous peasants, although the rural magistrates did render an important service to the state, their unpopularity among the revolutionaries testifying to the fact of their usefulness. Talking to the delegation of the peasants at his coronation in Moscow on May 15, 1883, the Czar asked them to express their frank opinion of the institute of the rural magistrates. Old and young alike—there were some ten thousand villagers from different parts of Russia— voiced their unanimous approval of the friendly "chinov-nicks" (government officials) and hoped to see them invested with additional judicial authority.

5

No outline of the reign of Alexander III could faithfully depict that new proud "imperial spirit" which characterized Russia in the eighties without describing the coronation of 1883. The foreigners who spent the unforgettable week of May 10-17 in Moscow carried away an impression of having seen history itself in the making. It was as though the new Russia with all its incredible possibilities had suddenly revealed its face in the ancient capital of the first Romanoffs.

As early as the end of April the influx of hundreds of thousands of visitors from the provinces and from abroad nearly tripled the population of the city. Special trains were coming in every hour of the day bringing the crowned heads of Europe, the members of the various royal families and representatives of the foreign Governments. The minister of the imperial court, appointed at the head of the reception committee, went without food and sleep rushing from station to station, overseeing the last minute preparations and satisfying the requirements of a complicated etiquette. The sovereigns of Europe expected to be met by their equals, which meant that we, the grand dukes, would have to place our entire time at the disposal of the visitors. I drew the Archduke Albrecht of Austria and his remarkably beautiful wife Maria-Theresa. We became friends at once, although it was tiresome for me to be their guide and to provide them with endless explanations dealing with the churches, the museums, the historical buildings, and the saints of the Kremlin. I must have acquitted myself rather well of this unenviable task because at the end of the celebrations they expressed a desire to visit St. Petersburg and asked the Czar for the pleasure of my escort.

An official state entry to Moscow headed the long program of celebrations. At half past nine in the morning on May 12, the Russian grand dukes and the foreign princes arrived on horseback at the Troitzky Palace to escort the Emperor to the Kremlin. At ten o'clock sharp Alexander III came out of the inner apartments, mounted his horse and gave the signal for departure. He rode in front of us, all by himself, a squadron of the Horse Guards forming vanguard and announcing his approach to the troops and to the civilian population lining the streets of our march. A long file of golden carriages followed our cavalcade, Empress Marie, her eight-year-old daughter Xenia, and Queen Olga of Greece occupying the first one, the others being reserved for the Russian grand duchesses, princesses of royal blood and elder ladies-in-waiting.

Stupendous shouts of "hurrah" accompanied us all the way to the Iverskaya Chapel where the Emperor dismounted and together with the Empress went inside for a short moment of worshiping at the shrine of the miraculous ikon of the Virgin. We entered the Kremlin through the "Spasskya Vorota" (the Gates of the Saviour) and rode straight to the Cathedral of the Archangels. A Te Deum officiated at by the metropolitan of Moscow and sung by the choir of the singers of the imperial opera concluded the official program of the day. The afternoon of May 12, and the whole of May 13 and 14 were occupied by an exchange of visits between the imperial family and European royalty and by all kinds of entertainment in their honor.

May 15 began with an imperial salute of one hundred and

one guns. Once more we assembled in the great hall of the palace at half past nine in the morning. This time we presented a colorful group, every one of the grand dukes and foreign princes wearing the uniform of his own regiment. I remember the Duke Alfred of Edinburgh, the younger son of Queen Victoria, strikingly imposing in his regalia of admiral of the British Navy. The Russian grand dukes for this occasion put on their diamond-studded chains of the Order of St. Andrew, which were worn around the neck and which supported a mammoth diamond double-headed eagle. The grand duchesses, the princesses of England, Germany, Austria, Denmark and Greece, and the ladies of the court displayed the biggest accumulation of glittering jewelry ever seen by me or anyone else, before or after May 15, 1883.

An uninterrupted, almost mystic silence filled the few minutes we had to wait for the sovereigns. We felt overawed by the deep religious significance of the approaching ceremony, and recognized that all words would have sounded false on the day the autocratic rights of the Russian Czar were to be bestowed upon him by an Act of God. No doubt, many a flamboyant republican would sneer at this last sentence of mine, but then the numerous scenes of the so-called "popular acclaim" witnessed by me in France and in the United States make me question the sincerity of democracy and the value of its opinions.

The Emperor and the Empress appeared as the clock struck ten. Accustomed to the simplicity of his pleasant life in Gatchino, the Czar showed his plain annoyance at the pompousness of the surroundings. "I know I have to do it," said the expression of his face, "but I want it to be distinctly understood that the sooner it is over the better I will feel."

The Empress, on the contrary, thoroughly enjoyed the proceedings. She liked meeting relatives. She loved to preside at solemn ceremonies. So miniature in comparison with the Czar, she had a radiant smile for everyone in the great hall. Covered with crown jewels and looking like some Oriental deity, she made her rounds, moving with small steps, the four court pages carrying her long, gold-and-ermine train. After the traditional "baise-main" (kissing of her hand by all parties present)—the Emperor standing in the center of the floor and watching this scene from under his heavy brows—the grand marshal of the court reported that everything was in readiness. The Emperor offered his arm to the Empress, and the procession started on its way out, through the halls filled with court dignitaries, ambassadors, ministers, and generals aides-de-camp.

According to the ceremonial, the imperial couple came out on the "Krasnoie Kriltzo" ("Red Porch"—"red" meaning "festive" in ancient Russian) and made the three traditional bows to the multitude of people packed in the large courts of the Kremlin. Deafening shouts of "hurrah" greeted the appearance of the sovereigns. It was the most touching moment of the coronation, bringing back to our minds the memories of the ancient Czars of Russia: beginning with Ivan III (fifteenth century) all masters of Russia expressed their close union with their subjects by making three bows from the steps of the "Krasnoie Kriltzo."

We now reached the stairs of an especially built wooden pathway covered with a red carpet which led into the Ouspensky (the Cathedral of the Assumption). From the place where I stood I could see the regalia of czardom, carried at the head of the procession by the highest officials of the state: the standard, the sword, the scepter, the globe, the shield, and the beautiful imperial crown.

Eight generals aides-de-camp were holding a red-and-gold canopy over the Emperor; eight chamberlains were holding a similar canopy over the Empress. The two field marshals of Russia—my father and my uncle Nicholas—walked immediately behind the Emperor, while the other members of the family and the foreign princes and princesses followed the Empress.

The Grenadier-Guards of the palace, wearing the uniforms

of 1812 and lined along the pathway, presented arms. The greatest bell of the Kremlin rang out once. The next moment the bells of the sixteen hundred Moscow churches started their joyous ringing, and the opening bars of the National Anthem gave the signal to a chorus of five hundred singers. Looking down at the ocean of waving hands and hatless heads I saw faces wet with tears. I tried to swallow the lump in my throat but failed in my efforts: the Russian triumphed over the Caucasian.

Three metropolitans and several scores of bishops met the sovereigns at the portal of the cathedral and escorted them to the two thrones mounted on special platforms. A large loge on the right was reserved for the members of the imperial family and the European royalty. The dignitaries of the court, the generals aides-de-camp, the ministers of the crown, and the foreign ambassadors found places in the loge on the left.

I listened impatiently to a lengthy divine service conducted by His Grace Isidor of St. Petersburg, the eldest metropolitan of Russia, anxiously awaiting the Great Climax.

At the end of what seemed to me several hours, the highest priest of the empire took the Crown of Russia, that lay on a red velvet cushion, and passed it to the Czar. Alexander III put it on his head with his own hands, and then taking another crown, the Crown of the Czarina, turned towards the Empress kneeling in front of him and placed it on her head, thus symbolizing the difference between the divine source of his power and the human origin of her prerogatives. The Empress stood up, and they both faced our loge, a supreme combination of stern majesty and graceful beauty.

Now the Emperor moved toward the center gate of the "Ikonostas" (a partition inlaid with ikons and separating the altar from the rest of the cathedral), ready for the holy communion. The Czar of Russia being recognized as the head of the Russian Church, he took the chalice from the hands of the metropolitan. The Empress was given the holy communion after him, and the ceremony of the coronation came to its conclusion.

Our procession returned to the palace in the same order as before, with the imperial salute booming, the bells of the churches ringing, and the population showing still greater enthusiasm at the sight of the crowns on the heads of the sovereigns. On reaching the "Krasonie Kriltzo" the Czar and the Czarina made once more their three traditional bows, after which they proceeded to the oldest part of the palace, where in a room known as "Granovitai Palata" they were to eat their meal by themselves, seated on an elevated platform and being served by the eldest dignitary of the court.

The remaining three days of celebrations left a memory of happy exhaustion. True to its traditional hospitality, the city of Moscow staged its festivities on a gigantic scale. We danced at the ball given by the Moscow nobility; we mixed among eight thousand guests invited to attend the ball offered by the imperial court in the Kremlin. We ate municipal lunches, state dinners and officers' mess suppers. We drove through the streets resounding with music and singing. We watched the distribution of presents to 500,000 workers and peasants gathered in the Khodynka Field. We paid honor to the talents of the cook of the metropolitan of Moscow renowned for the excellency of his all-fish meals. We received delegations, we sat through the two daily performances of the imperial ballet, we took the foreign princes and princesses to their trains, both the guests and the hosts nearly asleep on their feet.

On May 18 the Emperor left for a short rest in his Moscow summer residence "Neskuchnoe," situated on the shore of the Moscow River and surrounded by endless acres of centennial park. Lying in the tall dewy grass and listening to the nightingales singing right over our heads, we four—Nicky, Georgie, Sergei, and myself—discussed from all sides that new and fascinating feeling of security which came over us during the week of the coronation.

"Just think, what a great country Russia will have become by the time we will have to escort Nicky to the Cathedral of the Assumption!" said Sergei half-dreamingly.

Nicky smiled his usual, tender, shy, slightly sad smile.

CHAPTER SIX

A GRAND DUKE COMES OF AGE

Homme libre, toujours tu cheriras le mer!—BAUDELAIRE.

I

AT the age of ten I began to worry about my future.

"For my part I would naturally like to make good artillery-men of my sons," my father used to say each time I spoke of my different plans, "but then you have your own life to live."

It sounded magnificent. It meant in reality that in receiving my officer's commission I would be permitted to choose between several "eligible" regiments of the imperial guard. The very thought that any one of their sons would cast his ambitions outside the military service would have struck my parents as distinctly heretic. The House of the Romanoffs expected its members to wear a uniform of some description and cared little about their personal predilections and heart-felt desires.

The idea of joining the navy had first appeared on my clouded horizon around the year 1878, when through a sort of fortunate misunderstanding we obtained a cheerful and easy-going tutor in the person of Lieutenant Zeleny. Thoroughly incapable of giving lessons or making sour faces, he became putty in our hands, and we spent our usually gloomy mornings in listening to his highly colored descriptions of the gorgeous life led by the rugged men in the navy. To believe this excitable sailor, the fleet of His Imperial Majesty constantly went from one glamorous adventure to another, and an existence packed with thrills awaited a youngster aboard a Russian battleship.

"Now, listen to this," Zeleny would commence, "it happened in Shanghai . . ."

He would go no further, for his well-fed body would suddenly shake with fits of laughter. By the time he would get back into condition to explain what actually did happen in Shanghai, we ourselves would be rolling on the floor and giggling hysterically at the sight of the tears streaming down his sunburned face.

Zeleny's contagious gayety determined my choice. I dreamed of mysterious women driving in rickshaws in the narrow streets of Shanghai. I craved to behold the fantastic spectacle of fanatical Hindoos entering the holy waters of the river Ganges. I was anxious to encounter wild elephants charging through the jungle of Ceylon. My mind was made up. I decided to become a sailor.

"A sailor? My son a sailor?"

Mother looked at me in dismay.

"You are just a child. You do not understand what you are saying. Your father will never permit it."

Father frowned. The navy did not appeal to him in the least. The only two members of the imperial family who ever served in the navy did not do so well in his estimation. His brother Constantin was considered a "dangerous radical." His nephew Alexis chased after the women too much. It mattered not that the navy had but little to do with developing the political opinions of Constantin and the romantic inclinations of Alexis. My parents hoped to God that their son was not going to resemble either one of his two prodigal relatives.

This attitude of my parents failed to weaken my determination. There was always a streak of stubbornness in my nature. Again and again I broached the subject. Finally my parents promised to settle this troublesome question during our coming autumn stay in St. Petersburg. They thought that the splendor of the imperial palace and the beauty of the Sunday parades would fill my heart with envy for a brilliant uniform. They overlooked the fogs, the gray and dull days, the rawness of the air, the tension of the political moment. St. Petersburg made me turn my eyes toward the sea more than ever. What was a mere fancy of a dreaming boy in the Caucasus changed into a cry for escape in the north. And still, I doubt whether I would have succeeded in accomplishing my plan had it not been for the unexpected assistance of the new Czar. Unlike his father, Alexander III attached considerable importance to the part played by the fleet in the defense of the Russian Empire. Preparing to launch an ambitious naval program he believed that the fact of his cousin serving on a battleship would give a good example to the youth of the country. His friendly interference saved my life from being squandered in the stuffy atmosphere of the capital. I feel I owe him the greatest joys of my career, and I shudder at the realization of how perilously near I came to the possibility of becoming one of those self-satisfied stalwart Guardsmen who watched the world go by through the short end of their opera glasses fixed on the limbs of a twirling ballerina.

2

Logic and common sense demanded my entering the Naval Academy, but a grand duke was not supposed to "mix with the ordinary boys," and so I had to do my studies at home under the supervision of a special tutor, the gloomiest one to be found in Russia. Hired and paid to prepare me for the examinations that were to be conducted by a board of professors chosen by the Emperor, he must have formed a very low opinion of my abilities. Every day, for four years in succession, I heard him predict dismal failure for me.

"You will never pass the examinations," became the refrain of my naval tutor. No matter how conscientiously I prepared my lessons, he just shook his head, his weary harassed look transmitting his tragic thoughts. Sometimes I sat all night long trying to learn every word written in the text-

books. Even then he refused to give in: "You are just repeating, word by word, what other people have discovered
through endless years of study but you do not understand
what it all means."

The four-year program drawn by him included astronomy,
theory of the deviation of the compass, oceanography, theoretical and practical artillery, torpedo warfare, theoretical
and practical shipbuilding, military and naval strategy and
tactics, military and naval administration and regulations,
naval legislation, political economy, theoretical and practical
fortification, history of the Russian and principal foreign
navies, etc.

My professors, all of them highly qualified specialists, did
not share the opinion of my ferocious tutor. Thanks to their
encouragement I developed a genuine interest in my lessons.
The theoretical studies at home were accompanied by visits
aboard battleships and to building docks. Each summer I
spent three months on a practice cruise in company with the
cadets of the Naval Academy, my parents hoping that the
severity of naval discipline would change my decision at the
very last moment.

How clearly I can see the day when I left our summer
palace of Michailovsky to start the career of a sailor. Our
small chapel was packed with relatives, aides-de-camp, and
servants, and when the deep-voiced priest presented me with
an ikon at the conclusion of a Te Deum, my mother began
to cry. The beautiful words of a special prayer for "the
wandering and the voyaging ones" made her exaggerate the
perils awaiting her youngster. "Let us go, let us go," said
father nervously, and we all drove to the port of Peterhof
whence the yacht of Prince Eugene of Leuchtenberg was to
take me aboard H.I.M.S. *Varyag*. Feeling the ribbons of my
sailor's cap flutter gently about my face and casting an
admiring glance at my wide black trousers, I went perfunctorily through the ritual of kissing. My heart was already
far away. The faces of my parents and brothers seemed dim

and distant. They dropped out of my life right there at the pier of Peterhof never again to occupy their former place of prominence. I was gay as a prisoner at the dawn of his last day in jail. Even the presence of my tutor—he was to accompany me during this first practice cruise—failed to mar my happiness.

Toward evening we arrived at Twermine, a small lumber town in Finland, where the squadron of the Naval Academy lay at anchor. The admiral gave the signal and the *Varyag* lowered its steam launch manned by cadets of my age. They looked at me curiously, evidently speculating whether this unsolicited imperial addition to their crew was going to cause fuss and disturbance. A few words of welcome from Admiral Brilkin, and I was shown into my cabin. My dream came true but partially: although an indivisible part of the navy from now on, I was still being separated from the other boys and not permitted to bunk with them in their quarters. Another shock of disappointment came at dinner time. Instead of joining the cadets in their messroom, I was told to take my seat at the admiral's table in his private salon. This may have been to my advantage from the educational point of view, because while listening to the conversation of elder officers I learned many matters of importance, but at the moment I felt hurt. I feared that the cadets would resent my "exclusiveness" and would deny me their friendship.

The meal passed in an atmosphere of tenseness, everybody maintaining silence and exchanging warning glances. Several weeks elapsed before I succeeded in persuading those suspicious sailors that I had no intention of reporting their casual remarks to the Czar. I was facing a fight and I knew it. Back in my cabin I saw a large fat cat spread on my bed. He purred contentedly and demanded to be petted. His unerring animal instinct recognized a friend, for which I was extremely grateful. We spent that first night aboard the *Varyag* huddled together, his warm soft fur rubbing against my side. The cabin smelled of fresh tar. The sound of water chopping under the stern acted as a tonic for my strained nerves. I lay on my back listening to the hours being sounded by different ships on the right and on the left of us in different tones. Once in a while I heard the sleepy voice of the sentinel under the flag repeating his usual —"Who is rowing?" I was thinking of the new life that was to start tomorrow. I visualized the faces of the cadets seen by me in the steam launch and was working out various plans to conquer their friendship. The broad strong wooden beams over my head reminded me of the iron discipline of the navy, but my childhood had taught me to obey orders and expect no favors. I got up, opened my bag, and took a small yellowish engraving representing a bearded man with a gigantic shield. It was my saint—St. Alexander of the Neva, the first Russian grand duke of that name, who saved Russia from the pillaging Tartars in the thirteenth century. Now I had two friends protecting my sleep: a silent saint and a purring cat.

3

The sound of scraping woke me at sunrise. A moment of bewilderment, and then I realized that I was aboard a man-of-war. A look through the porthole disclosed the sight of numerous boats moving in all directions. I jumped up. I had a day full of excitement ahead of me.

Scrubbed with stone and sand, the decks of the ship shone brilliantly, making one almost ashamed to leave one's footprints on the wet surface. Tiptoeing along the aft deck I ran into a group of cadets gathered for the morning exercises. I stood still, searching my mind for an appropriate greeting.

"Hello, there," said a thin blond boy, "have you had a good night's rest?"

I answered that I had never slept so well in any other place in my life. The cadets moved closer. The ice was broken. They all had a question to ask. How late was I permitted to sleep in the palace? How many rooms did we have? Was it really true that I was going to become a sailor? How often did I see the Emperor? Is it true what people are telling about his physical strength? Was there a chance of any other grand duke joining the navy?

They listened to me with avid attention. They expressed first their stupefaction and then their delight at having discovered that even the heir apparent had to get up at six o'clock every morning. It appeared that the news of my arrival caused a sensation in the Naval Academy and that the cadets of the *Varyag* considered my choice of their boat a great honor.

"This will stop those Guardsmen from boasting about all the grand dukes serving in their regiments," proudly concluded the elder boy. "The navy now has its own representative in the imperial family."

I blushed with pleasure. I told them how sorry I was at having been forced to sleep and eat outside their quarters. They assured me that none of them ever thought of taking exception to this fact: "It's only natural that the admiral took additional measures of precaution in watching over your safety."

More questions were in order.

"How many servants are there in Gatchino?"

"How many people sit at the Emperor's dinner?"

"How many horses are there in the imperial stables?"

Up till eight o'clock I was satisfying their curiosity in regard to the imperial family and then we were called for the ceremony of raising the colors.

We stood with our heads uncovered while our white-and-blue-cross ensign was being hoisted. I noticed a slight blush of excitement appear on the indifferent face of the admiral, and a cold shudder crept down my back. In all my long years of service in the navy I could never become accustomed to witness this daily performance prescribed by the official routine without experiencing a genuine thrill. It always revived in my memory the mighty words of a laconic inscription placed by the French on the tombstone of the common grave of the Russian and French sailors who fought each other in 1854: "Unis pour la gloire, réunis par la mort, des soldats c'est le devoir, des braves c'est le sort!" ("United for glory, reunited by death,—'tis the duty of soldiers, 'tis the fate of the brave!")

The ceremony over, the order was given to man all boats. I was assigned to the boat sent from the corvette *Ghiliak* together with the cadets of my class. For an hour we exercised under sails and were instructed in rowing. Several times we had to pass under the stern of the admiral whose sharp eyes watched us critically. Our next lesson consisted of hoisting sails, the fore and main masts being manned by the sailors and the mizzen mast by the cadets. The turn of practical navigation came between ten and eleven. After luncheon and a short period of rest, four more hours of seamanship followed. Dinner was served at six. At eight we had to go to bed.

No favoritism was shown to me during the classes. My mistakes were pointed out with the same rough frankness applied to all other cadets. Once initiated to my duties I was supposed to work harder than anyone else, the admiral reminding me often that a member of the imperial family must show an example to his classmates. This equality of treatment pleased me tremendously. I learned easily. The irresistible attraction of the sea grew stronger every day. I kept all watches allotted to my service section, finding nothing unbearable in spending four hours in company with boys who became my friends and in the close proximity of the waves that rolled on their way to the mysterious lands of my dreams.

For obvious reasons I was never permitted to go ashore without my tutor, my mother having given strict instructions to bring my "morals" back to St. Petersburg in the same unspoiled state they had left that city. I would have loved to escape the old grouch to follow my friends to the out-of-the-way places from which they returned shortly before the evening tattoo, smelling of liquor and having many a story to tell.

"Did you enjoy your shore leave?" they asked me with a knowing wink.

"Oh, nothing in particular. Just walked around with my tutor."

"Poor boy! We had a much better time than that. If you only knew what we did."

But that I was likewise not permitted to know. The admiral had strictly forbidden the cadets to use "bad language" or describe "suggestive scenes" in my presence. Fortunately I had my imagination to rely upon. I was sixteen.

For three months we cruised around Finland and Sweden. Then we received orders to participate in the imperial review, which in itself rewarded me for all my efforts. I enjoyed this opportunity of showing my seamanship before the Emperor, the Empress, and my pals Nicky and Georgie. They came aboard our ship with a big party which included the Minister of the Navy and Grand Duke Alexis, the future bitter enemy of my naval reforms. Standing in my place, in the ranks of the cadets, I looked at the Emperor gratefully. He smiled. He was pleased to see me healthy and matured. As for Nicky and Georgie, all through the luncheon they had to listen to my incoherent ravings. The messages brought by them from my three elder brothers, who were doing their service in the Guards, left me unimpressed. I pitied the poor boys closeted in the awful capital. If they only knew what a chance they had missed by not joining the navy!

4

Four years passed, spent between the classroom of our palace in St. Petersburg and a man-of-war in the Baltic Sea. In September of 1885, the official governmental paper announced my promotion to the modest rank of sub-lieutenant of the navy. To the utter amazement of my tutor I had received the highest marks in all subjects with the exception of shipbuilding; up to this day I cannot see any sense in trying to make engineers out of sailors, for which reason my next-to-best mark received at that particular examination failed to cause me any anguish.

And now I was left to myself. For the first time in my life I faced the world without the benefit of tutors. My mother continued to consider me a mere child but I was rapidly approaching the most significant day in the career of a grand duke. On April 1, 1886, I became of age. At eight o'clock in the morning a special messenger of the Emperor brought me the uniform of aide-de-camp to His Majesty. Later in the day a reception (sortie) was held in the Peterhof Palace attended by ministers, deputations of the Guard regiments, court and state dignitaries, and headed by the Emperor, the Empress and all members of my family. A Te Deum was sung, and then the color bearer of the Sailors Guard Regiment advanced toward the center of the chapel. The Emperor beckoned to me. I approached the color bearer, accompanied by the priest who gave me two written oaths: the first was the special grand ducal oath in which I swore to obey the fundamental laws of succession to the throne and to uphold the institutions of the imperial family; the second dealt with the duties of Russian officers. Holding the colors in my left hand I read the two oaths aloud, kissed the cross and the Bible placed on the pulpit, signed both oaths, passed them into the hands of the minister of the imperial court, embraced the Emperor and kissed the hand of the Empress. We returned to the palace, where a luncheon in my honor was given for the immediate members of the imperial family. Royalty has an aversion for melodrama and nobody volunteered to lecture me on the meaning of the oath, as is the habit of the great democracies. No lectures were necessary. I intended to keep every word of my two oaths. Thirty-one years later I had occasion to recall this youthful determination of mine, when the majority of the grand dukes and the grand duchesses signed a paper prepared by the revolutionary government in which they renounced their rights. I refused to follow their example. I was born a grand duke and no dire threats could have made me forget that I promised to "serve His Imperial Majesty, not sparing my life and limb, until the very last drop of my blood."

In his very interesting memoirs, my nephew, the Crown Prince of Germany, relates a characteristic conversation which took place on November 9, 1918, between his father Kaiser Wilhelm and General Groehner—now a member of the German republican government but then an important staff officer of the imperial army. Wilhelm wanted to know whether he could depend on the loyalty of his officers. "Decidedly not," answered Groehner, "they are all bitterly opposed to Your Majesty." "But what about their oath?" exclaimed the Kaiser. "Their oath? What is an oath, after all," sneered Groehner, "it is only an idea."

I must admit that in this particular instance my sympathies were and are with Kaiser Wilhelm, although some of my relatives should be considered the legitimate predecessors of General Groehner's philosophy.

5

On reaching his twentieth birthday a grand duke of Russia gained financial independence from his parents. Usually a special trustee—chosen by the Emperor—was appointed for the period of the following five years to break the young man into the habit of spending money carefully and wisely. An exception was made in my case. It would have been incredibly foolish for a sailor preparing to go on a three-year cruise to have his trustee warm a chair in St. Petersburg. To be sure, I had to put up a fight but in the end my parents surrendered to my logic and I became a possessor of an annual income amounting to two hundred ten thousand roubles (around $110,000), of which amount one hundred fifty thousand roubles were being contributed by the Czar while the remaining sixty thousands represented a return from the moneys invested in my name during my childhood. I shall talk elsewhere of the financial arrangements prevailing in the imperial family. For the moment it would be sufficient to emphasize the difference between the two hundred ten thousand roubles received by me in 1886 and fifty roubles per month given to me by my parents during 1882-1886. Up to the year 1882 I was given no pocket money whatsoever.

The iron discipline of my upbringing being what it was, I continued to live in the same fashion. I knew no women as yet. I disliked gambling, and I took my liquor in moderate quantities. The bookdealers became the only direct beneficiaries of my newly acquired wealth. Back in 1882 I began collecting books dealing with the history of the navy, and this passion of mine was well known by now, both in Russia and abroad. Every bookstore in St. Petersburg, Moscow, Paris, London, New York and Boston felt it its duty to help me spend my two hundred ten thousand roubles, heavily wrapped packages arriving daily from all ends of the earth. Father gasped on entering my rooms filled from floor to ceiling with bulky leatherbound volumes but made no comment. His transfer from the Caucasus—the viceroyalty had been abolished in 1882—to St. Petersburg to the post of President of the Imperial Council helped to reconcile him with my service in the navy.

"Are you going to read all these books, Sandro?" he asked quietly though incredulously.

"Not exactly. I am merely trying to gather a library dedicated to the navy. Nobody has one in Russia and even our Minister of the Navy is obliged to write to London each time he is in need of a reference."

Father was pleased and promised to do all he could to increase my collection. In the years to come he saw it multiplied hundreds of times. On the eve of the revolution it consisted of over twenty thousand volumes and was recognized as the finest naval Library in the world. The Soviet Government turned my palace into the Club of Communistic Youth, and a fire caused by unswept chimneys destroyed every one of my books. It was a real pity because no money could buy some of the unique editions obtained by my English and German agents after long years of search and perseverance.

6

I did not entirely escape the service in the Guards, as, awaiting the launching of the good ship *Rynda,* which was to take me around the world, I had to perform my duties as an officer of the Sailors Regiment of the Imperial Guard. Not unlike the United States Marines, our regiment occupied a position " 'twixt and between." The army considered us as strangers. The navy called us landlubbers. Ours was the privilege of manning the imperial yachts in the summer and watching over the safety of various governmental buildings while ashore in the winter. Put in command of the first platoon of the first company I supervised its drills, gave the sailors lessons in reading, writing, arithmetic, and Russian history, and led them to all their assignments in the different parts of the capital.

Once each week we were ordered on a twenty-four-hour watch, a duty heartily disliked by both the officers and the sailors. The commander of our regiment, an uncompromising admiral of the old Germanized school, liked to pay us unexpected visits in the middle of the night, which meant that I had to walk for hours in deep snow checking up on the sentinels and trying to keep awake those strapping young fellows suffering from cold and hunger. In order to chase away my own temptation to fall asleep I used to work out the balance-sheet of what I called my "mental profits and losses." I compiled my assets and liabilities, grouping my numerous shortcomings under the title of "unfunded debt to be liquidated at the first opportunity." Trying to be honest with myself I concluded that I was handicapped in my "mental operations" by a terrific overproduction of hatred. Hatred for individuals and hatred for nations. I stood a fair chance of curing myself from the former: my animosity against individuals centered only on teachers, tutors and supervisors. But I felt helpless in the presence of the latter. It was not my fault that I hated the Jews, the Poles, the Swedes, the Germans, the British and the French. I blamed the Greek Orthodox Church and the monstrous doctrine of official patriotism—beaten into me by twelve years of study—for my inability to treat with friendliness all these nations that had never committed a crime against me personally.

Until I came into my first contact with the church, the word "Jew" signified for me an old smiling man who delivered chickens, turkeys, ducks and other poultry at our palace in Tiflis. I felt a genuine sympathy for the kind expression of his wrinkled bearded face, and could not believe that he traced his ancestry straight to Judas. But my reverend teacher persisted in his daily descriptions of the sufferings of Christ! He played on my childish imagination and succeeded in making me see a murderer and a torturer in every worshiper of Jehovah. My timid attempts at quoting the Sermon on the Mount were waved aside with impatience. "Yes, Christ did advise our loving our enemies," said Father Titoff, "but that should not affect our views of the Jews!" Poor Father Titoff! In his clumsy provincial way he was merely imitating the preachings of his betters who were promoting anti-Semitism for over eighteen centuries from the pulpits of the houses of God. The Catholics, the Episcopalians, the Methodists, the Baptists, all these supposedly Christian creeds and denominations have equally contributed to the despicable cause of fostering hatred, while the anti-Jewish legislation of Russia found its principal support among the high priests of the Greek Orthodox Church. In fact, the Jews began to suffer persecution in Russia only with the advent of the rulers whose blind obedience to the dictates of the church proved stronger than their understanding of the spirit of a great empire.

"The Czar of Russia cannot divide his subjects into Gentiles and Jews," blue-penciled Nicholas I across a project prepared by the bishops and suggesting to limit the legitimate activities of the Russian Hebrew; "he defends his faithful subjects and he chastises the traitors. No other criterions should guide his decisions."

Unfortunately for Russia, my grandfather's capacity for "imperial thinking" was not inherited by his successors, and my coming of age coincided with the introduction of cruel and dangerous measures inspired by the holy men of the Russian Synod. And yet, a comparison drawn between the limitations imposed upon the Hebrews in Russia and the present stupendous growth of the American anti-Semitism would prove most unfavorable to the presumably tolerant United States. For one thing, no St. Petersburg apartment house would have dared to broadcast its "one hundred per cent Gentile occupancy."

So much for my former hatred for the Jews which owed its origin to the teachings of the Greek Orthodox Church and which disappeared as soon as I discovered the hypocritical character of that quasi-Christian institution. I had to employ much greater efforts in extracting the roots of a general xenophobia firmly implanted in my soul by my teachers of Russian history. Their analysis of the events of our past made no allowance for the precipice invariably dividing a nation from its government and its politicians. The French were to be condemned for the many treacheries of Napoleon. The Swedes had to suffer because of the havoc wrought by Charles XII in the lives of Peter the Great's contemporaries. The Poles were never to be forgiven for the stupidity of their vain nobility. The British were always the same "perfidious

British." The Germans tolerated Bismarck in their midst. The Austrians had the misfortune of being ruled by Franz-Joseph, a man who had broken all promises given by him to Russia.

The world was full of my "enemies." The official conception of patriotism demanded my keeping the fires of hatred burning constantly.

What was I to do? How was I to reconcile the narrow-minded provincialism of my upbringing with the voice of the sea that talked of the joys of roving?

The endless St. Petersburg winter nights crept along slowly. The man was noticeably weakening in his struggle with the grand duke.

CHAPTER SEVEN

A GRAND DUKE AT LARGE

Pour l'enfant amoureux des cartes et des estampes
L'univers est égal à son vaste appetit,
Ah, que le monde est grand à la clarté d'une lampe,
Aux yeux du souvenir que le monde est petit!
—BAUDELAIRE.

I

ANOTHER winter; more nights of meditation. This time thousands of miles away from St. Petersburg.

Christmas Eve, 1886. H.I.M.S. *Rynda,* under combined power of steam and sails, enters the territorial waters of Brazil. Standing on the fore bridge—the Southern Cross blinking between the disjointed milk clouds—I am breathing deeply the fragrance of the tropical woods.

The stroke of 4 a.m. announces the end of the "dog-watch," allotted to me as a final endurance test. Below in the wardroom a cold supper and a decanter of iced vodka are waiting on the table.

The sputtering of the oil-lamp, the measured steps of the officer of the watch—silence. The divine silence of a man-of-war just before dawn. Full of meaning. Charged with the solemnity of the universe. Endowing its faithfuls with an eyesight capable of penetrating mist and fog.

It is difficult to realize that there is Russia, that there are somewhere far behind the Emperor, the family, the palaces, the churches, the marching soldiers, the galloping Cossacks, the pink-and-white beauty of bejeweled women.

I take out of my side pocket a tiny envelope containing a card. "Best wishes and speedy return! Your sailor Xenia." I smile. She is so sweet. Some day, perhaps. Unless the Emperor insists on his daughter marrying a foreign prince. In any event, Xenia is not twelve as yet. There is so much ahead for both of us. I have only begun my three-year cruise and must earn my promotion. I am just a simple sub-lieutenant. The fact of my being a grand duke and a cousin of the Emperor puts me in a dual position liable to breed hatred in our commander. Aboard ship he is my undisputed superior, but ashore he has to salute me, stopping five paces in front of me. Two well-painted ladies in the "Bar Américain" in Paris were amazed at seeing their awe-inspiring "Commandant Russe" jump up at the entrance of a youngster of no particular distinction. A shadow of encouragement on my part would have brought them to my table. Fortunately, I remained noncommittal. I had my hands full in Paris watching over the safety of Eberling. It looked as though he would miss the train for Le Havre and spend the next three years in the lobby of the Folies-Bergère.

Eberling is the first lieutenant of the *Rynda*. The day we left Russia he gave his word of honor to my mother that he would not let me out of his sight during our stay in such dens of corruption as Paris, Hongkong and Shanghai. This arrangement is the standing joke of our wardroom as Eberling is known to the entire navy for his ability to get into mischief. His kind blue eyes and "open" face inspired confidence in poor mother, but it appears that these very same features of his assure him a more than friendly welcome in all the countries visited by the *Rynda*.

"Remember, I promised Her Imperial Highness not to let you out of my sight," he tells me when ordering his fifth brandy-and-soda, "so you will have to stay with me wherever I go and whatever I do."

I laugh. So far I am still able to resist Eberling's provocations. Rio de Janeiro is our first "exotic" port of call.

2

A harbor challenging the haughty claims of Sydney, San Francisco and Vancouver. A white-bearded Emperor discussing the imminent triumph of democracy. A jungle preserving the atmosphere of the first week of creation. A narrow-waisted girl dancing to the strains of "La Paloma."

These four images will forever be associated in my mind with the word "Brazil."

"He who has tasted the water of Beykos shall return to Istanbul," maintain the Turks. I doubt it. I have had my fill of that glorified water, and yet I feel no desire whatsoever to revisit the city of European vices and Asiatic comforts. But I would pay almost any price to live once more through the thrill of being overcome by the spectacle of the beautiful Rio.

A cablegram from St. Petersburg awaited me ashore instructing me to pay an official visit to Emperor Dom Pedro of Brazil. January being the hottest month in South America, he was staying in his summer residence Petropolis, high in the mountains, an old-fashioned "funiculaire," zigzagging over the slope of a high hill, presenting the only means of transportation.

The jungle was upon us while we were still admiring the harbor. Far below, crystal streams were running at the bottom of precipices but the gigantic trees and the plants crowding around the funiculaire made them look like spots of silver. The palms, the lianas and all other twining colossi seemed interwoven with each other and were fighting for a breath of air and a ray of sunshine. Myriads of them were perishing before our eyes, but new myriads were being born, ready to join in this struggle for existence. Our miniature train crept ahead, breaking branches, pushing its way through the treetops and brushing the tall poisonous grass against our faces. The parrots yelled, the snakes crawled, the birds

96

circled in frightened packs, the large butterflies, colored to resemble the leaves, flew high above as though happy to remain in safety.

The voyage lasted three hours. It was awesome. Not one iota did the jungle change for three hours. It spoke of the millions of centuries of chaos bent on maintaining that chaos.

I trembled from head to foot. I understood what the Preachers of the Talmud meant by saying that there is nothing more terrifying than the unveiled face of the Creator. My companions—two young lieutenants of the *Rynda*—made the sign of the cross when on reaching the top of the mountain we saw Mr. Ionin, the Russian ambassador to Brazil. By that time we began to doubt the existence of human beings in this spot of the world.

Emperor Dom Pedro—his long white beard and gold-rimmed glasses gave him the appearance of an old university professor—listened sympathetically to my description of the jungle. The absence of political disputes and even of vital contacts between Russia and Brazil permitted him to converse freely.

"The Europeans talk so often about the so-called youth of the South American countries," he said with a great sadness in his voice. "No one of them realizes that we are hopelessly old. We are older than the world. Nothing is left, or at least nothing has been discovered so far pertaining to the peoples who inhabited this continent thousands of centuries ago. There is just one thing that will always remain in South America: the spirit of restless hatred. It comes from the jungle. It preys on our minds. The political ideas of today are connected with those of yesterday by no other link except that perpetual desire for a change. No government can endure because the jungle prompts us to fight. At the present moment there is a great deal of agitation in favor of a republican régime. Well, they shall have it. I know my people too well to attempt staging a needless bloodshed. I am tired. Let those future presidents try to maintain civil peace in Brazil."

A few years later Brazil became a republic. Dom Pedro did just as he had promised: he abdicated voluntarily and cheerfully, leaving his excitable subjects slightly taken aback by the disappointing ease of their victory. His memory is cherished in Brazil until this day, and a monument raised by popular subscription glorifies the quiet wisdom of that kind old man.

I liked him immensely, and as he was in no particular hurry, we stayed for over two hours in his unpretentious comfortable study with large windows opening on a vast garden, where innumerable honey-birds busied themselves in search of their afternoon meal. We spoke French. His very distinct, grammatically correct, though slightly uncertain phrasing added a touch of friendly shyness to this meeting between a tottering sovereign of the tropics and a representative of the then formidable reigning house of the North. When we were ready to go, he pinned the cross of the Great Order of Brazil on my breast. I appreciated the honor but admitted my preference for the Order of the Rose, a nine-pointed star in a crown of roses.

He laughed. "The Order of Rose is one of our humblest decorations. Practically everybody has it."

Even so. It fitted better my idea of Brazil. We compromised by my accepting both.

The remaining five days were spent by me in an atmosphere of enchanted laziness, on the "fazenda" of a Russian coffee merchant married to a very rich native woman. Each morning we rode to inspect his plantations spread over several square miles, and an improvised orchestra of slaves played for our enjoyment on peculiar instruments never seen by me outside of Brazil. In the evening, immediately after dinner, we sat on the balcony listening to the sharp screams of the jungle interrupting the monotonous beating of the tom-toms. We never lit the lamps, myriads of night beetles and fire-bugs providing plentiful illumination. The wife of our host had two nieces living with her on the fazenda. Both were young, tall, slim, dark-haired, narrow-waisted. For all I knew, both may have been beautiful. Any girl dancing to the strains of "La Paloma" played on a guitar in a tropical garden lighted by fire-bugs would have appeared beautiful to a youngster chilled by the fogs of St. Petersburg. I succumbed to the charms of the elder niece, voluntarily and eagerly. Possibly she liked me; possibly she wanted to ascertain how Brazil affects a Russian grand duke. Nothing could have been more innocent than that adolescent romance of awkward tenderness. If she is still alive, she must be sixty-three. I hope she remembers our January evenings of 1887 with the same feeling of gratitude that I do.

3

South Africa. A glimpse of the hard-working Dutch farmers. A monotonous landscape, doubly disappointing for one still reminiscing of Brazil. Luxurious country clubs of the British officers. Subconscious arrogance of a great power. Frequent quotations from Cecil Rhodes: "Think imperially."

And then the longest lap of our cruise: we are crossing from Capetown to Singapore. Forty-five days on the ocean with no sign of land. Our captain is delighted. He hates calling at ports where he has to surrender his authority to a pilot. "A pilot! What could be more ignorant than a blankety-blank pilot." Were it left to his choice, we would be sailing on and on for ages.

Singapore. I wish some of the very blasé ladies sipping tea on the terraces of their beautiful estates in England and complaining of the continuous absence of their husbands in the Orient would visit Singapore and witness the process of the making of that money which buys their jewels, their gowns and their castles. "Poor Freddie! He works frightfully hard all of the time. I cannot tell you what he does,

I am sure, but I know it has something to do with those queer Singapore Chinamen!"

Singapore's Chinatown. The main source of Freddie's revenue. Each second house an opium den. Degradation in full blast. Not that sort of degradation which serves vice on a golden platter in the European district of Shanghai, but dirt, filth, foul odors, depravity of the starving coolies buying their opium from the millionaires rated in Lombard Street. Blind beggars lying on wooden cots, each long pipe in their mouths representing perhaps several days of weary panhandling. Naked nine-year-old girls seated on the knees of lepers. A disheveled white man trying to pass an I.O.U. to the grinning proprietor of a den. The sickening smell of opium that nothing can get out of one's clothes. And just a short drive from this inferno—the charming lawns of an exclusive club for British residents, with white-clad gentlemen sipping their whiskey-and-soda under the shade of large umbrellas.

A week more in Singapore would have made me desperately ill. I blessed my stars when a cable from the Minister of the Navy ordered our immediate departure for Hongkong. My twenty-first birthday falling on April 1, the wardroom seized gladly upon this occasion to stage a celebration. As a rule we did not drink much aboard the ship, but this time the officers felt duty bound to propose numerous toasts to me and my relatives. The conversation, as invariably happens in the company of healthy young men, gradually drifted toward women. My "guardian" Eberling spoke at great length of his new conquests in Rio and Singapore; the second lieutenant praised the rustic charms of the South African Dutch; the eight sub-lieutenants modestly admitted having been treated quite well so far in all parts of the globe. Then everybody turned toward me. The fact of my innocence worried our wardroom considerably. They had dwelt upon it since the moment we left Russia, but now that I was twenty-one, it just did not seem possible! They found it

GRAND DUKE ALEXANDER WITH HIS FIRST-
BORN DAUGHTER IRENE IN 1896.

GRAND DUKE ALEXANDER AND GRAND
DUCHESS XENIA, SIX MONTHS AFTER THEIR
MARRIAGE.

THE CZAR AND THE CZARINA WITH THEIR
THREE ELDER DAUGHTERS IN 1900.

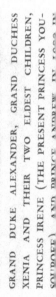

GRAND DUKE ALEXANDER, GRAND DUCHESS
XENIA AND THEIR TWO ELDEST CHILDREN,
PRINCESS IRENE (THE PRESENT PRINCESS YOU-
SSOUPOFF) AND PRINCE ANDREW, IN 1898 IN

both unnatural and extremely dangerous for my health. I had never been a hypocrite or a prude; I simply could not get accustomed to their manner of discussing such intimate subjects. This attitude of mine increased their determination, and all during our crossing from Singapore to Hongkong they talked of nothing else except the beautiful women of that city.

Eberling said he felt sorry for me:

"If you only knew what you are missing! What good is life without women? Now listen, I want to give you some sound advice, and I wish you would take it. After all, I am so much older than you are. You must meet women in Hongkong. I understand, you resented Singapore, and I appreciate that there were other interfering circumstances in Rio, but Hongkong! The women of Hongkong! The American girls!" He kissed his fingers with gusto. "The best in the world! Nothing like it! Why, I wouldn't exchange one American girl that lives in Hongkong for a thousand Parisian hussies. Please, do be reasonable and listen to me. I know a place in Hongkong where there are three of the nicest American girls. You understand, I would not think of taking you to one of those cheap five-a-day places. The one I have in mind is a very home-like apartment. Now, let me see, there was Betty. Yes, her name must have been Betty unless I am mixing her with a girl I knew in Shanghai. In any event, it's a tall, blue-eyed blonde. Exquisite! Then there was Joan, dark hair and green eyes. You'd be crazy about Joan, but wait, don't get crazy as yet, the best is only coming. Patsy! A girl of about five-feet-five, with a skin like . . . Well, what shall I compare her skin with? It's not exactly white, it's rather ivory. And the figure . . . The figure! Have you ever seen in the Hermitage Museum in St. Petersburg the statue of that, what do you call her? . . ."

Whichever statue Eberling meant—his knowledge of the Hermitage sculpture proved to be frightfully vague—my peace of mind was completely shattered. No boy of my age could have withstood the concentrated attack of the ward-room tempters. On the eve of our landing in Hongkong I gave in and consented to join in a "real party"!

On entering the apartment, where I was escorted by two of our officers, I was pleasantly surprised by the absence of the vulgarity one expects to encounter in such places. The rooms were furnished with a great deal of taste; the three hostesses were pretty and wore clothes of subdued elegance. The French would have called them "demi-mondaines," which is rather a far cry from the plain representatives of the oldest profession in the world, and which suggests a certain Du-Barryism of manner and policies. The after-armistice onrush of the crude gold-diggers dealt them a deadly blow but the late eighties saw them at their best.

Champagne was served and we began to chat. All three spoke in well-modulated voices. They discussed the current topics freely and amusingly; possessing a natural wit, they did not need the aid of profanity. The purpose of our call being perfectly obvious, a moment arrived when I was left alone with the prettiest of the three. She suggested she would show me her room. The inevitable happened.

Beginning with that evening we became friends. I felt no hesitation in taking her out to the restaurants and for long drives up the Pique from where we viewed the panorama of Hongkong. She behaved beautifully, a great deal better than the majority of the so-called "society ladies" belonging to the smart European set in China. Gradually she told me her story. She accused nobody. She did not complain. The spirit of adventure brought her from her native San Francisco to the Far East; the irresistible desire to possess "nice things" took care of the rest. It was life: one won or one lost, but one had to get hold of some chips to enter the game. She spoke of men without bitterness. Sober brutes, drunken angels, plain cads, big-hearted blackguards. It all depended on luck. She admired the passing show of the world, although she knew she had been run over by its band-wagon. Nothing at all could have been done to change her position.

It is impossible to enumerate all the nuances of love; no doubt, quite a few of them are fostered by pity. I felt considerable pangs of grief when I had to leave for Japan, and we kept up a correspondence for a year or so. Each time the *Rynda* returned to Hongkong, I hurried the rickshaw to the familiar house. When I revisited the Far East in 1890, her friends told me she had died of tuberculosis.

4

Once more there was a great to-do in our wardroom. The officers of the Russian clipper *Vestnik* came to visit us the moment we touched Nagasaki bringing thrilling tales of the two years spent by them in Japan. Nearly all of them had Japanese "wives." No ceremony of marriage had been performed but they lived with their native consorts in the miniature houses bearing the appearance of toyland because of small gardens full of dwarf trees, tiny streams, cardboard bridges and Lilliputian flowers. They said the Minister of the Navy gave them his unofficial blessing, for he understood the hardships awaiting a sailor separated from his home for a period of two years. It is necessary to explain that all of this happened long before Monsieur Loti and Signor Puccini had found an inexhaustible source for royalties in the heart-breaking stories of Madame Chrysanthème and Madame Butterfly. So, in this case at least, the arts had nothing to do with establishing moral standards for roving sailors.

About that time, a Japanese widow by the name of Omati-San ran a first-class restaurant in the village of Inassa, not far from Nagasaki. Considered a godmother of the Russian Navy, she employed Russian cooks, spoke Russian fluently, played Russian melodies on the piano and on the guitar, served hard-boiled eggs and spring onions with fresh caviar, and created in general the atmosphere of a typical Russian inn on the outskirts of Moscow. Outside of her culinary and entertaining activities, she likewise aided the Russian officers in making the acquaintance of their future Japanese "wives." She exacted no fee for this additional service, doing it from the sheer goodness of her heart. She thought she should help us to take back to Russia a pleasant memory of Japanese friendliness.

It was in her place that the officers of the *Vestnik* gave us a welcoming dinner attended by their "wives" who brought their unengaged female acquaintances.

Madame Omati-San outdid herself on that occasion, and for the first time in many months we ate an excellent Russian meal. The bottles of vodka sealed with the imperial double eagle, the unavoidable "pirojki," the "borsch," the blue boxes of caviar placed in huge blocks of ice, the mammoth sturgeon occupying the center of the table, the Russian music played in turn by the hostess and her guests—we could scarcely notice we were in Japan. We watched with natural curiosity the behavior of the toy-women. They laughed all of the time and participated in our singing, but they drank next to nothing. Their characters presented a strange mixture of utmost sweetness and thorough rationalism. Far from being ostracized by their country people, they regarded their present activities as a branch of civil service open to the members of their sex. Some day they intended to marry men of their own nationality, raise a family of children and lead a satisfied middle-class existence. For the moment they were willing to share the companionship of the gay foreign officers, provided they were treated well and with due respect. An attempt at flirting with the "wife" of an officer by his friends would have amounted to a grave breach of etiquette. No trace of the Occidental promiscuity touched their clear-cut conception of life; not unlike most of the Orientals, they preached moral purity and spiritual faithfulness, far superior, in their estimation, to the white man's ideal of technical virginity. Few of the American and European writers showed much, if any, understanding of this important feature of the Japanese rationalism. The heartbreak of Madame Butterfly brought a gale of laughter in the Empire of the Rising Sun because none of the wearers of the flowered kimonos were silly enough to expect to remain forever with their foreign "husbands." The usual "marital contract" called for a period of from one to three years, depending on the length of the stay of a cruising man-of-war in the harbor of Nagasaki. At the end of that time another officer came along, or if the first one was sufficiently generous, the "wife" had saved enough money to obtain a place in the community.

I visited frequently the houses of my "married" friends, and my situation as a bachelor was becoming quite compromising. The "wives" could not understand why that young "samurai"—they were told that "grand duke" was the Russian for "samurai"—should spend his evenings in front of another man's fireplace instead of establishing his own peaceful home. Whenever they saw me tiptoeing in my stockinged feet on the immaculately clean floors of their cardboard castles—one had to leave the boots outside—a shrewd smile of suspicion crossed the carmine-touched lips. Was that ridiculously tall "samurai" attempting to test their loyalty to their "husbands"? Or was he simply too mean to support a "wife"?

I decided to "marry." This news created a sensation in the village of Inassa and it was announced that a special review of the parties desirous to preside over the great Russian samurai's house would be staged on a certain day. In vain did I try to make arrangements less pompous. My friends were unanimous in supporting Madame Omati-San's claim that a fair chance should be given to every "eligible" girl and that an elaborate wedding dinner should be offered by me to the officers of the six Russian battleships stationed in Nagasaki.

The selection itself presented considerable difficulties. As far as I was concerned, they all looked alike. Smiling, fanning dolls, holding their cups with tea at a most exquisite angle. Not less than sixty of them responded to the invitation, and even the weatherbeaten experts of our wardroom stood completely puzzled in front of so much daintiness. I could not look at the flushed face of Eberling from fear of laughing, which would have been misunderstood by the "eligibles." Finally, I let my color-preference guide my decision, choosing a girl who wore a sapphire-blue kimono embroidered with large white flowers.

Now I had a home. A "pied-à-terre" in the full meaning of the word. The captain of the *Rynda* saw to it that we did not get "too soft" and made us work till six o'clock each day, but half past six found me in my Inassa residence, with a tiny creature seated at the dinner-table. The cheerfulness of her character was amazing. Never a frown, never dissatisfied, never irritated. I liked to see her dressed in kimonos of different colors and used to bring her yards and yards of silks, causing her to rush in mad delight into the street and invite all the neighbors to inspect the gifts. It would have been useless to attempt to restrain her from making so much fuss as she took pride in displaying to the village the generosity of her "samurai." She tried to make a kimono for me but even she had to scream looking at my six-feet-two wrapped in the national Japanese garb. I encouraged her passion for entertaining our friends because I could never get tired of admiring the serious dignity with which that doll received her guests and led them into the dining-room. On holidays we hired a rickshaw and went to inspect the rice plantations and the temples, finishing our evening in a Japanese restaurant where a great deal of respect was invariably shown to her. The Russian officers called her jokingly "our grand duchess," a title which was taken quite seriously by the natives. Elderly persons would stop me in the streets of Inassa and inquire whether I had any complaint to make against the treatment received by me at the hands of one of their own. It was as though the entire village had made a political issue of my "marriage."

Knowing that I would stay in and around Nagasaki for two years, I wanted to learn the Japanese language. There was no doubt as to the brilliant future of that country, and I thought at least one member of the imperial family should speak the language of Russia's progressive neighbors. My "wife" volunteered her services, and notwithstanding the considerable intricacies of the Japanese grammar I picked up a sufficient number of phrases to enable me to hold my own in a conversation on "simple" subjects.

One day a cable arrived from the Czar ordering me to pay a state visit to the Mikado. Our ambassador in Tokio prepared an elaborate program consisting of receptions, lunches and dinners, to be crowned by a state banquet at the palace. He showed great excitement and anxiety as I was to be the first representative of European royalty ever received by the Japanese Emperor. He explained to me that I would have to rely upon the services of interpreters because the Mikado spoke no other language than Japanese. I smiled discreetly; I thought my ability to converse with the Mikado directly would come in the nature of a great surprise to our ambassador.

The village of Inassa went sleepless from the realization that it contained in its midst a man who was to be entertained by their great Mikado. My Japanese friends became speechless in my presence. They just stood and bowed. Even my "wife" seemed to be frightened. She found my photograph in the local paper, with the caption explaining that the young Russian naval officer, who had stayed in Japan incognito for several months, happens to be the first cousin of the Emperor of Russia—and she wondered whether she should continue to call me "San" (the Japanese for my little name "Sandro"). It took fifty yards of green-and-pink silk to restore her peace of mind.

ONCE A GRAND DUKE

A former lord chamberlain of the Emperor of Germany was in charge of the "protocol" of the Japanese court at that time, which fact is sufficient in itself to suggest the pompousness of the reception extended to me in Yokohama and Tokio. From the moment the imperial salute of one hundred and one guns announced my arrival in Yokohama, for ten following days I ceased to be the modest sub-lieutenant of H.I.M.S. *Rynda* and had to be treated in the manner reserved by ceremonious Potsdam for visiting sovereigns. The special train of the Mikado waited for me in Yokohama, and all the members of the Government headed by Count Ito, then Prime Minister of Japan, came to meet me at the station in Tokio. I drove to the palace in a state carriage, preceded by a galloping squadron of the Mikado's guards.

The first imperial audience lasted but a few minutes. The Emperor and the Empress received me in the throne room surrounded by a dense crowd of princes and princesses. I made a short speech transmitting the greetings of the Czar. The Emperor expressed his delight at seeing me in Tokio and hoped for the continuation of the Russo-Japanese friendship. Both speeches were translated by the official interpreter of our embassy. I felt embarrassed in the presence of all these people who hardly reached my shoulder and I tried very hard to look smaller.

A week of sightseeing, visiting, reviewing troops, and then came the night of the state banquet. Placed on the right of the Empress, I gathered my courage, smiled pleasantly and addressed her in Japanese. For a second she looked astonished. I repeated my remark. She grinned. This initial success prompted me to tell her of my admiration for the progress made by Japan. It required some maneuvering on my part, and I tried to recall all the expressions used in identical cases by my Inassa friends. A strange sound came out of the Empress's throat. She stopped eating and bit her lip. Then her shoulders shook. She began to laugh hysterically. The Japanese prince seated on her left, who was listening to our conversation, dropped his head. Large tears were streaming down his cheeks. Next moment the entire table shrieked and guffawed. I wondered a little at this gayety as my speech was not purported to be humorous. When the gale of laughter subsided, the Empress made a sign to the prince and he addressed me in English.

"Where did you learn your Japanese, Your Imperial Highness?" he asked politely, his eyes still full of tears.

"Why? Do I speak it so badly?"

"Oh, not at all. You speak remarkably well, but you see, you are using a very special brand of Japanese, a brand which . . . Well, I am really at a loss . . . I do not know how I shall explain it to you . . . May I ask how long you have been in Nagasaki? Are you in a habit of visiting its Inassa district?"

Regardless of the opinion formed by the German lord chamberlain of the Tokio court, it must have been the gayest banquet in the history of the empire.

"I wish I knew her name," said the prime minister, escorting me to my carriage, "I would like to thank her in the name of His Majesty's Government for her brilliant methods of teaching the Inassa slang. How many lessons did you take from her, all told?"

5

With our main base established in Nagasaki—we returned there every three months—the *Rynda* proceeded on its itinerary which included the Philippines, India, Australia, and various islands situated in the Pacific and the Indian oceans. The memory of these places revives in me an acute feeling of homesickness that made me wish at one time I could surrender my title and leave Russia forever. The Molucca Islands, the Fiji Islands, Ceylon, and Darjeeling in the Himalayas, were particularly generous in their response to certain longings of my nature.

The tropical paradise of the Moluccas. The wide river

flowing through the palm woods of the Fiji Islands. The small, clean hotel in Darjeeling possessing a unique view of the proud Kunchinjunga.

And that early morning in the jungle of Ceylon: it rained all night long; the recently broken branches, the specific sharp smell and the mammoth tracks in the muddy ground disclose the proximity of the wild elephants; we are riding slowly and cautiously; the warning cry of the reconnoitering natives; "be careful, be careful! they are about to charge!" from our English escort; the whining sound of the bullets; the pride of bagging my first elephant!

I often thought of all of this after the revolution. It seemed to me that an island somewhere in the Pacific would be the most appropriate spot for one whose existence had been cut to pieces by the scissors of history. I spoke about it to my wife and sons, but they decided to remain in Europe, a continent which never appealed to me even in my youth. Some day I may still be able to fulfill my dream. Sorrowful as it is to return to the scenes of one's happiness forty years after, I do not believe that the ocean, the trees and the mountains could fail me. Only the humans do.

"Le voyage est une école du scepticisme," said Montaigne sententiously. In my case, the voyage proved an excellent school of "unlearning." In each country visited by the *Rynda* I succeeded in discarding some of the half-truths and commonplaces tacked to my mind by my education. The falsehood of official Christianity struck me most forcefully in the Far East, where its vulgar missionaries dared to pit their luke-warm mumblings against the sacred visions filling the existence of the Buddhist. We, the Christians, who were suffering bestial anguish at the thought of death and were crying in despair over the coffins of our departed relatives, what right had we to interfere with the peoples whose implicit faith in the immortality of the soul expressed itself touchingly in those cups with rice put on the graves of their beloved? Every one of those Chinese, Japanese, and Hindoos burned with the flames of that faith which deserted Christendom on the day of the Crucifixion, and which moved Goethe to write his most profound four lines:

> Und sobald du dass nicht hast
> Dieses "stirb und werde,"
> Bist du nur ein trüber Gast
> Auf der dunklen Erde.

The land of the White Man was the abode of the "trüber Gast," but there, in the "uncivilized" Orient, hope had preserved its fervor.

6

In the spring of 1889 the *Rynda* returned to Europe via the Suez Canal and Egypt. After short stops in Greece, where I enjoyed the reunion with my cousin Queen Olga, and in Monte Carlo, where I was met by father, mother, George and Anastasia, we proceeded on our way to England. Once more I was ordered to act as the personal representative of the Czar, conveying his greetings to Queen Victoria. The relations between the two countries being more or less strained at that moment, I did not relish my assignment. I had heard a great deal about the alleged coldness of the powerful Queen and was prepared to be frozen.

The invitation to the palace mentioning "the luncheon" only increased my fears. An audience has at least the advantage of brevity, but the thought of sitting through a long meal with a sovereign known for her distrust of Russia filled my heart with apprehension. Arriving at the palace ahead of the appointed time, I was shown into a large somber salon. I sat alone and waited for a few minutes. Two tall Hindoos appeared, bowed to me, and opened the double doors leading into the inner apartments. A short plump woman stood on the threshold. I kissed her hand and we began to talk. I was slightly taken aback by the very pronounced cordiality of her manner. At first I imagined it signified a coming change in Great Britain's Russian policy. The explanation was forthcoming, however.

"I have heard all sorts of good things about you," she said with a smile. "I must thank you for your kind treatment of one of my friends."

I looked surprised. I could not recall ever having met anyone capable of boasting of a friendship with Queen Victoria.

"Have you forgotten him already?" she asked laughingly. "Munchi, my teacher of Hindustani."

Now I knew the why of this warm reception, although Munchi had never told me of being the teacher of Her Britannic Majesty. I met him in Agra, while inspecting the Taj Mahal. He spoke most intelligently of the different religions of India and I was naturally pleased to accept the invitation to dine at his house. It never dawned upon me that the fact of my breaking Munchi's bread could elevate his standing in the eyes of the haughty Hindoo rajahs and that he would write a long letter to Queen Victoria glorifying my marvelous "kindness."

The Queen rang the bell. The door opened letting in of all people my friend Munchi in flesh and blood. We shook hands and wished each other good morning, the Queen watching this scene with obvious delight.

By the time luncheon was announced I felt completely at ease, being fortunately able to answer the Queen's very relevant questions about the political situation in South America, Japan and China. The British Empire had a right to be justly proud of that remarkable woman. Sitting at her desk in London she followed at close range the changing life of the far-away countries, her brief remarks disclosing sharpness of analysis and shrewdness of judgment.

Only the immediate members of the royal family were present at the table, the Prince and Princess of Wales—the future King Edward VII and Queen Alexandra—among them. The Princess of Wales dearly loved her sister, Empress

Marie of Russia, which coupled with her natural charming simplicity gave me further encouragement. She was slightly deaf and I had to raise my voice answering her queries about her sister, nephews and nieces. I glanced at the Queen to see whether she minded my seafaring volume of voice. She nodded understandingly: everybody was acting in the same manner when talking to the beautiful Princess of Wales, nobody more so than her own husband. A stranger walking into the dining-room of the palace would have thought he was witnessing a family quarrel.

Two days later I was invited to attend the family dinner, and from then on the Queen continued to favor me with her friendship, our meetings taking place in the Hotel Cimiez in Nice where she was in the habit of staying practically each spring.

For a sailor just off the ship the calendar of my social engagements in London looked quite imposing. The respects of the Czar had to be conveyed to all the members of the British royal family, which meant a series of luncheons, teas and dinners. I renewed my acquaintance with the Duke of Edinburgh whom I had met at the coronation in Moscow in 1883 and who was married to my cousin, Grand Duchess Marie Alexandrovna, the daughter of Emperor Alexander II. Their four daughters, although still in their early teens, already showed signs of their future remarkable beauty. The judges of pulchritude would have had a hard time choosing between "Missy," the present Queen-Dowager of Rumania; "Ducky," the wife of Grand Duke Cyril; "Sandra," the Princess of Hohenlohe-Langenburg, and "Baby B.," the Infanta Beatrice of Spain.

Then I met Mr. B., the last representative of the now extinct tribe of eccentric American millionaires. He lived on his yacht *Lady Torfrida*, a beautiful oceangoing craft that lay at anchor just outside London. When I say Mr. B. lived on his yacht, I mean that he remained aboard her for fifteen years and, what is more, was in a habit of staying in the same harbor from three to five years, never going ashore and very reluctant to receive visitors. The Russian naval attaché in London doubted whether I could reach an agreement with Mr. B. He thought that my desire to buy *Lady Torfrida* would only incense the American gentleman, causing him to use expressions capable of burning the delicate ears of Queen Victoria. I decided, however, to brave this danger and asked Mr. B. for the privilege of an appointment.

I found him sitting on the aft deck surrounded by a fine assortment of bottles placed in coolers. He felt irritated and was grumbling. He saw no reason why a grand duke should wish to possess his yacht. I explained that I wanted to revisit some of the attractive places of the Orient, traveling in a care-free fashion, not bound by the time-tables of the passenger steamers, and that as I intended to start my voyage next spring I would have no time to order a yacht.

"What do you expect me to do while you are having a hell of a good time?" he yelled in anger. "Am I supposed to sleep on the curb in the Strand? Or do you imagine you could stick me in a foul hotel, full of human smells and beastly noises?"

Decidedly not. The idea of making a miserable landlubber out of Mr. B. had never entered my intentions. I simply thought he could agree to sell me *Lady Torfrida* and buy for himself a similar yacht only of much larger tonnage that could be purchased immediately through my agents.

"Who's the looniest of the two?" he demanded to know. "You or me? Why, in the name of all sinners, is it too large for you to buy but not too large for me to sacrifice this noble craft of mine?"

"Well," I said modestly, "a man of your caliber should really possess a much larger yacht than *Lady Torfrida*." He sneered audibly and said something about my using a wrong kind of bait. I continued to argue. I must have worn him out, because at the end of two hours he announced that it was a matter requiring much greater consideration. Would I consent to be his guest on a week-end cruise?

"Just you and me and the wine."

At 5 a.m. on the following Monday, with both of us scarcely able to stand on our feet, an arrangement was signed whereby I became the proprietor of *Lady Torfrida* and Mr. B. consented to move his cellar to another yacht.

"Remember," he added, shaking his finger at me, "the deal goes through only provided the big thing is brought so close to *Lady Torfrida* that even a launch does not have to be lowered for me to move. And one condition more. You cannot have the name. *Lady Torfrida* stays with me. You will have to call her something else."

I readily agreed. I was going to rechristen the beautiful yacht *Tamara*, anyway.

"Who was she?"

"She used to be a Georgian Queen known for her habit of throwing her lovers from the tower of her castle."

"Quite a girl. Knew her personally?"

"Alas! She died without awaiting my arrival."

"They all leave us too early," said Mr. B. and opened another bottle of champagne.

While in London several years ago, I saw in the *Times* a short notice of Mr. B.'s sudden death aboard his yacht stationed as usual in the Thames. Wine and all, he lived to be eighty-two, which should be credited to the fact that he vigilantly kept the attempts at making a hole-in-one out of the circle of his eccentricities. "Torfrida" was the name of Mr. B.'s green-eyed fiancée, who went to purchase her trousseau in Paris where she met and married a stalwart British nobleman.

CHAPTER EIGHT

A GRAND DUKE SETTLES DOWN

I

SUMMER, 1889. The *Rynda* stands dismantled and forgotten in her dry-dock. I am back home, in the Michailovsky Palace.

I sit in my rooms and am bored. Nothing has changed in St. Petersburg. The same routine. The same three meals a day, with father always rushing the lunch through so as not to be late for the meeting of the Imperial Council. The same small chatter, the same shoo-shoo of the gossiping court ladies. The same tiptoeing servants. Even the same stubborn cook.

What is the matter with me? What makes me peevish?

Mother is suffering from heart disease. When walking with me, she stops often. She seems to be very glad to have me back. She tells me she worried constantly until a cable would come announcing our safe landing in this or that port of the Far East. I wish I could reciprocate her affection but it is not my fault that she has never shown me her love in the years when I needed it most.

All brothers, with the exception of kid Alexis, are doing their military service. They are in the summer camps of their respective Guard Regiments.

I meet Xenia. She is no more a tomboy. No more "your sailor Xenia." She is fourteen. I think she likes me.

I visit Nicky in his military quarters in the Kaporskoie village where he is passing his cavalry tuition in the very smart Hussar Guards Regiment commanded by Nicholasha. He lives in a small wooden bungalow built especially for him.

116

CZAR NICHOLAS II IN 1899.

THE LAST CZARINA IN 1899.

He is supremely satisfied to be an officer. We talk. I of the big hunt in India. He of the latest news in the Guards. His brother Georgie could not stand any more my raving letters and left on a practice cruise.

And so it goes. This life kills me. I must be off.

". . . Il est temps! Levons l'ancre! Ce pays nous ennuie . . ."

I and my brother Michael leave for Paris. We must see the International Exposition.

Paris. Crowds of foreigners and provincials gasping at the Eiffel Tower, the sensation of the exposition. Twenty thousand French mayors swallowing a free dinner in the Champs de Mars, scared lest they leave a bottle of wine or a piece of pastry not tasted. It nauseates me. We leave for Biarritz where our brother George Michailovich is recuperating from his recent illness. At least there is the ocean, and there are sands and sunsets in Biarritz.

Lazy evenings. Slight flirtation with two beautiful Russian girls whom we could never see in St. Petersburg as they do not belong to our "class." I think of Munchi and the nabobs of India. I am bored again.

"Look at our Buddha," laughs Michael; "he just cannot find a place for himself in the civilized part of the world." The new nickname flatters me, although I do not think it pays too great a compliment to the Divine Teacher.

Back in St. Petersburg. The "brilliant winter season." A big ball in the Winter Palace and a series of smaller balls at home. I am counting the days separating me from the spring when Mr. B. promised to send my yacht to Russia. I dance only with Xenia.

Thank God! The *Tamara* has arrived. There she is, her noble profile outlined against the Nicholas Bridge. I arrange a luncheon party for the family.

"Sandro, you are raving mad," decides father. "You mean to say you are going to cruise the world in a miserable shell like that?"

Poor father has never understood the enchantment of the sea. A sailor should not expect too much from an artillery-man! Only the Emperor, with his passion for all sorts of seagoing craft, showers the *Tamara* with compliments. Each summer he cruises in the Finnish waters aboard his majestic *Czarevna*. This summer he wants me to join him with my little *Tamara*.

Days of bliss. Severe beauty of the fjords. I take my meals with the Emperor's family, seated next to Xenia. The Emperor is enjoying his rest thoroughly. At night we play a silly card game called "the wolf."

September. Good-by, St. Petersburg! I hope not to see you for at least two years. The *Tamara* sails proudly down the Neva on its way to India. I persuaded my brother Sergei to accompany me. Somewhere in the Far East we are certain to meet Nicky, as the future Czar of Russia is about to proceed on his tour around the world. The spire of the Admiralty Building is growing smaller. My heart is beating a triumphant tattoo.

> Verse nous ton poison pour qu'il nous réconforte,
> Nous voulons tant—ce feu nous brûle le cerveau,—
> Plonger au fond du gouffre. Enfer ou ciel, qu'importe?
> Au fond de l'inconnu pour trouver du nouveau!

2

Fate was against us. Hardly did we reach the Far East when things began to happen back home. First, my brother Michael married a "commoner," a lovely girl of his choice, bringing the wrath of the Emperor and of our parents on his head. Then Georgie fell ill and the doctors diagnosed tuberculosis of both lungs, necessitating his immediate removal to Abbas-Tuman in the Caucasus. And finally, while we were traveling through India, a cablegram arrived announcing the passing of mother. She died of heart failure, taken ill on the train during her annual spring journey to our Crimean estate of Ay-Todor, where every tree and every flower had been planted under her personal supervision. Leaving the *Tamara* in the port of Bombay we jumped aboard a fast passenger steamer and hurried back to Russia. Never again was I to set foot on the sacred soil of India.

The Michailovsky Palace spelled desolation. Father walked aimlessly from room to room. He remained silent for hours, smoking thick black cigars, one after another, and staring through the long half-lighted corridors, as though hoping that a familiar voice would sound reminding him that he was not supposed to do his puffing in the drawing-room. He blamed Michael's marriage for aggravating mother's illness and he could not forgive himself for letting her go alone to the Crimea. He was fifty-nine. The sudden loss of his faithful companion made him look it. His Caucasus and his wife, nothing else ever mattered for him. Nothing at all was left for him to live for now that the jealousy of the petty courtiers and the Will of the Maker had separated him from both. Of course, there were the children, seven of us, but we grew up admiring him as a Tower of Strength, an Example of Duty, a Symbol of the glorious Empire of Nicholas I. When talking of him, we always referred to him as "Michael Nicholaevich"; when talking to him, we weighed our words and controlled our emotions. Our hearts went out to him in his present sorrow, but we could not find an appropriate way to express our sympathy. We all sat in silence, the words of the Scriptures pounding on my mind: "So they sat down with him upon the ground seven days and seven nights, and none spake a word unto him, for they saw that his grief was very great."

St. Petersburg seemed more loathsome than ever. I asked the Emperor for a commission in the Black Sea Fleet and was appointed officer of the watch on the battleship *Sinope*. I worked very hard for the next two years, concentrating entirely on my duties and taking but a two weeks' leave in February, 1892, to visit Georgie in Abbas-Tuman. He stayed alone in that mountainous place, the sweeping of the snow from the roofs of the houses providing his only amusement. The doctors thought that plenty of cool air would heal his affected lungs, and we slept under warm blankets with wide open windows, in a temperature of ten below zero. Georgie knew of my growing love for his sister Xenia, which combined with our old friendship and mutual interest in the navy made us consider ourselves two brothers. We never stopped talking, reminiscing over the days of childhood, trying to guess the future of Russia and discussing the character of Nicky. We both hoped that his father would reign for many years more. We both feared that Nicky's total unpreparedness would handicap him stupendously should he ascend the throne in the near future.

That spring I was transferred to the Baltic Sea. The Emperor expressed his satisfaction with my record in the navy and after two months in charge of a single hundred-ton torpedo boat I became commander of a squadron of twelve torpedo boats. During the summer naval review I received orders to "attack" the cruiser carrying the Emperor with his party. No man ever felt prouder, and no commander of a torpedo squadron ever attacked a battleship with greater zeal or more ferocious determination. The Minister of the Navy congratulated me on a "perfectly performed maneuver," and then came the biggest triumph of all: my gloomy naval tutor, who had predicted my dismal failure ten years earlier, sent me a letter saying that I was doing much better than he expected and that there was a slight possibility of my becoming a pretty decent officer in the long run.

In January, 1893, I learned that Russia's newest cruiser *Dimitry Donskoi*, about to return from China, would sail for the United States to thank the Americans for the help extended by them during the partial Russian famine of the previous summer. It was my big chance to visit the country of my boyish dreams. I decided to apply for a transfer to the

Dimitry Donskoi, but as long as I intended to solicit this one favor of the Czar I thought I might ask him for something else at the same time, "something else" being the hand of his daughter Xenia. I was not quite certain whether I would be able to return from America a bachelor unless engaged to marry at home. By that time I had seen and heard enough of the "belles Américaines" to realize that my knowledge of the severe regulations of the imperial family would lose its sting the moment I reached the harbor of New York.

The Emperor received me with his usual kindness. No matter how tall I grew, I remained for him "little cousin Sandro" who had played with his sons Nicky and Georgie in the garden of Livadia.

"What is the mystery?" he asked me with a smile. "Don't you see me often enough that you have to be received in an official audience?"

I am afraid I stated the purpose of my call not too eloquently. The penetrating look of his clear humorous eyes robbed me of my courage. I stuttered and stammered. The phrases that sounded beautiful when rehearsed at home, failed to produce a similar effect in this small comfortable room full of portraits and pictures.

"The matter of the transfer to the *Dimitry Donskoi* is sufficiently simple," he decided after a minute of thought; "in fact, I think it would be very appropriate if a member of my family should transmit my thanks to the President of the United States. As to the matter of Xenia and your proposition of marriage, I think you should talk to her before you talk to me."

"I did talk to her and she agreed that I should ask you for an audience."

"I see. Well, my boy, in principle I have nothing against you. I like you. If you love Xenia and Xenia loves you, I see no reason why you two should not be married. But you will have to wait for a while. Xenia's mother does not want her to marry so soon. Let us resume this conversation in a year or so."

I thanked him profoundly and rushed to Xenia to inform her of the results. Sooner or later, we expected to be able to get the consent of the Empress.

I felt I could leave for America with my heart relieved of anxiety.

3

I was just twenty-seven on that misty spring morning in 1893 when H.I.M.S. *Dimitry Donskoi* dropped anchor in the Hudson River.

Officially I came to express to President Cleveland the gratitude of my imperial cousin, Czar Alexander III, for the help extended by the American nation during the Russian famine. Unofficially I wanted to get an advance taste of the future and have the palm of my hand read by the spirit of a virgin race.

The World's Fair was about to open in Chicago, and the whole country was sizzling with excitement. Never before in the history of the Republic had so many nations sent their fleets to its shores. Great Britain, France, Germany, Italy, Russia, Austria, Argentina were all represented in the brilliant International Naval Review that took place in New York Harbor during the month of May.

The visit of the Infanta Eulalie being featured as the star attraction of the coming fair, Kaiser Wilhelm dispatched Germany's most famous composer Von Bülow to counterbalance this "Spanish intrigue"; the Scottish Highlanders sounded their bagpipes in Battery Place, and the French answered with a specially picked orchestra of the "Garde Républicaine." There was something tremendously significant in this spectacle of all the great powers fighting for American friendship and American good will. On a hot June night, while driving up gayly decorated Fifth Avenue toward the residence of John Jacob Astor, and looking at the endless row of illuminated mansions, I suddenly felt the mysterious breath of a new epoch.

So this was the land of my dreams! It was hard to believe that only twenty-nine years earlier this very land had had to go through the terrors and privations of a fratricidal war. In vain did I search for the traces of recent calamities along the streets that spelled joy, power, and wealth.

I thought of my grandfather, my uncle, and my cousin. They reigned over an empire which was even richer than this new country, confronting the same problems, such as an immense population incorporating in its midst several scores of nationalities and religions, tremendous distances between the industrial centers and the agricultural hinterland, crying necessity for extensive railroad building, etc. American liabilities were not smaller than ours, while our assets were bigger, if anything. Russia possessed gold, ore, copper, coal, iron; its soil, if properly cultivated, should have been able to feed the whole world. What was the matter with us? Why did we not follow the American way of doing things? We had no business bothering with Europe and imitating the methods befitting nations forced by their poverty to live off their wits.

Europe! Europe! It was our eternal fatal desire to mingle with Europe that had put us back God knows how many years.

Here, four thousand miles away from the cockpit of European strife, stood a living example of possibilities akin to ours, if we would only put a little common sense into our policies!

Right then and there, during the remaining few minutes of my ride, in 1893, I commenced working out a large plan for the Americanization of Russia.

It was intoxicating to be young and alive. It was a joy to repeat over and over again that the old, bloodstained nineteenth century was drawing to a close and leaving the stage clear for the irresistible efforts of coming generations. In any event, such were my feelings on that memorable night, and such was the tenor of my conversation at Mr. Astor's table.

My host and his friends looked at me with wide-open eyes. Had I not read the morning papers? Was I not aware of the bad news?

The National Cardage Company had suspended its payments, which in turn forced the Henry Allen Co., as well as various other Stock Exchange firms, into receivership.

"There is the devil to pay in the Street," said Mr. Astor. "I regret to admit that the whole country stands on the brink of a precipice."

A gentleman well known at the time for his astute judgment in important financial affairs asked for a copy of one of the great New York papers and handed it to me.

"I wish," he added rather severely, "you would glance at these gloomy headlines. They will give you a real idea of what's going to happen in America. I, for one, shall deem it my duty to advise my clients against any further commitments."

This took place on June 13, 1893.

The tragic copy of that newspaper is still in my possession. Its pages are ragged and yellow, but the message conveyed therein retains its vigorous meaning. For me it is a message of cheer. Whenever my friends express fear for the future of the United States, I read to them the newspaper printed on June 13, 1893, and let them decide for themselves whether the troubles of the moment are really of such unprecedented nature as their emotions would lead them to believe.

Financial crisis, industrial depression, blundering politics, sensational trials, administrative corruption, dangerous morals of the young generation, unkind remarks of visiting English authors, dearth of good literature, need for theatrical censorship, low batting averages of the ball players—there is hardly a phase of present-day American life which did not

cause sleepless nights to the readers and writers of that newspaper in 1893.

Glancing at the financial page we learn that Wall Street
is wrapped in gloom. "New York Central at 14½ reaches
a new low for the year. More bankruptcies expected within
the next twenty-four hours. Money on call is very scarce
at 12 to 15 per cent."

Under a glaring headline, "Lizzie Borden's Sensational
Trial in New Bedford, Mass., Creates an Enormous Amount
of Unhealthy Curiosity," we read the following slightly familiar communication:

"These people storming the local court house like wild
animals are not only urchins from the street and roughs and
toughs from the back alley, but well-dressed persons who
ought to know better."

The editorial writer advises us that "a fair notice is given
to the Democrats in the next Congress that they must redeem
all the pledges of their platform or be classed as admirers
of cowardice, instigators of knavery, liars and sneaks."

The Washington correspondent observes with a noticeable
degree of maliciousness that "although President Cleveland
was indisposed and remained at Woodley, many Senators and
Congressmen climbed the stairs only to find the President
away. Some of them poured the subject of their errands into
the ears of private secretary Thurber."

The burning of Ford's Theatre in Washington, accompanied by a heavy loss of human lives, creates a row between
the coroner and the investigating authorities. Three columns
of solid text are given under the headline which reads: "The
New Inquest Begun in Washington. The Inquiry into the
Ford's Theatre Disaster Threatens to Continue for Many
Weeks. Dr. Patterson Bluntly Refuses to Let Colonel Ains-
worth Participate in the Examination."

The fashion editor does not disguise his misgivings over the
extravagance of a "modern girl":

"Frou-frou might well be the name of the girl of this fantastic and daring period. She has frills on her shoulders and frills on her skirts and everywhere that a frill can be worn. On a pretty girl in a pink gown this writer counted fifteen separate gathered ruffles."

The tax collector is ever on the job, and "Jay Gould's Heirs Register a Strenuous Protest. Decided to Resist Payment of the Full Inheritance Tax."

Let us pass over a bitter remark of the baseball writer, referring to the "continuous slipping of the New York Giants," and see what is going on in the literary world:

"Mr. Robert Louis Stevenson's new story has the queer title of 'The Go Betweens.' We sincerely hope that the story reads better than its title sounds!"

A writer introducing himself as "the book buyer" confesses being thoroughly fed up with the arrogance of visiting British celebrities. In his estimation "the Englishmen who come to this country are too dull to appreciate the fact that the best English spoken in the world is spoken on this side of the Atlantic."

They are playing *Robin Hood* at the Garden Theatre in New York, but this fact does not prevent a righteous reader from writing a letter to the editor, expressing his distaste "at the frivolousness displayed on the modern American stage." He thinks that "something should be done to save the morals of our daughters who have to listen to all these remarks of decidedly bad taste."

The term "stenog" is not invented as yet, but we learn that the officers of the H.I.M.S. *Dimitry Donskoi*, taken on a tour of inspection through the Navy Yard, "exhibited much interest in and gave some sly glances to the young women typists who are employed in the offices and who are admitted to be pretty."

The history of humanity teaches us that the glorification of the Good Old Days has been invariably victorious in its struggle with the record of plain facts of the past. Each one of my three visits to America coincided with a period of serious financial disturbance. Each time I had been told that the nation was facing a veritable Armageddon. It makes me rather proud to think that even in 1893, having had no previous experience with Wall Street hysteria, I was inclined to disagree with the pessimistic conclusions of my alarmed friends: the unforgettable panorama of the World's Fair and Chicago itself in all the glamour of its boisterous youth made me realize that this was not a country to be despaired of.

My first stay in the United States taught me several useful lessons. I understood the advantages derived from the absence of frozen classes, and wished this important reform could be introduced at once at home. Unfortunately our best minds were in a habit of borrowing their ideas from France and imitating that age-old unwritten law—perhaps a survival of medieval guilds—which makes the son of a French janitor follow in the steps of his father: revolutions will come and go, but there is no doubt whatsoever that you will find him, in the years to come, standing on the threshold of that same dingy basement room where his parents have spent their whole lives. That is why, with all the eloquent talk about the United States of Europe, nobody as yet has been able to find a proper remedy for the incurable disease of the old continent.

At the end of that summer I left for Russia vowing to come back in the nearest future, but I was still a grand duke and as such had no right to dispose of my own time.

4

"When are you going to be married?" father asked me on my return to St. Petersburg.

"I have to wait for a definite answer from the Emperor and the Empress."

"Waiting and traveling seems the best you can do nowadays," said father impatiently. "Positively ridiculous! You must settle down. A full year has passed since you have talked to the Emperor. Go and see him again. Tell him you wish to have a definite answer."

"I won't do that, father. I would not think of annoying the Emperor. He may get very cross with me."

"Very well, Sandro. If such is the case, I am going to handle this matter in my own way."

And without another word father made for the Anichkoff Palace to have a plain talk with the Empress, leaving me in a state of distressed excitement. I knew that father adored Xenia and would do all in his power to get the consent of her imperial parents, but I likewise knew the Empress. She hated to be contradicted or rushed, and I feared she might say "no" in a manner precluding any further attempts on my part.

I remember having broken a dozen pencils in father's study awaiting his return. It seemed hours and hours since he left the house.

A bell rang in the room of father's valet, then I heard the familiar firm steps. He never walked fast up the stairs. This time he ran. His face radiated happiness. He nearly choked me in his arms.

"Everything is arranged. You are to go and see Xenia at half past four this afternoon."

"What did the Empress say? Was she furious?"

"Furious? It is too mild a word to describe her rage. She abused me in a most disgraceful way. She said I was trying to break her happiness. That I had no right to steal her daughter. That she would never speak to me again. That she never expected a man of my age would act in such an appalling manner. She threatened she would complain to the Emperor and would ask him to punish our entire family."

"What did you say?"

"Plenty, but what does it all amount to now? We won. That is the point. We won, Sandro, and Xenia is ours!"

His aide-de-camp who lunched with us that day admitted having never seen Michael Nicholaevich in such triumphant mood. "I am commencing to wonder," he whispered to me, "which one of you two is going to be married." Judging by our actions it must have been father, for while he enthused and made speeches, I sat quietly, hardly able to eat. After so many years spent in timid hopes of marrying Xenia, I was stunned by the suddenness with which my dream had become a reality. And then I could not get out of my mind the thought of my brother Sergei. He loved Xenia too. By a tacit agreement we never mentioned her name in our conversations, but what was he going to say now? He could not accuse me of any unfairness because it was Xenia's right to decide between him and me, and yet I realized that after today our relations would be bound to undergo a change. I pitied Sergei and wished something could be done to spare him this heartbreak but I could not sacrifice my love for Xenia.

At quarter past four I entered the Anichkoff Palace. I could not wait any longer. I looked at the guardsmen on duty and blushed. I had a feeling they already knew of my happiness. So as to avoid facing the elevator man I walked very slowly up the long flight of stairs.

Xenia's valet Beresin sat in a chair reading the newspaper.

"Will you please announce me to Her Imperial Highness."

Beresin opened his eyes in astonishment. It was something new for him as I always went in unannounced. He smiled, at least I thought he did, and led me to Xenia's salon. Only yesterday we all had a gay tea party in this beautifully furnished room, but today everything seemed different. I stood watching the door of Xenia's bedroom. "How funny," I thought, "that she should make me wait so long." She came in with her eyes fixed on the floor. A simple white silk blouse, blue skirt, brown stockings and brown shoes. She stopped in front of the window next to the door and waited. I took her hand and led her toward two large soft chairs. We talked in a whisper. I think we both talked at the same time. We used to kiss each other before but those were cousins' kisses. Now it was a kiss of possession.

"Let us go and see father and mother," suggested Xenia. "Be careful with mother. She is still furious. She wanted to annihilate your father for forcing her to consent."

I laughed brazenly. I would have faced ten Empresses at that moment.

Trying to look angry, the Empress kissed me and said:

"I know I should not kiss you for stealing my daughter, but what can I do? Please, tell your father not to dare to come near me for at least a year."

The Emperor winked at me: he had already telephoned to father to come immediately to the palace. A few minutes later the main culprit walked in, unabashed and grinning at the Empress. The Emperor gave orders to the valet to advise all the members of the imperial family that they were expected to be present at the engagement dinner at eight-thirty.

At the table Xenia and I were placed next to each other. Her father looked pleased and the atmosphere of sincere gayety prevailed. After many toasts, congratulations and family kisses, I glanced at Sergei. He smiled at me. He understood my fears and would not spoil my happiness. Nobody could have guessed his sufferings. His sportsmanship was superb.

5

The day of our wedding was set for the end of July. I tried to argue against this delay of nearly six months but was told to keep quiet and pray to God that the dressmakers would deliver Xenia's trousseau by that time. The honeymoon was to be spent in my beloved Ay-Todor, left to me in mother's will, and Lieutenant Chatelain, my friend of many years, undertook the task of redecorating and refurnishing the house. While a bachelor I never bothered to establish my court; as a married man I had to live up to regulations. Two ladies-in-waiting, a master of the court, and my personal aide-de-camp—any smaller number of perennial witnesses to our happiness would have incensed the Minister of the Imperial Court.

In the beginning of May Xenia and I accompanied the Empress to Abbas-Tuman. The approaching marriage of her daughter made the poor mother grieve with increased sharpness over the condition of her favorite son Georgie. He was delighted to see us, but his pale, worn-out face bore witness to the progress of his fatal illness. We passed every moment of four weeks together, driving into the mountains, organizing picnic parties, laughing, joking and dancing. We did our very best to cheer up Georgie. He was growing weaker and had a premonition he would never see St. Petersburg again. Our gayety failed to deceive him. The sight of two healthy happy people must have caused him additional pain, although externally he remained the same kind, generous, faithful Georgie. I thought it indecent to talk of our plans in his presence; listening to his hard uneven breathing—we occupied adjoining rooms—I lay awake and was choking with bitterness. What sense was there in this life of ours if nothing in the world could save Georgie?

In June we joined the Emperor aboard the *Czarevna* in the Finnish waters. He had lost considerable weight during our absence and was complaining of extreme fatigue. The doctors, the ever-optimistic court physicians, said he suffered the consequences of long months of hard work. They prescribed plenty of rest and fresh air. Hypnotized by his marvelous physique, they overlooked the development of his kidney trouble.

As in previous summers, we visited our favorite places ashore, did a great deal of fishing, entertained our friends, and played the game of "wolf." On July 20 we returned to the capital to attend the "exhibition of the trousseau" in one of the larger halls of the palace.

Dresses: morning, sports, afternoon, evening, and "grande soirée."

Coats: winter, spring, summer, and fall.

Fur coats and fur wraps: ermine, chinchilla, beaver, mink, seal, astrakhan.

Stockings, gloves, hats, umbrellas, and the mountains of accessories I do not pretend to know the exact names of.

Huge tables packed with dozens of sets of linen.

Silver plate for ninety-six persons. A gold toilette set of one hundred and forty-four articles. Gold-rimmed glass-ware, gold-rimmed cups, gold-rimmed dishes, etc., etc., eight dozens of each of these articles.

Jewelry: a pearl necklace consisting of five rows of pearls, a diamond necklace, a ruby necklace, an emerald necklace, and a sapphire necklace; emerald-and-ruby diadems, dia-mond-and-emerald bracelets, diamond breast ornaments, brooches, etc. All jewelry was made by Bolin, the best crafts-man of St. Petersburg. It represented, no doubt, a stupen-dous outlay of money, but in those days we judged the jewelry by the beauty of its design and colors, not by its value.

At the end of the hall stood a table covered with men's articles. I did not expect to be taken care of in Xenia's trousseau and was surprised. It appeared, however, that ac-cording to the tradition in the family the Emperor had to present me with a certain amount of apparel. There were four dozens of day shirts, four dozens of evening shirts, etc. Four dozens of everything. My particular attention was at-tracted by a silver dressing gown and a pair of silver slippers. The former struck me as being enormously heavy.

"Sixteen pounds," explained the master of ceremonies.

"Sixteen pounds? Who is going to wear it?"

My ignorance pained him. He explained that a bride-groom, belonging to the imperial family, must wear that monstrous gown and silver slippers when entering the bridal chambers on the wedding night. This ridiculous rule was included in the same set of regulations which forbade me seeing Xenia the day before the wedding. I sighed. What else could I do? The House of Romanoffs had no intention of changing its three centuries old traditions for the sake of pleasing poor Sandro.

Twenty-four hours of loneliness and cursing the originators of all traditions, and then came the Great Day. Our wedding was to be performed in the same Peterhof Chapel where I took my oath of allegiance eight years previous, this particular place being chosen as a concession to my superstitious hatred for St. Petersburg.

The procedure of dressing Xenia, supervised by the Empress and the eldest ladies-in-waiting, lasted three hours. Her hair was arranged in long curls and the crown jewels affixed in an order too complicated for me to understand or for any human to describe intelligently. For all I knew, she wore the same silver dress my sister Anastasia and all other grand duchesses wore for their weddings, and I remember seeing a diamond diadem on her head, several rows of pearls around her neck, and several diamond ornaments on her corsage.

Finally I was allowed to see my bride, and the procession started. The Emperor led Xenia. I followed with the Empress on my arm. Our relatives formed a long line behind us, occupying their places in accordance with the order of succession. Misha and Olga, the kid brother and kid sister of Xenia, were winking at me and I had to strain every muscle of my face to keep from laughing. Everybody afterwards said that the choir sang "divinely." My head was too occupied with the thoughts of our voyage to Ay-Todor to pay any attention to the prayers or to the singing. My mother had bought Ay-Todor, then a barren strip of land on the shores of the Black Sea, in the days of my early infancy. In a way we grew together. With the passing of the years it became a flourishing country estate covered with gardens, vineyards, lawns and coves. A lighthouse was built on its grounds to enable us to find our way on a foggy night. For us children that glaring strong light of Ay-Todor had become a symbol of happiness, and I wondered now whether

Xenia would feel about it the same way my brothers and I had for over twenty years.

Going back to the palace we marched in the same order as before, except that I changed places with the Emperor and was walking with Xenia on my arm.

"I cannot wait to get rid of this silly dress," she complained to me in a whisper, "it must weigh pounds and pounds. I wish we did not have to sit through that dinner. Look at papa, he is all in."

We all could see how worn out the Emperor was, but even he could not order the cancellation of the boring gala dinner.

Only at eleven p.m. were we able to change into more comfortable clothes, and off we drove in a court carriage to the suburban Ropsha Palace to spend our wedding night. On our way we had to change horses as the coachman was not able to control them.

The Palace of Ropsha and the adjoining village were brilliantly illuminated, so much so that our nervous coachman, blinded by the lights, overlooked a small bridge and landed us—three horses, carriage and two newlyweds—flat in the brook. Xenia fell at the bottom of the carriage, I on top of her, while the coachman and the footman were thrown into the water. Fortunately nobody was hurt and we were rescued promptly by the second carriage occupied by Xenia's servants. My wife's gorgeous ostrich-feathered hat and ermine-trimmed coat were covered with mud, my face and hands were absolutely black. We wondered what General Wiazemsky, who was to meet us at the entrance to the Ropsha Palace, would say, but that experienced courtier said nothing. As far as he was concerned, it may have been a new fashion among the newlywed members of the imperial family to take a swim fully dressed.

And now we were alone, for the first time since our engagement. We could hardly believe our luck. Could it be possible that we would be permitted to eat our supper undisturbed? We glanced at the door suspiciously and then burst out laughing. Nobody. Just ourselves. I took the box containing the jewelry of my mother and presented it to Xenia. As little as she cared about jewelry, she did admire a beautiful diamond diadem and a set of sapphires.

We parted at one in the morning to don our "wedding night uniforms." On my way to the bridal chambers I saw my figure, molded in silver, reflected in a mirror, and that ridiculous sight caused me another gale of laughter. I resembled an operatic Sultan in the grand finale.

Next morning we returned to St. Petersburg to face the rest of the ceremony, consisting of a reception for the members of the diplomatic corps in the Winter Palace, a visit to the tombs of our ancestors in the Fortress of Peter and Paul, and a prayer at the miraculous ikon of the Saviour. A special train was awaiting us at the railroad station. Seventy-two hours more and I would introduce its new mistress to Ay-Todor. Our plans mapped out for years in advance, we expected to lead a life of undisturbed happiness. Who could have thought on that pale-blue July evening of 1894 that but three months separated us from the greatest catastrophe in the history of the empire? Who could have foreseen that Emperor Alexander III would die at the age of forty-nine, leaving his work unfinished and placing the fate of one-sixth of the earth's surface in the trembling hands of a bewildered youth?

CHAPTER NINE

MY RELATIVES

I

THE premature death of Alexander III advanced the outburst of the revolution by at least twenty-five years. The Marxian historians are certain not to find this statement to their liking but one must not forget that each throne is only as strong as its weakest mainstay.

Beginning with October, 1894, three chief protagonists loomed in the arena of Russian internal strife: the Czar, the imperial family and the patron saints of the revolution. The sympathies of the remaining one hundred fifty million odd Russians swung between throne and anarchy, and it depended entirely on the cleverness of either one of the two adversaries to secure their somewhat lukewarm support.

I shall commence with the imperial family, which is appropriate because the lack of experience of Nicholas II made him solicit first of all the advice of his relatives. I have dealt upon several occasions with the different members of the family. This time I shall draw an unbiased characteristic of those who had reached maturity by 1894.

Nicholas II had three living granduncles, brothers of his grandfather, Emperor Alexander II: Grand Duke Constantin Nicholaevich who had retired by that time to his estate in the Crimea and was enjoying the companionship of his second wife, a former ballerina; Grand Duke Nicholas Nicholaevich Sr. who occupied the post of inspector-general of the Russian Cavalry and who was exceedingly popular among the officers but whose advanced age precluded active participation in the affairs of state; Grand Duke Michael Nicholaevich—my father—who was presiding over the Imperial Council and who was also inspector-general of the Russian Artillery. Of the three my father had by far the widest governmental experience, his twenty-two years at the head of the Caucasian administration having taught him the science of ruling. He would have made an ideal adviser for the young Czar had it not been for his unyielding attitude of an old disciplinarian. His grandnephew was his sovereign: as such he had to be obeyed implicitly. Whenever Nicholas II said to him: "Uncle Misha, I think we should follow the suggestion of the Minister of Foreign Affairs," my father bowed and followed the suggestion of the Minister of Foreign Affairs. Accustomed to seeing men of mature mind and iron will on the throne of Russia, he never doubted the ultimate wisdom of his grandnephew's decisions, which nullified the potential value of his thorough understanding of the problems of the empire.

Next in line came the four imperial uncles, who were the four brothers of the late Czar Alexander III.

Grand Duke Vladimir Alexandrovich, father of the present pretender to the throne, Grand Duke Cyril, possessed a hidden talent for all arts. He painted well, he was a patron of the ballet and the original financial backer of Mr. Sergei Diaghileff, he collected ancient ikons, he visited Paris twice a year, and he adored giving elaborate parties at his splendid palace in Czarskoie-Selo. A kind-hearted man, he fell a victim to his eccentricities. A stranger meeting Grand Duke Vladimir Alexandrovich was certain to be taken aback by the roughness and by the shouting voice of this grand seigneur of Russia. He treated the younger grand dukes with a maximum of contempt. None of us could have engaged him in conversation unless prepared to discuss subjects of art or the finesses of French cooking. His visits to Paris meant a red-letter day for the chefs and maîtres-d'hôtel of the Ville Lumière, for after making a terrific row about the "inadequacy" of the menu he would invariably finish the evening by putting a lavish tip in every hand capable of being stretched out. By virtue of his age and birth he occupied the important post of commander of the Imperial Guard Corps, although he resented the interference of military duties with his pursuit of the arts. His wife, Grand Duchess Maria Pavlovna Sr., belonged to the German reigning house of Mecklenburg-Schwerin. Her brother Friedrich married my sister Anastasia. She was a delightful hostess and her entertainments deserved the reputation she enjoyed throughout Europe. Emperor Alexander III disliked her because of her refusal to join the Greek Orthodox Church, which caused the legend about her "strong German sympathies." After the death of her husband she finally changed her religion but the gossipers persisted in accusing her of lack of patriotism.

Uncle Alexis, Grand Duke Alexis Alexandrovich, was admitted to be the best-looking man in the imperial family, although I am afraid his tremendous weight would have handicapped him with the modern girls. A man of the world to his finger tips, a Beau Brummell and a bon vivant hopelessly spoiled by women, particularly by those of Washington, D. C., he traveled a great deal. The necessity of spending a year away from Paris would have caused him to resign his post. He had a post. Strange as it may seem, he was the grand admiral of the Russian Navy. His knowledge of naval affairs could not have been more limited. The very mention of the pending naval reforms brought a hostile frown on his handsome face. Not interested in anything that did not pertain to love-making, food and liquor, he invented a convenient way of staging his weekly conferences with the admirals. He invited them to dinner in his palace, and after the Napoleon brandy would find its way into the stomachs of the appreciative guests, the host would open the naval conferences with a story going back to the antediluvian days of the sailing ships. Each time I sat at his table, I heard him repeat the self-same recital of the shipwreck of the frigate *Alexander Nevsky* which occurred many years ago on the rocks of the Danish coast, near Skagen. I learned by heart every detail of this involved narrative and took the precaution of moving my chair a few inches away just at the moment when, according to the scenario, Uncle Alexis had to bring his fist down on the table, exclaiming in a thundering voice: "And only then, my friends, did the bloody captain recognize the silhouette of the rocks of Skagen!" His cook was a real artist. The admirals were perfectly willing to keep the debates within the limits of the days of H.I.M.S. *Alexander Nevsky*. Tragedy marred the end of this joyful existence: disregarding all signs of the approaching war with Japan, the grand admiral continued his rounds of revels, waking one morning to find that our fleet encountered a crushing defeat in the battle with the modern dreadnoughts of the Mikado. He resigned his post and died shortly afterwards. His was a case of fast women and slow ships.

Uncle Sergei, Grand Duke Sergei Alexandrovich, played a fatal part in the downfall of the empire, having been partially responsible for the Khodynka catastrophe during the coronation of the year 1896. Try as I will, I cannot find a single redeeming feature in his character. A very poor officer, he commanded the Preobrajensky Regiment, the crack regiment of the Imperial Guard. A complete ignoramus in administrative affairs, he held fast to the general governorship of the Moscow area, which should have been entrusted to a statesman of exceptionally seasoned experience. Obstinate, arrogant, disagreeable, he flaunted his many peculiarities in the face of the entire nation, providing the enemies of the régime with inexhaustible material for calumnies and libels. The generals visiting the messroom of the Preobrajensky Regiment listened with stupefaction to the chorus of officers singing a favorite song of Grand Duke Sergei, with its refrain consisting of the words—"and peace, and love, and bliss." The august commander himself illustrated those not very soldierlike words by throwing his body back and registering a tortured rapture in his features.

The Czar should never have allowed Uncle Sergei to retain

his post in Moscow after the storm of indignation caused by the Khodynka catastrophe. As though to accentuate his repugnant personality on a background of virtue, he married Grand Duchess Elizabeth, the elder sister of the young Czarina. No two human beings could have offered such a contrast. Ravishing beauty, rare intelligence, delightful sense of humor, infinite patience, hospitality of thought, generous heart, all gifts were hers. It was cruel and unjust that a woman of her caliber should have tied up her existence to a man like Uncle Sergei. Everybody fell in love with "Aunt Ella" the very first moment she arrived in St. Petersburg from her native Hesse-Darmstadt. One evening in her company, and the memory of her eyes, her skin, her laughter, her genius for putting one at ease, threw us all into the depths of despair at the realization of her approaching betrothal. I would have given ten years of my life to stop her from entering the church on the arm of haughty Sergei. I liked to think of myself as her "cavaliere servente," and I despised the condescending grimace of her husband when exaggerating his St. Petersburg drawl he would address "Aunt Ella" as "my child." Too proud to complain she stayed by his side for nearly twenty years, her loyalty undiminished by the passing of time and her sorrow adding a spiritual halo to her beauty. No mere pose but a genuine pity for all humanity moved her to visit the assassin of her husband in his death cell in the Moscow prison. Her subsequent retirement to a convent, her heroical though unsuccessful efforts to guide her younger sister, the Czarina, and her final martyrdom at the hands of the Bolsheviks, justly entitle her to canonization. No nobler woman has left the imprint of her personality on the blood-stained pages of Russian history.

Uncle Paul, Grand Duke Paul Alexandrovich, was the nicest of the four uncles of the Czar, although he too possessed an inclination for "mounting the high horse," which trait he owed to his close friendship with his brother Sergei. He danced well, he was greatly admired by women, and he looked quite attractive in his dark-green-and-silver dolman, raspberry tight breeches and low boots of a Grodno Hussar. Satisfied with the care-free life of a brilliant officer, he never occupied a position of responsibility. His first wife, a Princess of Greece, died when he was still very young, and he married for the second time the divorced wife of a colonel, thus committing a double breach of the regulations prevailing in the imperial family, no grand duke being permitted to marry a commoner and no divorced woman being received at court. He had to leave Russia for an indefinite stay in Paris. I believe he benefited considerably by his forced exile through meeting people of intelligence and importance. It changed his character, bringing out human traits formerly hidden under a mask of nonsensical haughtiness. During the World War he commanded for a short time the Guard Corps on the German front but exercised no influence on the affairs of state.

There is not much to add to what I have already said about Georgie (Grand Duke George Alexandrovich) and Misha (Grand Duke Michael Alexandrovich), the two brothers of Nicholas II. Georgie was the cleverest of the three but he died too early to develop his brilliant abilities. Misha was eleven years younger than the Czar. He fascinated everybody by the wholehearted simplicity of his manner. A favorite of his family, of his fellow officers, and of all his countless friends, he possessed a well-organized mind and would have succeeded in any branch of the service had it not been for his marriage to a commoner. It happened just at the time he reached maturity and it put the Czar into a most embarrassing position. He wished his brother all possible luck but in his quality of head of the imperial family he had to follow the course prescribed by law. Misha left Russia, married Mrs. Woulfert (the divorced wife of Captain Woulfert) in Vienna and settled in London. So he too was absent from Russia and estranged from his brother during the tense years that preceded the conflict.

And now I am coming to the sons of the Czar's three granduncles. In Russia we were considered his "second uncles"; according to Anglo-Saxon ideas of relationship we were his cousins.

First of all, there were two sons of Grand Duke Constantin Nicholaevich, the third one (Wiacheslav) having died in his early youth and the fourth (Nicholas) having spent his life in exile in Turkestan. The eldest "Constantinovich," Grand Duke Constantin Constantinovich, was a talented poet and a very religious man, which in a measure both broadened and narrowed his outlook. He was the author of the best translation of *Hamlet* that ever appeared in Russia and himself played the title rôle in a series of private performances given at his palace. He presided with great tact over the Imperial Academy of Sciences, being the first to recognize the genius of Pavloff. He wrote poems, essays, plays, short and long stories, using the pen name of "K. R." and receiving favorable notices even in the papers opposed to the régime. He organized a club for the officers of his regiment supplanting former drinking with a healthy interest for modern Russian literature. Thoroughly understanding the soul of a peasant, he achieved marvels in reforming the methods of teaching adopted by our army. Nothing pleased him more than a morning spent in the military barracks where he personally conducted a class for the recruits. While in charge of the Russian military schools he did a great deal to humanize the barbarous mentality of the tutors, who thought that a cadet should be led to his commission via fear and punishment.

All this was very laudable. One would have fancied that a man like Grand Duke Constantin Constantinovich should prove invaluable in assisting the Czar, but Mr. K. R. hated politics and feared politicians. He wanted to be left alone with his books, his plays, his scientists, his soldiers, his cadets, and his own happy family consisting of his wife (Princess Elizabeth of Saxe-Weimar), his six boys and his two daughters. His wishes were respected, the throne missing thereby a golden opportunity.

His younger brother, Grand Duke Dimitry Constantinovich, was a confirmed woman hater and an enthusiastic horseman. "Beware of skirts!" "The war with Germany is imminent!" "I would like you to see my yearlings!" No other subjects touched the heart of Dimitry Constantinovich. He did remain a bachelor and he did possess excellent yearlings. As to the war with Germany, predicted by him fifteen years in advance, his nearsightedness, which developed into a practical blindness by 1914, kept him in the rear, cursing his fate and supervising the training of the cavalry.

Of all the members of the imperial family, Grand Duke Nicholas Nicholaevich Jr., the elder son of my uncle Grand Duke Nicholas Nicholaevich Sr., exercised the greatest influence on the conduct of the affairs of state. The two pivotal acts of modern Russian history—the Manifesto of October 17, 1905, and the abdication of Nicholas II on March 2, 1917—should be credited to a peculiar aberration of his political foresight. No bitterness guides my pen in describing the personality of cousin Nicholasha. The feud between him and my brother Nicholas Michailovich belongs to the world that is no more. Both of them are dead and both have long since entered the Hall of History. Far be it from me to try to minimize his thorough honesty and good intentions. The men of the type of Grand Duke Nicholas Nicholaevich Jr. could be used to a distinct advantage by any organized state, providing its ruler was conscious of the natural limitations of a single-track mind.

Cousin Nicholasha was a superb army officer. He had no peer in maintaining discipline, in drilling soldiers and in preparing military reviews. When attending a parade of the St. Petersburg garrison, one was certain of witnessing the brilliant performance of a perfectly trained military unit: each company in prescribed formation, each button in its proper place, each move delighting the hearts of the past masters of routine! Had he been left undisturbed in his position of commander of the St. Petersburg military area, Nicholasha would have justified all expectations and possibly would have prevented the revolt of February 28, 1917. Looking back at the twenty-three years of the reign of Nicholas II, I can find no logical explanation why, in the name of God, the Czar should have sought Nicholasha's advice on any matters of state importance. Like all army men accustomed to tackling clearly defined tasks, Nicholasha felt dizzy when confronted with a complicated political situation where his habit of raising his voice and threatening punishment failed to produce the desired effect. The general strike of October, 1905, left him bewildered, his beloved military status prescribing no remedies for that sort of collective insubordination. There was obviously no way of arresting several million strikers! The next best thing to do, in his estimation, was to ascertain the nature of the demands of the "commanders of the strikers." An attempt at explaining to Nicholasha that the revolt of 1905 was marked by its anarchistic character and that there were no "commanders" to negotiate with, would have proved useless. As long as the world existed, all armies, revolutionary or otherwise, had been led by their commanders! And so on October 17, 1905, in the face of a general strike promoted by the Bolshevik section of the Social-Democratic party, and in the presence of an agrarian revolt conducted by the peasants clamoring for additional land, Nicholasha persuaded the Czar to sign a manifesto demanded by the garrulous leaders of the intelligentsia. The latter had no connection with the Bolsheviks and the peasants: they were nevertheless "the commanders," commanders without an army. The strikes continued and the peasants, not satisfied with the convocation of a parliament, which consisted of talkative weaklings, went on burning the estates of their landlords. The Czar was obliged to order a pitiless suppression of the revolt but the régime itself never recovered from the humiliation caused by the fact of a sovereign capitulating before a mob.

"Nicholas II would have never signed the Manifesto of October 17," relates Witte in his memoirs, "had it not been for the insistence of Grand Duke Nicholas Nicholaevich Jr."

The experience of 1905 did not cure Nicholas II of his inclination to consult Nicholasha. Twelve years later, preparing to take the most important decision in the history of Russia, he turned once more to the sponsor of the notorious Manifesto. Had Nicholasha advised the Czar on March 2, 1917, to remain with the army and to accept the challenge of the revolution, Mr. Stalin would not have been entertaining G. B. Shaw in the Kremlin in 1931. But the former commander-in-chief of the Russian Army was still looking for the "commanders of the revolution" and thought he recognized one in Mr. Kerensky. The real significance of the tragedy dawned on him only a week later, when arriving at G.H.Q. to resume his exalted post he learned that the St. Petersburg Soviet would not permit Mr. Kerensky to employ his services.

Think of the simplicity of the man who crosses a continent gone drunk with revolt, observing nothing of the crowds, the demonstrations and the riots, and remaining totally unshaken in his belief that the "new commanders" would appreciate his unselfish patriotism and military judgment!

Overshadowed by the splendor of Nicholasha's numerous titles and positions, his younger brother Grand Duke Peter Nicholaevich led the unassuming life of an officer in the Guard Lancer Regiment. His grave illness, tuberculosis of the lungs, forced him to stay for several years in Egypt. He abandoned the service and became interested in architecture. He was a shy man deprived of conversation, letting his wife Militza Nicholaevna (a daughter of King Nicholas of Montenegro) do all the talking in the family. Militza and her sister Stana (Nicholasha's wife) exercised an exceptionally bad influence on the young Czarina. Superstitious, gullible, excitable, those two Montenegrin grand duchesses fell an easy prey to native and foreign adventurers. Each time they ran across a "remarkable" man, they dragged him to the imperial palace, which happened in the case of "Doctor" Philippe and Rasputin. They talked freely and irresponsibly. Seated across the table from Poincaré, then President of the French Republic, during his visit to Russia in July, 1914, Militza attacked Austria in the most tactless manner and said she was "rejoicing" at the coming war. The Czar reprimanded her severely but nobody and nothing could have stopped the two Montenegrins from interfering with affairs of state and serving as mouthpieces for Balkan schemers.

Continuing my review of the imperial family in the order of succession to the throne, I arrive at my own five brothers. Raised and educated far away from the capital, we "Michailovichi" differed considerably from our uncles and cousins. Although faithful subjects of the Emperor, we did not approve of everything occurring in the palace. We spoke frankly and criticized constructively. We were called "dangerous radicals," the "danger" part of the cognomen reflecting the bitterness of the courtiers, the "radical" part possibly corresponding to the truth but depending on the meaning one put into that greatly abused word.

My eldest brother, Nicholas Michailovich, was, no doubt, the most "radical" and the most talented member of our family. Mother mapped out a distinguished military career for him, and in order to please her he graduated from the War College. His real interests lay in the direction of pure historical research. He consented to serve in the Chevalier Guards simply because of his friendship with Empress Marie (my mother-in-law), who was its Honorary Commander. His intellectual superiority over his fellow officers took all enjoyment out of his regimental contacts; gradually he drifted away from his military environment toward the archives and the libraries of St. Petersburg and Paris. His monumental biography of Emperor Alexander I, written after years of gathering material and verifying data, remains unsurpassed in the historical literature of Russia. No student of the first twenty-five years of the nineteenth century could ignore the analysis of the events and the general survey of the period given by Nicholas Michailovich. When translated into French it created a stir among the Napoleonic experts, causing many a treatise to be revised, changed or rewritten. The French Academy elected him a member,—an honor seldom, if ever, accorded to a foreigner,—and he was always besieged with invitations to lecture before the French historical societies. His profound knowledge of French culture and his mature appreciation of the spirit of Roman civilization helped to develop his friendships with the French writers and scientists. He felt at home in Paris, although the majority of the Parisians could never get over the shock of seeing a Russian grand duke trace his steps to the Collège de France in preference to Montmartre, while his modest manner of living in the old Hotel Vendôme caused maîtres-d'hôtel and casino directors to express open fears for the future of the grand ducal trade.

It must have been painful for Nicholas Michailovich to explain some of the things that were happening at home to his friends in the Collège de France and in the Chambre des Députés. I cannot say that I approved unreservedly of his very "Frenchified" political views. An enthusiastic admirer of the parliamentary régime and an inveterate follower of the Clemenceau-Jaurès duels, he hated to admit that a constitution patterned after the Third French Republic would prove a dismal failure in Russia. The truth was that he had been born in the wrong country. They nicknamed him "Philippe Egalité" in the Chevalier Guards, not realizing that their imperial friend went much further in his republicanism than that brother of the King of France who attempted to use the revolution as a stepping stone for his personal ambitions. My brother had all the necessary qualifications of a loyal president of a civilized republic, which led him often to mistake the Nevsky Prospect for the Avenue des Champs-Elysées. A long letter sent by him to Nicholas II in July, 1916, contained several paragraphs written in French. "Dear Nicky, please excuse my French," he added in postcriptum, "but I think it enables me to find more adequate expression for my thoughts . . ." A brilliant stylist possessing the secret of harmonious prose, he must have realized, perhaps reluctantly, that his Gallicized thoughts would sound strange indeed in Russian.

Poushkin's epigram dedicated to the famous Russian philosopher Tchaadaeff can be easily applied in the case of my elder brother:

> He would have been a Pericles in Athens,
> He would have been a Brutus in Rome,
> He is but a Hussar Officer in Russia!

I know of no one who would have surpassed him at the post of Russian ambassador to France or Great Britain. His clear mind, his cosmopolitan outlook, his innate dignity, his understanding of foreign mentalities, his broad tolerance and his sincere pacifism would have gained him love and respect in any capital of the world. Petty jealousies and silly regulations kept him from taking a prominent place in the ranks of our diplomats, and so instead of helping Russia where it needed his assistance most, he was condemned to political inactivity by persons who could not forgive him his talents and who would not forget his contempt for their ignorance. From this point of view his life should be considered wasted. In his early youth he fell in love with Princess Victoria of Baden, daughter of our uncle the Grand Duke of Baden. It broke his heart as neither the Russian Emperor nor the Greek Orthodox Church would countenance a marriage between two first cousins. She married the future King Gustav-Adolph of Sweden; he remained a bachelor and stayed alone

GRAND DUKE ALEXANDER IN A XVII CENTURY COSTUME
WORN BY HIM AT THE COURT BALL IN JANUARY 1903.

GRAND DUCHESS XENIA, WIFE OF GRAND DUKE ALEXANDER,
IN A XVII CENTURY DRESS WORN BY HER AT THE COURT BALL
IN JANUARY 1903.

in his very large palace, surrounded by books, manuscripts and botanical collections.

My second brother, Michael Michailovich, had none of Nicholas Michailovich's talents. He adored the military service and enjoyed himself immensely in the Egersky Regiment of the Guards. His good looks, generous heart and dancing ability endeared him to St. Petersburg society, and very soon "Miche-Miche" became a recognized favorite in the capital. Unfortunately he was a marrying man. At the age of twenty, immediately after coming into possession of his money, he started building a luxurious palace. "We must have a decent place to live in," he told his architects. "We" meant him and his future wife. He did not know as yet whom he was going to marry but he wanted to marry someone as soon as possible. In constant search for the "girl of his dreams" he made several attempts at marrying outside of the ranks of royalty. It created painful scenes between him and our parents and it led nowhere. Finally he concluded a morganatic marriage with a morganatic daughter of the Duke of Nassau whose maternal grandfather was the celebrated Russian poet Poushkin. That put an end to Miche-Miche's elaborate plans of lavish entertainments in the beautiful brand-new palace. He was asked to leave Russia and remained the rest of his life in London. One of his daughters, known under her present title of Lady Milford-Haven, married Prince Battenberg, cousin of the Queen of Spain.

My third brother, George Michailovich, showed in his childhood the signs of a talent for painting. He shared my passion for the Caucasus and expected to do his military service in Tiflis, in the Grouzinsky Grenadier Regiment. The transfer of our father to St. Petersburg played havoc with George's intentions and talents. While serving in the Horse Artillery of the Guards he struck up a friendship with Grand Duke Peter, which proved fatal to his colorful personality. Imitating his cousin Peter, he lost all individuality and began living in an atmosphere of riding schools, race

149

horses, and cavalry officers. On my return from the Far East I found that a new human being had taken the place of the chum of my Tiflis days. I was not interested in this stranger, and our relations lost their former character of mutual admiration. George had two daughters by his marriage with Princess Marie of Greece; the elder, Xenia, married and later divorced Mr. William Leeds, Jr., of New York; the younger, Nina, is married to Prince Paul Chavchavadse and lives likewise in America.

My fourth brother, Sergei Michailovich (he was three years younger than I), gladdened our father's heart by becoming a good artilleryman. As inspector-general of the Russian Artillery he did all in his power to impress upon the sluggish minds of the Imperial Government the inevitability of a war with Germany. His advice was ignored but later on he was pointed out to the opposition party in parliament as "the man responsible for our unpreparedness." This ingenious scheme of thrusting the knife in his back did not surprise Sergei Michailovich. Brought up by Colonel Helmersen, an ex-aide-de-camp of our father, he seemed to have taken as his motto "tant pis" (so much the worse)—the favorite expression of that venomous descendant of German barons. Whenever Helmersen thought something had gone wrong, he shrugged his shoulders and said "tant pis" with the final air of one who enjoyed going to the devil. The tutor and the pupil vied with each other in maintaining that silly attitude, and it took my brother a long time to get over his habit of looking perennially hurt, a pose which earned him the nickname of "Monsieur Tant Pis." Like myself, he had been an intimate friend of Nicholas II for over forty years, and it is to be regretted that he did not succeed in transmitting some of Colonel Helmersen's critical methods to his pal of the Czarskoie-Selo Palace. He never married, although his faithful companion, a famous Russian ballerina, provided him with a substitute of family life.

My youngest brother, Alexis Michailovich, died of tuberculosis at the age of twenty.

A few lines dedicated to the so-called "half-sovereigns"—the Leuchtenbergs, the Oldenburgs and the Mecklenburg-Strelitz'—will conclude this posthumous review of the imperial family of Russia. We used to call them "half-sovereigns" because, although possessing the title "Imperial Highness," they were not grand dukes but simply dukes and princes.

Of the three Dukes of Leuchtenberg, sons of Grand Duchess Marie Nicholaevna of Russia by her marriage with the Prince of Leuchtenberg, only Eugene was sufficiently known in Russia, owing his prominence to the beauty of his wife Zina, who was a sister of the famous General Skobeleff and who had received the title of Countess Beauharnais. When I say that Zina was "beautiful" I am fully aware of the utter impossibility even remotely to convey the physical endowments of that woman. I have never seen anyone like her, in all my travels throughout Europe, Asia, America and Australia, which is extremely fortunate because women of her maddening pagan appeal should really not be permitted to roam at large. Her entrance into the room always sent me running out of it. I knew of her habit of coming close to people, when talking to thém, and I felt I could not be responsible for my actions. All the younger grand dukes sympathized with me wholeheartedly. They suffered, every one of them. The proper thing to do was to crush Zina in one's arms and let the Minister of the Imperial Court do his worst, but somehow we could not muster sufficient courage for this logical action. To make matters worse, our Beau Brummell, Grand Duke Alexis Alexandrovich, was an inseparable friend of the Leuchtenberg couple, his love for Zina having long since defeated his fear of causing a scandal. They were known throughout the world as the "ménage royal à trois," all remonstrations of the Emperor failing to impress his passionate uncle. I think Alexis Alexandrovich would have torn down the whole navy for the sake of staying with Zina.

The poor health of Eugene's two brothers, Nicholas and George, necessitated their staying abroad most of the time. George occupied a prominent position in Paris society, basking in the reflected glory of the Romanoffs and recognized as the most generous host of the French capital. His second wife, Stana of Montenegro, had divorced him and married Grand Duke Nicholas Nicholaevich Jr.

The head of the clan of the Oldenburgs, Prince Peter, came to Russia during the reign of my grandfather, married a Russian grand duchess and liked it so much in St. Petersburg that neither he nor his children ever went back to Germany. His eldest daughter married Grand Duke Nicholas Nicholaevich Sr., changed her religion and received the title of Grand Duchess Alexandra Petrovna of Russia. As usually happens with neophytes, she became a bigoted adherent of the Greek Orthodox Church and turned her life into an endless worshiping of living bishops and dead saints. She wound up by taking the veil.

Her brother, Prince Alexander of Oldenburg, was the greatly feared commander of the corps of the Guard troops. His severity verged on insanity. The news of his approaching inspection produced nervous breakdowns among the officers and caused a panic among the soldiers. He could not keep quiet for a second, jumping from town to town and pyramiding rows in the manner suggestive of a provincial actor engaged for the rôle of Frederick the Great. His weakness for scientists provided an unexpected counterpart for his maniacal features. A lavish supporter of laboratories, institutes and various expeditions, he was beloved by struggling young scientists who felt sorry for the "poor unbalanced prince." His appointment to the post of inspector-general of military hospitals in 1914 spelled catastrophe for the negligent surgeons. This time, however, the army appreciated his severity.

Prince George and Prince Michael of Mecklenburg-Strelitz were the two sons of my aunt Grand Duchess Catherine by her marriage with the Duke of Mecklenburg-Strelitz. Half-Germans by birth but thoroughly Russian in their sympathies, they entered our military service after their graduation from the universities of Germany. Neither of them occupied a post of importance.

2

Such were the Romanoffs who stood around the throne of Russia in the most critical years of its existence. With all their shortcomings, their loyalty to the dynasty and their innate patriotism could have been used by the Czar to distinct advantage had he understood the urgent necessity of letting his relatives choose their careers outside the military service. Even the least gifted of them would have made much better executives of the imperial administration than those treacherous robots who succeeded in getting hold of the portfolios during the second part of the reign of Nicholas II. The self-same Uncle Alexis, an unsurpassed joke as grand admiral of the navy, would have fitted perfectly a position requiring his knowledge of foreign countries and his ability for "mixing."

No ruler, be he emperor, president, prime minister or dictator, can afford to ignore his closest supporters in the distribution of the controlling posts of the Government. Picture a President of the United States, elected on a Republican ticket, telling the loyal members of his party that they would have to learn how to command an army corps while the Democrats would sit in his cabinet. Imagine Stalin showing preference to strangers of vague political views and brushing aside the old chieftains of the Bolsheviks. Visualize Mussolini announcing to his Fascists that he intends to bring Nitti back to Italy.

There is no element of exaggeration in my comparison. No man is stronger than his party. No man can rule without a party. The last Czar of Russia should have acted as the head of the party of the existing régime when the attacks of the revolution made a minister's loyalty to the throne more valuable than his talents. Viewing the crowd of hypocritical noblemen, scheming courtiers and worthless bureaucrats filling his palace, he should have recognized that he could count only on the loyalty of his immediate relatives for the execution of his orders and for the transmission of his wishes to his subjects, who had kept their faith in the crown long after losing confidence in the ministers. Not that we expected him to form a hundred-per-cent grand ducal cabinet; far from it. We simply wanted to be permitted to serve in the different departments of the government, preferably in the provinces, where we could have been of use in establishing direct contacts between the Czar and the nation.

He met our arguments with a reference to the tradition:

"For nearly three hundred years it was a habit of my ancestors to insist upon military careers for their relatives. I am not going to break this tradition. I will not permit my uncles and cousins to interfere with my Government."

This decision of his was partly inspired by the jealousy of the ministers and partly influenced by the annoyance caused to him by the behavior of his uncles. As always happened with Nicholas II, logic was crushed by emotional complexes, but then most of his actions would present an unsolvable puzzle for anyone not familiar with the circumstances of his childhood, his upbringing and the first ten years of his reign.

The character study of the last Czar of Russia should be preceded, however, by a short excursion into the realm of finance: too many people continue to believe that the maintenance of the imperial family overburdened the taxpaying capacity of the nation.

CHAPTER TEN

MILLIONS THAT WERE

I

IT had always been conceded by financial experts and awe-stricken laymen alike that the late Czar was one of the ten richest men in the world. Even now, thirteen years after his tragic death, we are still occasionally being informed by the gentlemen of the American press that the Bank of England remains in possession of the "vast fortune of the Romanoffs."

Not so long ago a poor unbalanced girl arrived in New York, was introduced as Grand Duchess Anastasia, the youngest daughter of Nicholas II, and declared her intention to sue for "her share of her father's millions." This badly conceived plan disclosed an amazing lack of practical purpose: beginning with the summer of 1915 there was not a farthing left in the Czar's name in the Bank of England nor in any other bank outside of Russia. Twenty million pounds sterling, that were being kept in London since the days of Emperor Alexander II (1856-1881), had been entirely spent to support the hospitals and various other charities patronized by the imperial family during the war (1915-1917). This fact remained unknown to the general public for the simple reason that the Czar was not in a habit of having his good deeds press agented. Had he reigned longer, Nicholas II would have found himself a rather poor man at the close of the great European conflict. In his best days he could never have come anywhere near the wealth of the Rockefellers, the Mellons, the Bakers, the du Ponts, the Harknesses, the Rothschilds, the Mendelssohns and the rest of the multi-millionaires, but having parted with the family deposits in

England he would have compared quite unfavorably even with the exiled Kaiser Wilhelm or the vacationing King Alfonso.

In fact his entire revenue was derived from the following three sources:

1. The annual governmental appropriation for the needs of the imperial family which amounted to eleven million gold roubles (slightly less than six million dollars);
2. proceeds of the exploitation of the so-called "oodely" (estates belonging to the imperial family);
3. interest from deposits kept abroad in English and German banks.

The "oodely" consisted of hundreds of thousands of acres of land, cotton plantations, vineyards, breeding farms, fruit gardens, champagne and wine plants, etc., purchased mostly in the second half of the eighteenth century by the far-sighted Catherine the Great, and given a special status by the suspicious Emperor Paul I. Their aggregate value, estimated in 1914 at about fifty million dollars, did not correspond to their comparatively modest earnings balancing between one and two million dollars per annum. The trouble was that too many reasons of diplomatic and political nature interfered with their management. No proper advertising had ever been given to the champagne "Abrau-Durso" lest it would hurt the feelings of France, then the principal ally of the Russian Empire. No railroad could be built along the southern coast of the Crimean Peninsula lest the radical press should see in it a disguised assistance to the sales of imperial apples, peaches and pears, and the latter had to be marketed locally at the ridiculous price of some five cents per barrel.

An identical situation existed with regard to the money earned by the deposits in the foreign banks. The Minister of the Imperial Court and the managing director of the Department of "Oodely" were strictly forbidden to invest in any foreign or domestic securities, in order to keep the gossipers from saying that the Czar was personally interested in this or that particular industry.

The frozen assets of the imperial family represented an outlay of some eighty million dollars covering the cost of rarest diamonds, pearls, emeralds, rubies and other crown jewels that had been purchased during the three centuries of the reign of the Romanoffs.

The Great Imperial Crown, made by the famous Posier, jeweler to the court of Catherine the Great in 1762, was in the shape of a miter and carried on its top a cross of five enormous diamonds held together by an uncut ruby; the band surrounding the head contained twenty-eight large diamonds, and there were eleven equally large diamonds in a foliated arch which supported the cross and the ruby, with a hoop of thirty-eight perfect "rosy" pearls on either side.

The Imperial Diadem, finished during the reign of Emperor Alexander I, contained thirteen mammoth "ancient" pearls, 113 "rosy" pearls, 500 diamonds of different sizes and 84 brilliants.

Among the other highly valued treasures were: the Orloff diamond of 194½ carats purchased by Count Alexis Orloff in Amsterdam in 1776 and presented by him to Catherine the Great; the Moon of the Mountain uncut diamond (around 120 carats); the Shah diamond (around 85 carats); and the Polar Star, a magnificent 40-carat pale red ruby.

It would be idle speculation to try to guess even the approximate sum that could have been obtained from the sale of these famous jewels. The experts had always been of the opinion that nobody outside the Russian, the German and the Austrian Emperors could possibly have been interested in acquiring such prodigious gems. That is why the disappearance of the three empires put the present possessors of the Russian crown jewels in the somewhat paradoxical position of merchants who have succeeded in obtaining certain goods through the process of eliminating the only logical customers.

2

All in all, the Czar could have counted on receiving each first of the year from ten to twelve million dollars. A very comfortable income for a private individual of even the most fastidious tastes but a sum entirely out of proportion to the colossal demands made on the Czar's exchequer.

To begin with, he had to think of his relatives and of the maintenance of the palaces. Each one of the grand dukes was entitled to one hundred thousand dollars per annum; each one of the grand duchesses was given a dowry of five hundred thousand dollars; each one of the princes and princesses of imperial blood * received five hundred thousand dollars at their birth, as a settlement precluding all further claims. This item of the Czar's expenses consumed from two to three millions, depending on the varying number of grand dukes, the frequency of their marriages and the birth rate in the imperial family.

Outside of the smaller imperial residences scattered all over Russia, five big palaces had to be taken care of.

The Winter Palace in St. Petersburg, an enormous dwelling built by Rastrelli for Empress Elizabeth and facing the river Neva, employed about twelve hundred servants. Although uninhabited for the last twelve years of the Romanoffs' reign and used for balls and special occasions only, it had to be kept in perfect order on account of its art collections and the crown jewels displayed in its "White Salon."

The Czar usually spent the greater part of the year in his Czarskoie-Selo Palace. Constructed by Empress Catherine I and enlarged during the subsequent reigns of Empress Elizabeth and Catherine the Great, it presented the appearance of a little city with its large park occupying eight hundred acres,

* The title of grand duke and grand duchess ("Imperial Highness") was given to the children and grandchildren of an Emperor; further generations received the title of prince and princess of imperial blood ("Highness").

its artificial lakes, elaborate stables, etc. Six hundred employees were permanently working on its grounds.

In the summer the Czar stayed either in the Peterhof Palace or in Livadia on the Black Sea. Both places naturally required a considerable amount of servants and a small army of experienced gardeners. Peterhof, situated on the shores of the Gulf of Finland, was often compared with Versailles, for it possessed a beautiful network of waterfalls, fountains, canals and lakes.

The Dowager-Empress Marie lived in the gigantic Anichkoff Palace in St. Petersburg; the palaces in Moscow and Gatchino likewise made their existence felt by the overtaxed payroll of the Czar. Three thousand hired persons had to be given their monthly salaries, nourishment, uniforms and special allowances.

Grand marshals of the court, masters of ceremonies, masters of the hunt, equerries, chamberlains, hunters, coachmen, butlers, chauffeurs, valets, gardeners, cooks, assistant cooks, maids, etc., etc.—all of them expected to get a present twice a year, at Christmas and on the Czar's saint's day. Thus, quite a fortune was being annually spent on heavy gold watches with the Imperial monogram made of diamonds, gold cigarette cases, brooches, rings and other trinkets.

Next in line came the imperial theaters, three in St. Petersburg and two in Moscow. The world-wide reputation and the huge success of the imperial ballet did not seem to affect their receipts, and all five of them were losing money steadily. The deficit had to be covered by the Czar out of the budget of the imperial court. Possibly we needed a Gatti-Casazza to teach us how to combine the promotion of beauty with financial success. As it was it cost the imperial family around a million dollars per year to keep up the standards of Russian art. Beginning with 1905 Mr. Diaghileff joined the list of the subsidized theaters. His spectacular "seasons" in Paris and London were made possible through the generosity of

Czarskoie-Selo as this impresario extraordinary never cared to waste his valuable time in the box office.

A similar support had to be given to the Imperial Academy of Arts. Officially financed by the Government it could never make both ends meet, and the members of the imperial family who were registered among its sponsors found it extremely hard to ignore the dire need of the young artists.

Then came charity. Charity of all kinds and descriptions.

The Red Cross wanted to build an annex to a hospital in a large industrial center but was seventy-five thousand short of the necessary sum.

The King of Montenegro dropped in at the Czarskoie-Selo Palace to pay the compliments of the season to the great Slavonic sovereign which meant that a check for not less than three hundred thousand gold roubles would have to be prepared well in advance, for the old chap was invariably in a hurry to get back home to his starving subjects and his barefoot army.

The director of the Academy of Cadet-Pages called the attention of the Czar to the deserving case of a young man who had the makings of a splendid officer but needed to be assured ten thousand roubles per annum to enable him to keep up the pace required of a guardsman.

A favorite aide-de-camp displayed signs of distress: he had gambled again and had but twenty-four hours to settle that debt of honor. A mere bagatelle of twenty-five thousand.

A grandson of a famous general wrote a letter asking for fifteen hundred roubles to help him continue his education.

A Russian artist who had scored a marvelous "moral" success in Paris, came back to Russia and exhibited his works. He felt certain that his entire career depended upon his selling a "still life" to the imperial family.

A brave policeman was killed in the performance of his duty and left his family penniless.

And so on and so forth.

While still the heir to the throne, Nicholas II received

from his great-grandmother a legacy of two million dollars. He decided to "put it aside" and to use its income for particularly deserving charities. The principal was gone within three years!

Considering all the other expenses of the imperial family the money appropriated for entertainment will appear surprisingly small. The comparatively modest cost of the spectacular balls and state dinners given several times during the season finds explanation in the fact that no particular purchases had to be made and no additional help hired for these functions. The wine and the flowers were provided by the Department of "Oodely," and even the musicians figured on the monthly payroll. It was the brilliancy of surroundings rather than the actual expenditure of money that struck visiting strangers who received invitations to the court balls.

Extremely modest and simple in his private life, the Czar had to bow on such occasions to the requirements of etiquette: the ruler of one-sixth of the surface of the earth naturally received his guests in an atmosphere of lavish splendor.

The enormous high-ceilinged mirrored halls of the palace were filled with statesmen, courtiers, foreign ambassadors, officers of the various guard regiments and visiting Oriental potentates. Their glittering uniforms embroidered in gold and silver provided an impressive background for the ladies resplendent in their court gowns and jewels. Troopers of the Chevaliers Guards and of the Horse Guards wearing helmets surmounted by the imperial double-headed eagle, and Cossack Life Guards in their picturesque "cherkeskas," were stationed at the entrances and along the stairways. Numerous palm trees brought from the imperial hothouses were placed all over the palace. The bright lights of the mammoth chandeliers reflected in the mirrors gave to the whole scene a touch of unreality. A look at the main ballroom made one feel as though the matter-of-fact twentieth century had suddenly slid back into the fastidious days of Catherine the Great.

And then a hush would fall over the crowds. The grand master of ceremonies would appear and give three taps on the floor with his ivory-handled staff, which announced the arrival of Their Imperial Majesties.

The heavy doors of the inner apartments were thrown open and the Emperor and the Empress stood on the threshold accompanied by the members of the imperial family and the most important court dignitaries on duty. The sovereign led the first dance which was always the polonaise, and then the ball commenced. A series of waltzes was followed by the cotillon, with the Emperor and Empress watching but never taking part. The Czar left immediately after the supper thus enabling the younger set to dance less restrained by etiquette.

3

There was hardly one hundred thousand dollars left for the personal needs of the Czar by the time he had distributed the annual allowances to his relatives, paid the salaries of the employees, settled the bills of the contractors engaged in the perennial alterations of the palaces, straightened out the problems of the imperial theaters and attended to the charities. Fortunately for his children, their allowances were kept intact during their infancy and reached sufficiently important proportions by the time they came of age to permit the luxury of a steady extra income. However, such was not the case of the last imperial family. An overcareful Minister of the Imperial Court, acting against the orders of the Czar, had decided shortly before the war to transfer abroad the sums belonging to the imperial children. Of all places he chose Berlin, and seven million roubles (about sixteen million gold marks in 1914) dwindled during the period of German currency inflation to a small fraction of one cent, for it took in the fall of 1923 *five billion* marks to buy one dollar! The generous Berlin bankers expressed a desire to settle with the heirs of the Czar any time they were ready.

They were willing to give the remaining grand dukes a choice between seven million paper Romanoff roubles or sixteen million paper marks "1923."

Incredible as it may seem, the Czar of all the Russias used to be "broke" regularly, long before the end of the fiscal year. It stands to reason that he needed much more than one hundred thousand dollars to take care of the "unexpected expenses." Two ways were open to him for the solution of his difficulties. He could draw on the twenty million pounds sterling in the Bank of England, or talk to the Minister of Finance. He preferred to avoid both these channels and simply would remark: "We will have to live very modestly for the next few months."

Raised and educated to recognize his responsibilities toward the empire, the Czar did not hesitate for a second to give the whole twenty million pounds to the hospitals during the war but nobody could persuade him to touch even a particle of that fortune in peace time. When automobiles made their appearance in Russia he was one of the first to display enthusiasm over this new form of transportation, but for several years he could not see his way clear to obtaining the money necessary for establishing an imperial garage. There were seven hundred horses in the stables of Czarskoie-Selo waited upon by an impressive number of equerries, trainers, coachmen, stablemen, etc. Horses could not be sold nor the employees fired just because a new invention had proven its value in far-away Michigan. At last the Czar ordered two cars from the French factory of Delauney-Beleville and engaged a Belgian chauffeur by the name of Kegretz. Not until the outbreak of the war did he consent to increase the rolling stock of the imperial garage.

Looking back at the life led by the imperial family, I cannot help comparing it with that of the American magnates. I doubt whether any one of the steel, automobile or oil kings would ever be satisfied today with a yacht as modest in its appointments as H.I.M.S. *Standard,* and I feel quite certain that no head of a powerful American concern would retire as poor as the Czar was on the day of his abdication. His palaces, estates and jewels nationalized by the new Government, he had nothing left that he might have called his own. Had he succeeded in reaching England he would have had to work for a living.

CZAR NICHOLAS II DRESSED AS A XVII CENTURY CZAR, ON THE
DAY OF THE COURT BALL IN JANUARY 1903.

THE LAST CZARINA OF RUSSIA IN A XVII CENTURY DRESS WORN
BY HER AT THE COURT BALL IN JANUARY 1903.

CHAPTER ELEVEN

NICHOLAS II

I

AN ignorant nurse and a negligent physician were responsible for Nicholas II wearing the crown, having overlooked the illness that attacked his elder brother, a lusty infant named Alexander. Thus, he had become heir apparent by virtue of an accident. The disappointment of his parents could be well imagined. He felt it keenly and developed a pronounced shyness of manner. He never cried. He rarely laughed. He did not like to play. The surroundings of his childhood were gloomy. Constant talk about attempts on the life of his grandfather. Absence of boys of his age. Low-ceilinged rooms in the suburban Palace of Gatchino which seemed to have been planned by Emperor Paul I to serve as an ugly contrast to the spacious luxury of the Winter Palace in St. Petersburg.

He drew as his teachers a simple-minded Russian general, a sentimental Swiss tutor, and a young Englishman who was extremely fond of outdoor life. None of the three had the remotest idea of the task facing the future Czar of Russia. They taught him all they knew, which proved to be little.

At the end of his tuition and on the eve of getting his commission in the Hussar Guards, Nicholas II could have fooled an Oxford professor into mistaking him for an Englishman and possessed a similar command of German and French. But that was all. The rest of his knowledge consisted of loose bits of information never to be of any practical use in his future life. According to the general, the mysterious forces emanating during the sacrament of taking the oath on the day of the coronation provided all the practical data required by a ruler.

He developed an immense liking for the military service. It appealed to his passive nature. One executed orders and did not have to worry over the vast problems handled by one's superiors. He commanded a squadron in the Hussar Guards. He spent two years as an officer of the first Horse Battery. The death of his father found him in the Preobrajensky Regiment of the Guard, at the head of a battalion and wearing the stripes of a colonel. He kept that comparatively modest rank during the rest of his life. It reminded him of his care-free youth and he never consented to promote himself to a general. He thought it would not be playing fair to take advantage of the throne for his personal glorification.

His modesty made him popular among his fellow officers. He participated full-heartedly in their festivities, and the small chatter of the messrooms increased his natural provincialism. Colonel Romanoff may have felt at ease but the heir apparent had nothing to gain from a constant association with a jolly crowd of healthy young men discussing horses, ballerinas and the latest French songs.

Appointed member of the Imperial Council he listened twice a week to a coterie of moth-eaten bureaucrats competing in unabashed catering to the Czar. The procedure bored him. His thoughts were far away.

At home he lent a hand in building snow-houses, chopping wood and planting trees, the physicians having prescribed plenty of exercise for his father. The conversation dwelt upon the pranks played by his young brother Michael or the progress of my courtship of his sister Xenia. Never a word about politics. Never a chance to improve his mind. It had been silently agreed that the cares of the state should not be permitted to enter the private life of Alexander III. The autocratic one-man-government needed rest. The ruler capable of handling the temperamental Kaiser shook with laughter at the bright repartee of his youngest children. He rejoiced in pouring cold water on the head of the unsuspecting Michael, who never failed to return the compliment later on during the dinner.

Every second summer they went to Copenhagen for a reunion with our Danish, English and Greek relatives. They exchanged greetings and shed a tear over the passing of time. Aunt Alexandra—later Queen of England—commented on the approaching marriage of her son George. Aunt Olga— the late Queen of Greece—sighed in bewilderment: it seemed she had carried him in her arms only yesterday.

In 1890, with but four years standing between him and the throne, Nicholas II was sent on a voyage around the world, presumably to complete his education. We met in Colombo on the Island of Ceylon. The message announcing his arrival reached me in the heart of the jungles while chasing a pack of elephants. I must have appeared wild to him with my three weeks' growth of beard, tales of dangerous encounters and trophies of the big hunt spread on the deck on my yacht *Tamara*. The stillness of the tropical night interrupted once in a while by the cries of the frightened monkeys made him unusually talkative. He envied my thrilling vacation. He found no pleasure in traveling as he did, aboard a battle cruiser flying the standard of the heir apparent to the crown of Russia.

"My trip is senseless," he said with a great deal of bitterness; "palaces and generals are the same all the world over, and that's all I am permitted to see. I could just as well have stayed at home."

Next morning I rejoined my elephants and tigers while Nicholas proceeded on his way to Japan. At the railroad station of Kioto he was struck by the saber of a fanatic and would have been killed had it not been for the quickness of Prince George of Greece. His voyage of studies came to an abrupt end, leaving a sizable scar on his head and increasing that presentiment of tragedy which first visited him on the day of his grandfather's assassination.

He longed to be back in Gatchino protected by the iron-and-steel figure of the Czar. The physical prowess of Alexander III seemed to convey a message of safety to this pale-faced heir apparent, and there was, no doubt, something reassuring in the spectacle of a solid silver rouble being bent by the vise-like imperial thumb. On October 17, 1888, the whole nation witnessed still bigger display of that Herculean strength when the Emperor saved his children and relatives by holding on his shoulders the roof of a wrecked dining car in the train derailed by the revolutionaries. The world gasped. The hero himself remained indifferent but the terrific strain did affect his kidneys. On October 20, 1894, Nicky and I stood on the veranda of the beautiful palace in Livadia armed with bags of oxygen and watching the end of the Colossus. Even the salty sea air failed to restore the life spent in one continuous effort to prevent the revolution from following its merciless course. He died as he lived, a bitter enemy of resounding phrases, a confirmed hater of melodrama. Just muttered a short prayer and kissed his wife.

People die every day, and we should not attach any undue historical importance to the death of a man we loved, but the passing of Alexander III decided the ultimate fate of the Russian Empire. Everyone in the crowd of relatives, physicians, courtiers, and servants gathered around his now lifeless body realized that our country had lost the only support which kept it from falling down a precipice. Nobody understood it clearer than Nicky. For the first and last time in my life I saw tears in his blue eyes. He took me by the arm and led me downstairs into his room. We embraced and cried together.

He could not collect his thoughts. He knew he was the Emperor now, and the weight of this terrifying fact crushed him.

"Sandro, what am I going to do," he exclaimed pathetically. "What is going to happen to me, to you, to Xenia, to

Alix, to mother, to all of Russia? I am not prepared to be a Czar. I never wanted to become one. I know nothing of the business of ruling. I have no idea of even how to talk to the ministers. Will you help me, Sandro?"

Help him! I, who knew even less than he did of governmental affairs. I could have advised him on questions pertaining to the navy, but the rest! . . .

I tried to quiet him, mentioning the names of the persons on whom he could rely, although in my heart I felt that his despair was only too well founded and that we all were facing an imminent catastrophe.

2

The fiancée of the new Czar, Princess Alix of Hesse-Darmstadt, had arrived from Germany on the eve of the death of Alexander III. The Minister of the Imperial Court was too excited to think of ordering a special train and she traveled as an ordinary passenger. Taken to the Palace Chapel of Livadia she was baptized according to the rites of the Greek Orthodox Church. The wedding was performed in St. Petersburg, scarcely a week after the funeral. The honeymoon consisted of attending two masses a day and receiving visits of condolence. The whole thing looked grotesque. I doubt whether the greatest of theatrical producers could have staged a more appropriate prologue for the tragedy of the last Czar of Russia.

The young Empress spoke Russian with difficulty. Her predecessors used to benefit by the lapse of time between their betrothals to the future Czars and their ascension to the throne. The wife of Alexander III had lived in the country for seventeen consecutive years preceding her coronation, but Princess Alix was given exactly ninety-six hours to study the language and get acquainted with the national customs. Unable to grasp the relative standing of the innumerable courtiers she made errors, irrelevant in themselves but tantamount to formidable crimes in the eyes of St. Petersburg society. It frightened her and created marked reserve in her treatment of visitors. This in turn gave circulation to comparisons between the friendliness of the Dowager-Empress and the "snobbish coolness" of the young Czarina. Nicholas II resented this malicious matching of his mother against his wife, and very soon the relations between court and society became antagonistic. Then we all went to Moscow for the ceremony of the coronation.

The day of the "Khodynka Massacre" drew nearer. The causes of the tragedy may have remained a puzzle to the foreign correspondents—Richard Harding Davis being one of them—but the experienced officials anticipated the worst long in advance. The ability of the Czar's uncle, Grand Duke Sergei Alexandrovich, then Governor-General of Moscow, to handle millions of people attracted by the festivities, was questioned on all sides.

"Are you certain, Nicky," I asked the Emperor before leaving St. Petersburg, "that Uncle Sergei realizes the difficulty of the task?"

He made a gesture of impatience:

"Of course, he does. Please, Sandro, try to be fair to Uncle Sergei."

"I am fair, Nicky, but I remember how concerned your father was on this occasion. He supervised every detail personally. It is not so easy to distribute gifts to half a million people packed into a field that was really never planned to hold such crowds. Think of all the agitators anxious to exploit this opportunity to create a disturbance."

"I believe, Sandro," he answered coldly, "that Uncle Sergei knows it all just as well as you do, if not better."

I bowed my way out.

The first two days in Moscow gave the lie to the gloomy prophets. Beautiful spring weather, ancient city decorated with flags, bells ringing from the domes of sixteen hundred churches, cheering multitudes, the young Czarina radiant in her crown, scores of European royalty driving in their spectacular carriages—no official planning could have created the effect of this spontaneous rejoicing.

In accordance with the program, the distribution of the gifts to the population was to take place at eleven o'clock on the morning of the third day of the festivities. All night long the ever-increasing groups of peasants and workers were gathering in the narrow approaches to the Khodynka Field roped off by a thin cordon of police. By sunrise not less than five hundred thousand people stood packed within a few city blocks pushing their way ahead and exerting considerable pressure on a lonely squadron of bewildered Cossacks. For some mysterious reason the impression prevailed that the Government had underestimated the number of the celebrants and that the majority was bound to return home empty-handed.

The pale light of dawn disclosed pyramids of large cups with imperial monograms mounted on especially constructed stalls. A mighty roar came from the crowd. In an instant the Cossacks were lifted in the air together with their horses, and everybody surged forward.

"For God's sake, careful, careful," shouted the commanding officer, pointing toward the field. "It is full of ditches and trenches."

His gesture was taken for an invitation. Few, if any, remembered that the Khodynka Field provided in ordinary times a training ground for a battalion of engineers. The people running in front understood their fatal error but by then it would have taken at least an army corps to stop the stampede. They fell into ditches, one on top of the other, women clutching their children, men fighting and cursing.

Five thousand people were killed, a still greater number wounded and mutilated. At three o'clock in the afternoon we drove to the Khodynka Field, passing on our way wagons laden with dead bodies. The cowardly chief of police tried to distract the attention of the Czar by asking him to acknowledge the cheers. Each "hurrah" sounded to me like a slap in the face. My brothers could not control their indignation and we four demanded the immediate dismissal of Grand Duke Sergei and the calling off of all festivities. A painful scene ensued. The elder grand dukes rallied around Uncle Sergei.

"Don't you see, Nicky," said Uncle Alexis, "that the 'Michailovichi' (the intimate name given to us, the sons of Grand Duke Michael) "are inclined to play to the radical grandstand. They are openly siding with the revolution. They are trying to get the Moscow governorship for one of their own."

My brother, Grand Duke Nicholas Michailovich, answered this infantile remark by a long, clear-cut speech. He explained all the horror of the situation. He evoked the shadows of the French sovereigns dancing in the Park of Versailles and ignoring the signs of the approaching storm. He appealed to the heart of the Emperor.

"Remember, Nicky," he concluded, looking him straight in the eyes, "the blood of those five thousand men, women and children will remain forever a blot on your reign. You cannot revive the dead but you must show your sympathy with their families. Do not let the enemies of the régime say that the young Czar danced while his murdered subjects were taken to the Potter's Field."

That night Nicholas II attended a big ball given by the French ambassador. The broad smile on the face of Grand Duke Sergei led the foreigners to believe that the Romanoffs had lost their minds. We four left at the moment the dancing commenced, thus committing the gravest breach of etiquette and making Uncle Alexis exclaim with venom: "There go the four imperial followers of Robespierre."

✦✦✦

3

A slender youth, five-feet-seven, Nicholas II spent the first ten years of his reign sitting behind a massive desk in the palace and listening with near-awe to the well-rehearsed bellowing of his towering uncles. He dreaded to be left alone with them. In the presence of witnesses his opinions were accepted as orders, but the instant the door of his study closed on the outsider,—down on the table would go with a bang the weighty fist of Uncle Alexis or Uncle Nicholas. There was really but little choice between the two hundred fifty pounds of the former packed in the resplendent uniform of Grand Admiral of the Fleet, and the six-feet-five of the latter decorated with the imperial monograms and gold cords of General A.D.C.

Uncle Sergei and Uncle Vladimir developed equally efficient methods of intimidation, and the last Czar of all the Russias used to sigh deeply on hearing one of these four names announced during the busy hours of a crowded morning.

They always wanted something. Nicholas fancied himself a Great Warrior. Alexis ruled the waves. Sergei tried to turn Moscow into his private domain. Vladimir advocated the cause of the Arts.

They all had their favorite generals and admirals who were supposed to be promoted ahead of a long waiting list; their ballerinas desirous of organizing a "Russian Season" in Paris; their wonderful preachers anxious to redeem the Emperor's soul; their miraculous physicians soliciting a court appointment; their clairvoyant peasants with a divine message.

By six o'clock in the afternoon he was worn out, subdued, disillusioned. He looked at the portrait of his father and wished he had learned to talk the language used by that formidable first country squire of Russia.

They all were afraid of Alexander III.

"Stop playing the Czar," he wired to that self-same Uncle Sergei.

"Throw that swine out!" he wrote on the report describing the strange activities of a high official involved in a public scandal with another man's wife.

"Europe may well afford to wait while the Russian Czar is fishing," he replied to a courtier urging him to receive at once the ambassador of a great power.

An overambitious minister, threatening to quit, was taken by the collar and shaken like a puppy. "You shut up," Alexander III thundered; "when I choose to kick you out you will hear of it in no uncertain terms."

Kaiser Wilhelm proposing to "divide the world between Russia and Germany" was met with the curt remark: "Don't act like a whirling dervish, Willy, look at yourself in the mirror."

It was too bad that this outspoken man had to die at the age of forty-nine. God knows Nicholas was in no hurry to ascend the throne. If father had only lived twenty or thirty years more! Everything would have been different, everything . . . including those bumptious uncles and boisterous cousin Willy.

4

I attempted to make Nicky see the impositions of our relatives. Being as much his uncle as any one of the elder grand dukes and capable of matching their height inch for inch, I did not mince my words. I talked for hours. I quoted history, economics, native and foreign precedents. I failed dismally. My voice lacked that shouting quality. I was "Sandro," the pal of his childhood, the husband of his beloved sister Xenia. He knew how to cool my temper by a joking reference to bygone days. He noticed my habit of crouching in my chair so as to look smaller. He was not afraid of me.

How often, while fighting for a complete reorganization

of the navy run by Uncle Alexis in a manner befitting the eighteenth century, I saw him raise his shoulders in despair and heard him say in a monotone:

"I am sure he won't like it. I am telling you, Sandro, he won't stand for it."

"Well, Nicky, if such is the case, you will have to make him stand for it. You owe it to the empire."

"What can I do with him?"

"Great guns, Nicky, you are the Czar. You can do whatever you feel is necessary for the protection of our national interests."

"It sounds awfully good, Sandro, but I know Uncle Alexis. He will be acting up terribly. Everybody in the palace will be certain to hear his voice."

"I have no doubts about that, but so much the better. Then you will have an excellent alibi for discharging him on the spot and refusing to grant him any further audiences."

"Fancy my discharging Uncle Alexis! The favorite brother of my father. Do you know, Sandro, I believe that my uncles are right and that you did turn Socialist during your stay in America!"

This went on for months and years. I threatened to resign from the navy unless my advice was heeded. He smiled. He felt sure I would never cause him additional troubles. When finally I did quit, Uncle Alexis expressed his keen delight by keeping his voice down for almost a week. On May 14, 1905, our fleet was smashed to pieces by the Japanese, but nothing could have mattered to Nicholas II by that time: the glory of the reign had not materialized. He was going through a peculiar change of life and was steadily drifting in the direction dictated by his numerous complexes. He had lost confidence in everybody. Good and bad news left him equally indifferent. The welfare of his only son became his sole interest. The French would have diagnosed his case as that of a man suffering from "les défauts de ses vertus" (the defects of his virtues), for he possessed all the qualities praiseworthy in a simple citizen but fatal in a Czar. Had Nicholas II been born in an ordinary family, he would have spent a harmonious existence, rewarded by his superiors and respected by the whole community. He worshiped the memory of his father, he was a devoted husband, he believed in the inviolability of his sacred oath of office, and he endeavored to remain honest, polite and unassuming till the very last day of his reign. It was not his fault that ironical history turned each one of these sterling virtues into a deadly weapon of destruction. It never dawned on him that a ruler has no right to be human.

5

The hypothetical question, "What would father have done in this case?" worried Nicholas II a great deal. My tongue itched to say that measures wise in the nineteenth century would never fit into the surroundings of our epoch. However, one does not argue with emotions, and grave statesmen wasted long hours guessing as to the decision which would have been made under similar circumstances by Emperor Alexander III.

Pobedonostzeff, the former tutor and minister of the late Czar, usually presided over these foolish conferences. His cynical mind excelled in permeating the young Emperor with a fear of everything even remotely suggestive of modernism.

"Whom would you recommend, Mr. Pobedonostzeff, for the post of Minister of the Interior?" asked Nicholas II when the turn of the century brought forth a new wave of revolutionary activities. "I must find a forceful man. I am tired of figureheads."

"Well," said Mephistopheles, "let me see. There are two men trained in the service of your father, Pleve and Sipyagin. I can think of no one else."

"Which one of the two shall I take?"

"It's six of one and half a dozen of another, Your Majesty. Pleve is a scoundrel, Sipyagin is a fool. Both will do."

Nicholas II frowned.

"I do not follow you, Mr. Pobedonostzeff, I am not in a joking mood."

"Neither am I, Your Majesty. I realize that the continuation of the régime depends on our ability to keep Russia in a frozen state. The slightest warm breath of life would be certain to cause the whole thing to rot. That is why the task could be performed only by persons of Pleve's or Sipyagin's peculiar characteristics."

Sipyagin, appointed Minister of the Interior on the strength of this unique recommendation, was killed by the revolutionaries on April 2, 1902. His successor in office, Pleve, met a similar fate on June 3, 1904. Pobedonostzeff asked God to bless their "worthy souls" and suggested letting Witte decide upon the choice of a "best available man."

"Witte is a revolutionary under the skin, Your Majesty. He dreams to become the first President of the Russian Republic, he is a quarrelsome fellow, a noisy reformer, but with all of it, he is a deserving pupil of the administrative school created by your father. He did make an excellent job of putting the Russian currency on a gold basis and has so many friends among the moneylenders in Paris that he may succeed in restoring our credit abroad."

Mr. Witte was given carte blanche. In less than eighteen months he forced the Czar into signing a peace with Japan, into granting important amendments to the constitution and into convoking the first Russian Parliament (the so-called "first Duma"). True enough, he obtained an important loan of five hundred million dollars in France but the revolutionary activities developed stupendously under his administration threatening the very existence of the régime.

On July 8, 1906, the presidency of the Council of Ministers passed into the hands of Mr. Stolypin, a remarkable man of real genius, who realized that the Russia of the twentieth century had to be handled in a manner entirely different from the methods practiced in the days when the "red" movement was limited to the big cities. Peace and order in the empire were restored by him, and a powerful impetus given to the growth of the industries. On September 14, 1911, a young lawyer Bogroff killed Stolypin in Kieff during a theatrical performance in honor of the Czar's visit to this flourishing capital of Southwestern Russia. At the ensuing cross-examination Bogroff admitted having combined for many years the duties of undercover agent of the Imperial Secret Police with those of a member of the Terroristic Organization in Paris. His presence in the theater, in close proximity to the box occupied by the Imperial Family, was made possible through an official order dispatching him to "protect the person of the Czar."

Once more Nicholas II turned toward the shadows of the past and appointed an old bureaucrat to succeed the dynamic Stolypin. Mediocrity regained lost ground and dragged Russia into a nonsensical war followed by a triumph of the revolution. Fifteen million peaceful peasants had to leave their homes in 1914 because Alexander II and Alexander III were in the habit of protecting the Balkan States against Austria. The opening words of a manifesto issued by the Czar on August 1, 1914, told the tale of an obedient son crucified on the cross of his loyalty: "Faithful to its historical traditions, our empire cannot view with indifference the fate of its Slavonic brethren . . ." No greater lack of logic could have been condensed within the limits of a short sentence! Even the most powerful empire ceases to be an empire precisely at the moment when sentimental faithfulness to the traditions of the past is permitted to interfere with its victorious march toward the future.

6

Nicholas II was polite. He was exasperatingly polite. I suppose he was the most polite man in Europe. Therefore, the skeptical statesmen left his presence thoroughly convinced of having discovered an impish desire for mischief behind this impenetrable wall of civility.

"Our Czar is an Oriental, a hundred per cent Byzantine," said Witte shortly after his dismissal from the post of President of the Council of Ministers. "We talked for two solid hours. He shook my hand. He embraced me. He wished me all the luck in the world. I returned home beside myself with happiness and found a written order for my dismissal lying on the desk."

Kaiser Wilhelm and Grand Duke Nicholas, the commander-in-chief of the Russian armies in 1914-1915, would have eagerly agreed with Witte's opinion. Both of them attempted to make full use of the Czar's politeness and both became embittered as a result of their experience.

On July 11, 1905, Nicholas II invited the German Emperor to a luncheon aboard the imperial yacht *Polar Star* anchored at Bjoerke in Finland. Cousin Willy decided to combine pleasure with a little business and came carrying in his pocket the detailed project of a Russo-German alliance. One glance at that tricky document frightened the Czar.

"It is a pretty clever piece of work, if you want to know my opinion, Nicky," volunteered the Kaiser. "It will bring innumerable blessings not only to our countries but to the rest of the world as well."

"Very nice project, indeed," politely agreed his host.

"Will you sign it, Nicky?"

"I may. Leave it with me. I will naturally have to show it to my Minister of Foreign Affairs."

"Now, Nicky," commenced the Kaiser, and the Czar lowered his head. The eloquence of Cousin Willy being well, though unfavorably, known throughout the world, Nicholas II endeavored to change the subject. Nothing doing. The "boy orator of Potsdam" delivered a marvelous speech, at the end of which only two possibilities remained open to his listener: to talk sharp and plain, or to sign the document.

The politeness of the Czar being even stronger than his desire to imitate his father, he reached for a pen.

"That's fine, Nicky," complimented the Kaiser. "One little formality more, and the most important treaty in modern history is going to become a reality. Who is going to witness your signature? Is there any one of your ministers aboard?"

"I shall ask Count Lamsdorf, my Minister of Foreign Affairs, to do it tomorrow."

"But I think I saw Admiral Birileff, your Minister of the Navy, on my way to your study."

"Yes, he is aboard, but I really prefer to have the signature of Count Lamsdorf."

Another burst of the Kaiser's eloquence followed, and Admiral Birileff was summoned into the study. So prepared was Nicholas II to cancel this improvised treaty immediately after his return to Czarskoie-Selo that he did not care to let his minister read the document.

"Admiral Birileff," said the Czar blushingly, "have you faith in me?"

"Your Majesty knows that I am always willing to do my utmost for the crown and Russia."

"Very well. Will you then sign a paper for me? I would rather not show you its contents. I have my reasons."

Admiral Birileff bowed and signed the Treaty of Bjoerke.

In due time, an appropriate letter was dispatched to Berlin stating firmly that it would be impossible for Russia to enter into any such arrangement with Germany owing to previous treaties concluded with France. Kaiser Wilhelm called God to witness this "treachery" of the Russian Emperor and swore never to believe him again. It is practically certain that the exchange of telegrams between the two imperial cousins in July, 1914, would have prevented the war, had it not been for the bitterness stored by the Kaiser during the intervening nine years.

The episode of the forced resignation of Grand Duke

Nicholas is equally characteristic. To begin with, the Czar did not want to put him at the head of the Russian armies realizing only too well that the amateurish talents of "Uncle Nicholas" would be a poor match for the military genius of Ludendorff and Mackensen. The retreat of our forces during the summer of 1915, largely due to the errors of the Supreme Command, made an immediate change imperative because the shaken confidence of fifteen million soldiers had to be restored at once. Nicholas II tried to lead his proud relative toward a dignified solution, but his hints were ignored and his politeness misunderstood as usual. Finally on August 23, 1915, he signed an order dismissing Grand Duke Nicholas and appointing himself commander-in-chief.

7

The figure of Rasputin captivated the imagination of the civilized world. Serious historians and prolific novelists wrote many a thick volume dedicated to the part played in the Russian debacle by that illiterate Siberian "moujik" whose long black beard assumed devilish proportions under the pencil of cover designers.

The "truth about Rasputin" is sufficiently simple. He rose to power because of another "sterling virtue" of Nicholas II which stamped the character of the Czar as strongly as his unfortunate politeness. The Czar was a devoted husband and a loving father. He wanted to have a son. Four girls were born, one after another, within seven years of his marriage to Princess Alix of Hesse-Darmstadt. It preyed on his mind. He all but reproached me for having had five sons within the same period of time. Unbelievable as it may sound, my friendship with the Empress suffered a slight setback on account of this difference in the sex of our children.

A mysterious gentleman appeared in the palace. "Doctor Philippe of Paris," he was introduced by the two Montenegrin grand duchesses (daughters of King Nicholas of

Montenegro married to Grand Duke Nicholas and Grand Duke Peter). The French ambassador warned the Government against this soft-spoken stranger but the Czar and Czarina were of a different opinion. People anxious to be deceived are easy dupes. The pseudo-scientific eloquence of Dr. Philippe reached its mark. He claimed to possess the power to influence the sex of an unborn child. He prescribed no medicines that could have been checked by the court physicians. His great secret consisted of a complicated series of "hypnotic passes," something akin to the modern theory of "twilight sleep." At the end of a two months' cure he pronounced the Empress pregnant. All festivities were called off. The European papers mentioned the approach of an "important event in the family of the Czar of Russia." Six months passed. The Empress had an acute attack of nerves, and the court physicians were called in, against the strenuous protest of Dr. Philippe. Their verdict was swift and formidable: they found no sign of pregnancy. Dr. Philippe packed his bags and returned to Paris.

Two years passed. On July 30, 1904, the Empress gave birth to the long awaited son, and he was named Alexis. The defeats on the Japanese front faded into insignificance next to this joyful event. At the age of three, while playing in the garden outside the palace, Alexis fell and started to bleed. The court physician on duty applied the usual remedies, prescribed in such cases, all of them failing to bring relief. The Czarina fainted. She did not need to hear the opinions of the learned specialists to know what that stubborn bleeding meant: it was the dread "hemophilia," hereditary illness of all the male members of her father's family for the past three hundred years. The strong blood of the Romanoffs failed to outbalance the weak blood of the Dukes of Hesse-Darmstadt, and an innocent boy was going to suffer the consequences of the stark negligence displayed by the Russian court in finding a fiancée for Nicholas II. The régime that exiled grand dukes for marrying healthy women outside the ranks of royalty did not bother to look up the history of the House of Hesse-Darmstadt.

Overnight the Czar had become ten years older. He could not bear the thought that his only son, his lovable Alexis, stood condemned by medical science either to die at an early age or lead the existence of an invalid.

"Is there no specialist in Europe that can cure my son? Let him name his own price, let him stay for ever in my palace. Alexis MUST be saved."

The court physicians felt miserable. Their answer was a plain "no." They could not have misled the Czar into any false illusions. They had to admit that the greatest specialists in the world were helpless against the ravaging power of hemophilia.

"Your Majesty must realize," said the chief court physician, "that the heir apparent will never be completely cured of his disease. The attacks of hemophilia will recur now and then. Strenuous measures of protection will have to be taken to guard the heir apparent against falls, cuts and scratches, because the slightest bleeding may prove fatal to persons affected with hemophilia."

A gigantic sailor, Derevenko, received orders to watch over the safety of poor Alexis and to carry him in his arms on all occasions requiring excessive walking.

Life lost all meaning for the imperial parents. We were afraid to smile in their presence. When visiting the palace, we acted as we would in a house of mourning. The Emperor buried himself in work but the Empress refused to surrender to fate. She talked incessantly of the ignorance of the physicians. She professed an open preference for medicine men. She turned toward religion, and her prayers were tainted with a certain hysteria. The stage was ready for the appearance of a miracle worker, and the two Montenegrin grand duchesses encountered no difficulty in persuading the Empress to receive Rasputin.

"He is marvelous. He is a new saint. He cures all ills.

He is a simple peasant from Siberia, but you know, Alix, God never entrusts His power to the spoiled children of sophistication."

The rest of the Rasputin epic hardly needs telling. It is still open for discussion whether the absence of attacks of hemophilia merely coincided with his visits to the palace, or whether that scheming fakir successfully used mysterious methods known to the Mongolian medicine men of his native Siberia. As far as the Empress was concerned, he saved her son from death. Nicholas II despised Rasputin and took great exception to his repeated visits. Shortly before the war, Rasputin was obliged to leave for Siberia, where his former peasant mistress stabbed him and he nearly died. The attacks of hemophilia recurred! The Czarina cried and begged her husband to authorize the recall of the "savior of Alexis." Rasputin returned in triumph. This time he intended to extract considerable profit out of his curative powers. He concluded a business alliance with a group of unscrupulous adventurers. His letters of introduction signed in an appallingly illiterate hand made their appearance on the desks of high government officials and in the private offices of prominent bankers. The same society that demanded his blood a few years later invited Rasputin to its receptions and asked him for all sorts of favors.

On December 25, 1916, nine days after Rasputin was assassinated in the palace of my son-in-law, Prince Felix Yousoupoff, I sent the Czar a long letter predicting the revolution and demanding drastic changes in the ranks of the Government. My concluding paragraph read as follows:

"Strange as it may sound, Nicky, we are witnessing the unbelievable spectacle of a revolution being promoted by the Government. Nobody else wants a revolution. Everybody realizes that the moment is too dangerous to afford the luxury of internal troubles, while there is a war to be fought and won,—everybody with the exception of your ministers. Their criminal actions, their indifference to the sufferings of the people, and their continuous lies, will force the people to revolt. I do not know whether you will take my advice or not, but I do want you to understand that the coming Russian Revolution of 1917 is a pure product of the efforts of your Government. For the first time in modern history, a revolution is being engineered not from below but from above, not by the people against their Government, but by the Government against the welfare of the people." *

8

I was not alone in diagnozing the situation. Eight weeks before, on November 1, 1916, my eldest brother, Grand Duke Nicholas Michailovich, presented to the Czar a sixteen-page memorandum classifying the crimes committed by Stuermer, then the head of the Government.

On November 11, 1916, my other brother, Grand Duke George Michailovich, put on paper the impressions of his visit to General Brussiloff, at that time commander of the armies of the southwestern front. "My dear Nicky," wrote George, "unless a new Government, responsible for its actions before the Parliament, is created within the next two weeks we are all headed for a debacle."

On November 15, 1916, still another brother of mine, Grand Duke Michael Michailovich, who had resided in London since 1891, joined his voice to the chorus of warnings: "I just came back from Buckingham Palace. Georgy" (familiar name for King George of England) "is very much upset over the political situation in Russia. The usually well-informed agents of the British Secret Service predict a revolution in the very near future. I sincerely hope, Nicky, you will find it possible to satisfy the just demands of our people before it is too late."

* All my documents having been confiscated by the Bolsheviks during my imprisonment in Crimea, in 1918, I am quoting this and following letters from the book of SECRET IMPERIAL PAPERS published by the Soviet Government in Moscow in 1921.

"What is it? Treachery or stupidity?" exclaimed Professor Paul Milukoff, the popular leader of the liberal party, from the parliamentary tribune.

Alas, it was neither the one nor the other. It was something considerably deeper and extremely more dangerous: Nicholas II, Czar of all the Russias, commander-in-chief of fifteen million soldiers, maintained with all the fervor of a passive Christian that "God's wishes shall be fulfilled." I nearly swooned on hearing this stupefying formula.

"Who, in Heaven's name, Nicky, has taught you this unique way of worshiping your God? Do you call it Christianity? No, Nicky, it sounds more like the Mohammedan fatalism of a Turkish soldier, who is not afraid of death because the wide-open gates of Paradise are awaiting his arrival in the Great Beyond. True Christianity, Nicky, means Action even more than it does Prayer. God entrusted to you the lives of one hundred and sixty million men, women and children. God expects you not to leave a stone unturned in order to improve their lot and assure their happiness. The pupils of Christ, Nicky, never sat with folded arms. They went from one end of the earth to the other, bringing something infinitely valuable into the tottering pagan world."

"God's wishes shall be fulfilled," he repeated slowly. "I was born on May sixth, the day of Job the Sufferer. I am ready to accept my doom."

It *was* final. No warnings could have impressed him. He was walking toward the precipice thinking that such was the will of his God. He was still fascinated by the divine rhythm of the lines describing the Sufferer glorified by Christendom on May 6 of each year: "There was a man in the land of Uz, whose name was Job; and that man was perfect and upright, and one that feared God and eschewed evil."

With a possible difference in the methods of "eschewing evil," Nicholas resembled his ideal in every detail. He forgot he was a Czar. And so, instead of dying "old and full of days," he met his doom in a dark cellar in Siberia, trying in vain to talk to the bloodthirsty soldiers of a Bolshevik firing squad. Knowing him as I did, I am certain he cared little about himself but wanted to ask them to spare the lives of his wife and children.

CHAPTER TWELVE

TIN GODS

I

OUTSIDE the imperial palaces lay Russia; "an icy desert and the abode of the Bad Man," to quote Pobedonostzeff.

A roll call of the events of 1894-1917 shows the intensity of that Bad Man's activities.

May, 1896—Khodynka catastrophe.

1897-1901—partial strikes in St. Petersburg, Moscow and throughout the provinces; numerous attempts on the lives of ministers, governors and chiefs of police; extraordinary measures of precaution are taken to guard the young Czar.

1902—assassination of Sipyagin, Minister of the Interior.

1904—assassination of Pleve, Minister of the Interior.

1904-1905—disastrous Russo-Japanese war.

January 9, 1905—revolutionary agents, ignoring the order forbidding all demonstrations, lead St. Petersburg workers toward the palace, supposedly to present a petition to the Czar although the latter is absent from the capital. After many warnings, the troops are obliged to fire. Two hundred workers are killed and wounded.

February 5, 1905—assassination of Grand Duke Sergei Alexandrovich in Moscow; the members of the imperial family are asked by the police not to attend his funeral because the ancient capital is crowded with terrorists.

June 6, 1905—revolt in the Black Sea Fleet.

October 12, 1905—declaration of the general strike by the first short-lived St. Petersburg Soviet.

October 17, 1905—Nicholas Nicholaevich, Jr., and Witte

persuade the Czar to capitulate before the mob. A manifesto is issued convoking the Parliament ("Duma").

October 20-25, 1905—Jewish pogroms.

Autumn, 1905—extraordinary measures have to be taken to assure the unhindered return of the army from the Japanese front and to protect the safety of the Trans-Siberian Railway from the assault of the revolutionaries.

December, 1905—the revolt in Moscow assumes tremendous proportions. The Semenovsky Regiment of the Imperial Guard is sent from St. Petersburg to restore order.

April 27, 1906—the opening of the First Duma, made of talkative professors, journalists, lawyers and "moderate" revolutionaries.

Spring-summer, 1906—the so-called "illumination" lights up the Russian continent from one end to the other,—the peasants are burning their landlords' estates. A score of governors and generals are assassinated.

July 7, 1906—the Czar dissolves the First Duma. Several hundred parliamentarians refuse to quit and issue a proclamation advising the population to stop paying taxes. Stolypin, appointed President of the Council of Ministers, inaugurates an organized offensive against the revolutionaries.

August 12, 1906—the explosion of a bomb planted by the revolutionaries in Stolypin's summer house causes grave wounds to his children.

Winter, 1906-1907—an epidemic of robberies—organized by the revolutionaries to replenish the exchequer of their executive committee—necessitates the proclamation of martial law in most of the larger cities.

June 3, 1907—the Czar dissolves the Second Duma, which surpassed even its predecessor in arrogance, the Russian Army having been insulted from its tribune.

Autumn, 1907—the new elections are being held in accordance with the new electoral law which assures larger representation for the agricultural elements of the nation. The members of the Third Duma appear to be slightly less talkative but all of them are suffering from a peculiar inferiority complex.

1908-1911—the measures taken by Stolypin succeed in restoring order, the industries and the banks are flourishing as never before. Stolypin is preparing a new law tending to increase the land holdings of the peasants and to do away with the community property of the villages.

September 14, 1911—Stolypin is assassinated in Kieff.

1912-1914—the Government is headed by Kokovtzeff, a colorless bureaucrat frightened of his own shadow and incapable of constructive ideas. Sazonoff, the Minister of Foreign Affairs, is a puppet in the hands of the French and British Governments; his policies involve Russia in all sorts of Balkan adventures and are liable to cause trouble with the Central Empires.

July 30, 1914—Sazonoff and Nicholas Nicholaevich, Jr., advise the Czar to sign the order for a General Mobilization.

1915-1916—the revolutionaries dominate the "auxiliary organizations of the front" and lead a hidden propaganda against the régime. St. Petersburg is flooded with defeatist literature which exploits the "influence of Rasputin" as means for poisoning public opinion.

February, 1917—German agents conduct propaganda in the breadlines of St. Petersburg and organize strikes in the factories working for national defense.

March, 1917—the abdication.

2

This very brief summary of blood, terror and flames, fails to depict the utter stupidity and the boundless irresponsibility of the clique that for twenty-three years persisted in their efforts to cause the collapse of the empire. It is significant that none of those leaders, who loomed largely on the Russian horizon in 1894-1917, succeeded in riding the storm of 1917-1918. Every one of them had either been shot by the Bolsheviks or obliged to seek refuge abroad. Only the vacillating government of Nicholas II could have tolerated them in Russia. To quote one of their own ideologists, Mr. Michael Gershenson—"The Russian intelligentsia should be grateful to the Czar's government for protecting them by its jails and bayonets against the furor and anger of the nation; woe to us all, if we ever live to see the day of the fall of the Czar." This was written in 1907!

Who were those men and women plotting incessantly against the existing régime? What queer logic led them to believe that the chaos once unchained would limit its fury of destruction to the imperial palaces? Their membership in the various political parties, such as "social-revolutionary," "social-democratic," "popular-socialistic," "constitutional-democratic," etc., meant little to themselves and it would be certain to mean still less to a student of Russian history. A flamboyant leader of the "social-democratic" party and an intimate friend of Lenin, Mr. Malinovsky, was drawing his monthly allowance as an undercover agent of the Department of Imperial Police. On the other hand, Mr. Alexander Gouchkoff, presumably the head of the conservatives, did all in his power to bring about a military revolt in the Russian Army.

The veneer of political nomenclature would have to be washed off the face of the Russian revolutionary movement to enable us to see the heterogenous features of its tin gods, its fanatics, its adventurers, its would-be ministers, its blue-blooded followers and its zealous government-baiters.

The name of Leo Tolstoi headed the crowded list of the tin gods of the revolution. For no special reason, except his unfortunate authorship of platitudinous political pamphlets and his infantile feud with the Greek Orthodox Church, the greatest literary genius of modern Russia was revered as an Apostle by the revolutionary youth of the country. Students and laborers traveled for thousands of miles to his aristocratic estate in "Yasnaya Poliana," and his sermon of New Christianity was mistaken by them for the clarion call of the revolt. Once in a while, his poetic soul moved by so much worship, Tolstoi felt the urge to address a threatening letter to the Czar. He dreamed of being persecuted, arrested, exiled to Siberia. Neither Alexander III nor Nicholas II ever thought of doing anything so silly: their profound admiration for the author of *War and Peace* helped them overlook the many theatricalities of an old man, pathetic in his determination to use the pen of a genius for writing pamphlets suggestive of a tyro. He specialized in denouncing the "cruelties" of Emperor Nicholas I. One day, my brother Nicholas Michailovich pointed out to him in a letter of respectful denial the extreme absurdity of his accusations. A curious answer arrived from Yasnaya Poliana: Tolstoi was confessing his "deep respect for the patriotic policies" of our grandfather and was thanking Nicholas Michailovich for the "interesting historical data." In the meanwhile, the sales of the nauseating pamphlet continued undisturbed, the traditions of the imperial family preventing the publication of my brother's polemic with Tolstoi.

Immediately on receipt of the news of Tolstoi's death, Nicholas II sent a friendly telegram to his widow, expressing his sincere sorrow and extending condolences. The intelligentsia frowned at this simple human act of the sovereign, thinking that it might spoil the monstrous political demonstration staged by them on the day of the funeral. Endless speeches were made on that November afternoon of 1910, denouncing the existing régime and dwelling upon topics thoroughly irrelevant to the occasion. Had it not been for the tear-stained face of Countess Tolstoi, the participants of that revolutionary rally would have entirely forgotten that they were witnessing a funeral, the funeral of a man who was glorified by the world purely for his literary achievements and who had been born in a family that owed its title and opportunities to the greatly hated Czars of Russia. "Dear Leo Nicholaevich, your memory shall always live in the hearts of the grateful peasants of Yasnaya Poliana," read the inscription of a sixteen-foot banner carried by the pallbearers. Seven years later, the "grateful peasants of Yasnaya Poliana" desecrated the grave of dear Leo Nicholaevich and burned his ancestral home. This time they listened to a different speech made by the representative of the soviet. The latter explained that, after all, Tolstoi was an "aristocrat and a landlord," i.e., an "enemy of the people."

Next to Tolstoi, among the ranking saints of the revolution, were Prince Peter Kropotkin, Madame Vera Figner, Madame Breshko-Breshkovskaya (the so-called grandmother of the Russian revolution), and the numerous political assassins who served their sentences in the Fortress of Schlüsselburg near St. Petersburg. Aristocrat Kropotkin preached his sufficiently harmless theory of pink-water anarchism from the safety of his comfortable abode in London; all others, mostly women, qualified for red canonization in a series of terroristic acts staged by them as far back as the late seventies. An enthusiastic feminist would be inclined to rejoice at this ascendancy of the weaker sex, but the biographers of Charlotte Corday would find little inspiration in the characteristics of those bloodthirsty Russian spinsters who seemed to have been molded by the hands of Krafft-Ebing and Freud. The rigid etiquette of the intelligentsia prescribed, however, for an eighteen-carat liberal to stand up at the mention of Vera Figner's name: the venerable lady participated in the assassination of the Czar-Liberator, and the "cruel" Emperor Alexander III had dared to imprison his father's murderess. Curiously enough, the Bolsheviks refused to recognize the divine prerogatives of the revolutionary tin gods, and the first anniversary of the soviet régime found them either back in jail or in exile. One may say that the Law of Retribution has a habit of choosing strange emissaries to execute its warrants.

Pleve's assassin, Sazonoff, and the moronic youngster

Kalyaieff (who threw a bomb into the carriage of Grand
Duke Sergei Alexandrovich) should both be classed among
the revolutionary fanatics. They and their likes served as
cannon fodder for Boris Savinkoff, the greatest adventurer of
modern times. "A Prince Hamlet who tried to do a Cesare
Borgia," said Bolshevik Radeck of Savinkoff during the
latter's trial in Moscow in 1925. Add to this deft portrayal
a dash of Casanova and a sprinkling of Baron Münchhausen,
and the figure of that most un-Russian of all Russian revolutionaries is complete. A soldier of fortune, a poet, a
"great lover," a story teller, a fantastic liar, a gourmet, a
high liver, a master and a slave of resounding words—Boris
Savinkoff fought all régimes for the sake of fighting. He
organized the assassination of Grand Duke Sergei Alexandrovich, he plotted against the life of Nicholas II, he in-
trigued against the Provisional Government with General
Korniloff, he "sold out" General Korniloff to the Provisional
Government, he worked as an agent of the Allied Secret
Service against the Bolsheviks, he rode on a white horse side
by side with Pilsudsky at the head of the Polish legions pillaging the cities of Southwestern Russia, he preached a holy
war against the soviets, he surrendered to the soviets and
denounced their enemies, he dreamed of becoming a Dictator
of Peasant Russia, and he finished his career by jumping out
of the window of a Moscow jail.

"The revolution and the counter-revolution are all alike
to me," he confessed to an acquaintance of mine in 1918.
"I am craving for action. My only ambition is to keep the
self-satisfied morons from loafing in their backyards and
watching the amorous antics of a rooster."

Popular imagination, ignorant of Savinkoff's real personality, saw in him a St. Patrick of the Russian revolt and
credited him with almost every political murder of the first
decade of the twentieth century. In truth, he had killed
with his own hands but one single elderly policeman caught
by him unawares and unarmed. He always found hysterical

youngsters willing to listen to his eloquent speeches and ready to die for the greater glory of the revolution. And die they did—while Savinkoff himself hurried back to his pleasant life in Paris and to his favorite restaurant Larue where he used to fight all the existing governments from twelve to two each afternoon, washing down the memories of his miraculous escapes with a bottle of excellent Mouton-Rothschild. In the case of Grand Duke Sergei's assassination he had a touching alibi to offer: "I would have killed the Grand Duke with my own hands had it not been for the fact that two children were seated with him in the carriage when he drove past the corner where I stood with my bomb." This very attractive story made a great hit at Larue's; years afterwards, one of the two children—Grand Duchess Marie—expressed a desire to meet the man who had "saved" her life. The fact remains that the death-dealing bomb was thrown by Kalyaieff, who went to the gallows, and that the fancier of children returned to the Rue Royale.

He was a novelist of considerable talent, and in an indirect way the Russian Imperial Government had financed his terroristic acts by allowing his books to be sold throughout the country and his weekly articles to be run in the Moscow newspapers. It never dawned on our Minister of the Interior that a goodly fifty per cent of the Russian revolutionaries—Savinkoff, Trotzky, Tchernoff and Zenzinoff among them—were able to continue their activities only thanks to the royalties and the salary-checks paid to them by the Russian publishers. I do not believe that the postal authorities of any other country, even the United States or England, would extend their facilities to a newspaper known to support the assassins of the members of the Government. And yet, Russia was accused by the world of having established a "barbarous censorship of the press."

The miraculous escapes of Savinkoff, some of them eclipsing Casanova's Venetian adventures from the point of view of pure showmanship, were largely due to his close collaboration with the notorious Azeff, the official leader of the terrorists and the unofficial agent of the Department of Police. I do not claim to possess the ultimate solution to the Azeff mystery. The revolutionaries described him as an "agent provocateur extraordinary"; the Department of Police accused him of displaying a greater fealty to the red cause. In any event, he did not advise St. Petersburg of the plots against the lives of Pleve and Grand Duke Sergei Alexandrovich, although all the details were known to him weeks in advance. His fear of the revengeful Savinkoff must have overwhelmed his passion for money, and his secret dispatches from Paris failed to mention even the whereabouts of his garrulous collaborator. Testifying before a self-styled Investigating Committee of the revolutionaries in Paris, Savinkoff threatened at first to kill any "blackguard" who would dare to "throw mud" in the face of his dear friend Azeff. He said that had it not been for the absolute loyalty of Azeff, he would have been caught by the police the night before the grand duke's assassination. He may have added too that the payroll of the Secret Imperial Police had always been crowded with names of prominent revolutionary leaders and that there was no point in singling out Azeff's case.

"We could have hired almost every red celebrity, provided we were willing to meet his or her price," wrote a former director of the Department of Police in his posthumous memoirs. The revolutionaries hastened to provide a confirmation of this amazing statement by burning the archives of the Moscow Political Police twenty-four hours after their triumph in March, 1917.

3

The imperial régime could have rested comfortably on its laurels were the "red peril" limited to applause-seekers like Tolstoi and Kropotkin, to theoreticians like Lenin and Plekhanoff, to insipid old women like Breshko-Breshkovs-

THE LAST CZARINA IN THE UNIFORM OF HER OWN GUARD REGI-
MENT.

THE HEIR APPARENT AND ONLY SON OF THE LAST CZAR, GRAND DUKE ALEXIS NICHOLAEVICH, AT THE AGE OF EIGHT IN 1912.

kaya and Figner, and to adventurers like Savinkoff and Azeff. As happens with every contagious disease, the real danger lay in the multitude of its unregistered transmitters: the mice, the rats, the insects. Or to employ more dignified terms, the bulk of the Russian aristocracy and intelligentsia formed the army of germ-carriers. The throne of the Romanoffs was destroyed not by the future leaders of the soviets and not by the bomb-throwing youngsters, but by the titled persons who wore resplendent court uniforms and by the bankers, editors, lawyers, and university professors who lived off the bounty of the empire. The Czar would have satisfied the workers and the peasants; the police could have taken care of the terrorists; but there existed no way of pleasing the would-be ministers, the blue-blooded followers of the revolution, and the government-baiters bred by the Russian universities.

What was to be done with those princesses and countesses who spent their days going from door to door and spreading monstrous lies about the Czar and the Czarina? What was to be done with that scion of the ancient family of Princes Dolgorouky who solidarized with the enemies of the empire? What was to be done with the president of Moscow University, Prince Troubetzkoi, who turned that famous institution of learning into a radical campus? What was to be 'done with that brilliant Professor Milukoff who felt it his duty to denounce the régime in foreign lands, undermining our credit abroad and gladdening the hearts of our foes? What was to be done with Count Witte—raised by the Czars from clerk to prime minister—who specialized in providing reporters with scandalous tales discrediting the imperial family? What was to be done with the average professors of our universities who educated their pupils in the belief that Peter the Great lived and died a scoundrel? What was to be done with our press which met with rousing cheers every news of our defeat on the Japanese front? What was to be done with the members of our Duma who listened with radiant faces to the gossipers swearing to the existence of a wireless station connecting Czarskoie-Selo with Hindenburg's headquarters? What was to be done with the commanders of our armies, put in their high positions by the Czar, who were more interested in helping to increase the anti-régime feelings of the population of the rear than in scoring victories over the Germans on the front? What was to be done with our veterinarians who, while gathered at their annual convention in Moscow supposedly to discuss new means of fighting hoof-and-mouth disease, wound up by passing a resolution demanding the establishment of a radical cabinet?

The anti-régime activities of the Russian aristocracy and intelligentsia could easily make a thick volume of "Boners," to be dedicated to the former Russian liberals now crying over the "good old days" in the streets of Paris and New York, but the first prize for arrogant stupidity should be given to the Russian press of the period. A man's achievements counted for nothing with the Russian newspapers unless his antagonism to the existing régime had been plainly expressed by him, both verbally and in writing. Scientists and musicians, actors and writers, painters and bridge builders were judged according to the intensity of their radical sentiments. I need not go further than quote the sad experience of philosopher Rosanoff, columnist Menshikoff and novelist Lesskoff.

All three refused to follow the dicta of the liberals for various reasons of their own. Rosanoff, because he cherished his independence of thought. Lesskoff, because he maintained that literature had nothing in common with politics. Menshikoff, because he doubted the possibility of a Czarless Russian Empire. All three were subjected to a merciless punishment by the leadings newspapers and book publishers of the country.

Lesskoff's manuscripts were returned unread, his name was sneered at by cub reporters acting as literary critics, and a few published novels of his (printed at his own expense) were boycotted by the prejudiced readers. The Germans and the Danes, led by Georg Brandes, happened to be the first to discover Lesskoff and to speak of the superiority of his craftsmanship over that of Dostoievsky.

Menshikoff spent the life of a veritable leper, snobbed by the contemporary luminaries and avoided even by the staff of his own newspaper *Novoie Vremia*. The name of that greatest journalist ever produced by Russia had become a synonym for all that was low, vile and contemptible. Such was the tyranny of the self-appointed liberal censors of public opinion that on the occasion of the fortieth anniversary of Menshikoff's column no writer dared send him a congratulatory wire for fear this act would become known to the public. And so the old man sat alone in his deserted office, frothing at the mouth and writing still another one of his brilliant unappreciated articles.

As for Rosanoff, even the unique originality of his philosophy and his universally recognized genius did not save him from being ostracized by the newspapers, the magazines, the clubs and the literary associations. The voluminous "Rosanoffiana"—by now it has grown into hundreds of volumes—began to appear only after his death, when the arrival of the Bolsheviks made all feuds of the past look supremely ridiculous. During his lifetime the man who had anticipated Freud by a whole generation was reduced to the writing of small pieces for Menshikoff's paper. Shortly before the war, a prominent Russian publisher revolted at the sight of this talent being wasted in such an ignominious fashion and engaged Rosanoff to write under the pen-name of Varvarin for his well-known Moscow newspaper *Russkoie Slovo*. It does not take long for a pack of sheep to smell the approach of a lion. The very first article by Varvarin caused a row among the collaborators of the *Russkoie Slovo*. A delegation headed by Dimitry Merejkovsky (the author of *Leonardo Da Vinci*) called on the brave publisher and presented him with an ultimatum: he had to choose between them and Mr. Rosanoff-Varvarin.

"But, gentlemen, gentlemen," begged the publisher, "surely, you cannot deny Rosanoff's genius."

"We are not interested in his genius," replied the delegation. "Rosanoff is a reactionary and we cannot afford to work with him on the same newspaper."

Mr. Merejkovsky is to be found at present in Paris, shedding tears of regret over the golden age of the Russian reactionaries and overburdened with admiration for the memory of the philosopher he deprived of a chance to earn a living.

In a delightful piece entitled "The Revolution and the Intelligentsia" and written immediately after the victory of the soviets, Rosanoff described the predicament of Mr. Merejkovsky and all other former Russian liberals in the following manner: "Having thoroughly enjoyed the gorgeous spectacle of the revolution, our intelligentsia prepared to don their fur-lined overcoats and return to their comfortable houses, but the overcoats were stolen and the houses burned."

CHAPTER THIRTEEN

DRIFTING

I

THE events of my personal life during the twenty-three years of the reign of Nicholas II were closely interwoven with the tragic dates of the Russian history.

In the beginning I took things as they came and tried to build my home against a background of chaos. I owed it to my wife. I was prompted to it by my love for her.

Our honeymoon interrupted by the death of her father, we returned to St. Petersburg anxious to assist Nicky and Alix in their initial steps as sovereigns. No two newlywed couples could have been more intimate. At first we occupied adjoining apartments in the enormous Anichkoff Palace, all four of us wishing to be near the Dowager-Empress. Then we moved together to the Winter Palace, a place of depressing magnitude, with its bedrooms reminding one of American convention halls. In the spring we stayed in Gatchino, in the summer in Peterhof. In the fall we voyaged to Abbas-Tuman to be near Georgie and to the Crimea where my estate of Ay-Todor was adjoining Nicky's palace in Livadia. Always together, never tiring of our friendship. When my daughter Irene was born in July, 1895, Nicky and Alix shared my joy and sat for hours at Xenia's bedside admiring the beautiful features of the future Princess Yousoupoff.

A newcomer in Russia, Alix felt a natural desire to spend her time with the people she trusted and understood, which brought our intimacy to a point rarely reached by relatives-in-law. Long after meals we would remain at the table going over the reports presented to Nicky by his ministers.

In my anxiety to be of value to the throne I emphasized the urgent necessity of building a large battle fleet. Ten years of service in the navy had opened my eyes to the inadequacy of our national defense. I knew my subject well and was able to supply Nicky with carefully verified data. He decided that I should prepare a short pamphlet, to be printed in one hundred copies only and to be distributed among the elder officers of the navy. This project amounted in a way to a plot hatched by the Czar and his brother-in-law against the Minister of the Navy Tchichacheff and the Grand Admiral of the Navy Grand Duke Alexis. As long as my actions corresponded to Nicky's wishes I was quite willing to bring their wrath on my head. Alix took an active part in our "scheme." I remember her whispering to me during a court luncheon in April, 1896: "Did you mail your pamphlet to the admirals?" "I did, this morning," I whispered back, bending to kiss her hand. Our neighbors at the table pricked their ears and looked mystified. Next morning Alix called me into her apartment to say that Uncle Alexis and Tchichacheff were threatening to resign until I offered them my official apologies. I went straight to Nicky.

"I hope you remember that I have written and mailed my pamphlet with your consent and blessing."

"Quite so, quite so," sighed Nicky. "But don't you see, Sandro, there is a great deal of truth in what Uncle Alexis says. After all, I cannot permit my brother-in-law to destroy the discipline of the navy."

I stood aghast.

"Good gracious, Nicky! Were you not the first one to whom I read the rough draft of the pamphlet?"

"Of course, of course, but let us have peace in the family, Sandro. Be a good boy and accept the suggestion of Uncle Alexis."

"What is his suggestion?"

"That you should be put in command of the battleship *Emperor Nicholas I* stationed in Chinese waters."

"I see. So I am to be exiled to China because I executed your orders."

His face twitched uncomfortably.

"It is purely a question of maintaining discipline."

"And if I refuse to accept this appointment?"

"Well, I really don't know what we can do then. I suppose Uncle Alexis will insist that you should be dismissed from the service in the navy."

"Thanks, Nicky," I said, praying to God that He would help me to control my temper, "I would much rather prefer this second suggestion of yours."

He brightened up immediately and embraced me.

"I knew, Sandro, that you would take this news in a proper spirit. Just leave Uncle Alexis alone for a while, and then, in a year or two, we shall see what can be done to give you full satisfaction. Only think, Sandro, how happy Xenia will be when she finds out she can have you now for herself."

Xenia was delighted. Thanks to Nicky's unwillingness to stand by me in the "Battle of Peterhof" we enjoyed the happiest years of our married life. The children were coming in rapid succession. My son Andrew, the eldest of six boys, was born in January, 1897, the others followed between 1899 and 1906. I could never sympathize with the fathers who act like helpless lunatics the day of the birth of their children. I myself invariably remained by Xenia's side till it was over. The court physician used to administer to her a small dose of chloroform to ease the pains, causing her to laugh and say all sorts of funny things, in consequence of which all our children were born in an atmosphere of gayety. Each time I made it a point to follow the ancient Russian custom: a father is supposed to light the two candles, which were held by him and his wife during their wedding ceremony, just at the moment when the first shrieks are heard in the room, and to wrap the newly-born baby in a shirt worn by him the previous night. Call it a silly superstition, but it seemed to give Xenia more self-confidence.

The growth of Ay-Todor accompanied the enlargement of my family. I took an immense pride in planting new trees, working in my vineyards and supervising the marketing of my wines, fruits and flowers. There was something hopeful and encouraging in being able to get up at sunrise and to say to myself, while riding along the bridle-path lined by jungles of wild roses: "This is real. This is mine. This will never turn on me. This is the place where I belong and where I should stay forever."

Very soon, in the natural course of developments and improvements, it became necessary to buy the adjoining lands from the Crimean Tartars. The acquisition of each additional acre of rich soil gave me as much of a thrill as the birth of a son. A very picturesque trail built by me across my new properties, and connecting Ay-Todor with Livadia, became known as the "Imperial Trail" because Nicky and Alix liked to use it for their daily visits to our house. I never held against Nicky my dismissal from the navy. I felt sorry for the weakness of his character but I did not care to spoil our Crimean idyll by referring to a matter unpleasant for both of us.

Princess Zinaida Yousoupoff often joined us in our picnics and parties. Our friendship dated back to the late seventies in St. Petersburg when we used to go skating together each Sunday. A woman of rare beauty and culture, she bravely bore the burden of her stupendous wealth, giving millions to worthy charities and trying to satisfy each deserving plea. She married several years ahead of me and came to Ay-Todor escorted by her handsome boy Felix. Little did I think in those days that eighteen years later my small Irene was to walk with him to the altar.

Three years passed. I had every reason to be grateful as far as my personal life was concerned. Unfortunately I could not remain entirely idle when in St. Petersburg and

I gave my time to the editing of the Naval Year Book and to collaboration in other books dealing with the problems of the navy. That was rather disturbing because it proved the impossibility of making a landlubber out of a sailor. I suppose I should have stayed all year round in Ay-Todor, satisfied with cruising in my yacht *Tamara* and admiring the waves lit by the rays of the Ay-Todor lighthouse. But I had the navy in my blood. In vain I tried to become interested in general politics and to do something outside the navy. Sooner or later, I found myself charting the course of an imaginary cruiser or heatedly engaged in playing the "Naval Game," a game invented by me in 1897 and adopted by the Naval College.

By 1899 I could not stand it any longer. I asked Nicky to make a careful examination of Uncle Alexis' hurt feelings. I hoped that three years of fine food and attractive women had healed the grand admiral's wound.

Uncle Alexis grinned pleasantly: "So, that Caucasian rebel, that troublemaker Sandro has finally understood his mistake."

"Yes, Uncle Alexis," confirmed Nicky, "there is no doubt but that Sandro has repented."

"Well, well . . . That's good news. Tell him I am willing to overlook his impossible behavior of three years ago. I shall appoint him second in command on a coastguard battleship."

In the summer of that year we lost Georgie. He suffered a hemorrhage while taking his morning ride on a motorcycle, and passed in the hands of a peasant woman, several miles away from his Abbas-Tuman house. He was the third victim of tuberculosis in the imperial family. The same illness accounted for the death of my youngest brother Alexis Michailovich in 1895 and of my cousin Wiacheslav Constantinovich in 1882.

2

The new year of 1900 saw the realization of my ambitions, the ambitions of every sailor. I was promoted a full-fledged captain and put in command of the new battleship *Rostislaff* stationed in the Black Sea. This appointment coinciding with the beginning of the new century and coming to me at the age of thirty-four seemed a lucky omen for my future career. It would possibly have proven such had I been left alone with my ship and my family.

One summer cruise aboard *Rostislaff* and back in St. Petersburg, Nicky asked me to double up my duties of captain with the chairmanship of an important industrial enterprise in the Far East. It appeared that a group of Vladivostok business men had acquired a concession from the King of Korea for the exploitation of all the Korean forests situated between our border and the river Yalu; in need of large working capital they had approached the minister of the imperial court soliciting the Czar's financial backing. Experienced investigators dispatched by the court to Korea spared no superlatives in describing the benefits to be derived by Russia from that concession. According to their testimony, the existence of the richest gold mines in the world was suspected in and around the Yalu district. The proposition looked quite attractive if handled carefully and tactfully. In talking to Nicky I emphasized the word "tactfully"; I feared the arrogance of our Foreign Office that had always combined its catering to the Occidental powers with a clumsy attempt at bullying Japan. Completely ignorant of the military strength of the Far Eastern Empire, our diplomats sat at their desks in St. Petersburg dreaming the dreams of Hastings and Clive. They intended to do to Manchuria what the British had succeeded in doing in India. Under their strenuous pressure our Government decided to occupy Port Arthur a few years previous and to continue the Trans-Siberian Railway straight through Manchuria. This bold seizure of the port, taken by the Japanese in 1894 but ceded by them to the Chinese, was followed by the just and indignant protests of the Tokio cabinet. Count Ito came to St. Petersburg and proposed a peaceful settlement. He failed in his mission and there was nothing left for him to do but to conclude an anti-Russian alliance with Great Britain. It was an open secret in diplomatic circles that the Czar of Russia gave his consent to a series of adventures in the Far East because he listened to the perfidious advice of the young Kaiser. Nobody doubted likewise that Russia was bound to have a war with Japan, should she persist in claiming rights to Manchuria.

"Do we want to have a war with Japan?" I asked Nicky. "If we do, then we should immediately begin building the second track of the Trans-Siberian Railway, concentrating our troops in Eastern Siberia and launching a large number of modern battleships."

He just shook his head and said I was paying too much attention to gossip. No, he did not expect to have a war with Japan, nor with anyone else, at least not so long as he remained Czar. His words sounded reassuring. I accepted his offer to head the Yalu Concession Committee.

A year went by. First thing I knew, everybody was discussing the imminence of a new adventure by our diplomats. This time they wanted to prolong the Trans-Siberian Railway up to the Korean border and to declare the annexation of a part of Korea by the Russian Empire. I sat down and wrote a very harsh letter to the Minister of the Imperial Court Baron Fredericks, resigning from the chairmanship of the Yalu Committee and predicting a war with Japan in the immediate future. I minced no words in expressing my disapproval. I declared that as "a faithful subject of the Emperor and as a person not entirely bereft of my senses I shall have nothing further to do with a shameful scheme jeopardizing the lives of hundreds of thousands of innocent Russians."

Fredericks complained to the Czar. Nicky felt exceedingly hurt by my plain language and asked me to change my decision. I said "no" in a rather excited fashion.

In any other case the retirement of the chairman of an important undertaking would have been made public, but Baron Fredericks thought my disagreement with the Czar could affect unfavorably our interests in the Far East. Outside of our small circles of relatives and friends nobody ever learned that Grand Duke Alexander Michailovich had ceased to participate in the work of his committee. This happened in 1902. Two years later the politicians said that the war with Japan was caused by the Czar's brother-in-law and "his adventure" in the Yalu Peninsula. Not until the Bolsheviks published the contents of the archives of the imperial court, did my real part in the events that led to the war of 1904-1905 become known to the nation.

3

Once more I found solace aboard the *Rostislaff* and in the vineyards of Ay-Todor, and once more I consented to take an official position in the Government. This time, however, I had myself to blame.

During my frequent conversations with Nicky I often asked him to do something for the development of our Merchant Marine and for the improvement of our commercial ports. I suggested that he create a special Ministry of the Merchant Marine, freeing that vital part of our national life from the routine of an overcrowded Ministry of Finance. It took Nicky several months to make up his mind. Then he decided that I should be the Minister of Merchant Marine. On December 6, 1902, I was promoted rear-admiral and ordered to take my seat in the cabinet of ministers, the youngest member of the Government in the history of the empire.

Up to that time I maintained friendly relations with Minister of Finance Witte. He seemed to like me, while I respected the broadness of his vision and the originality of his methods. We often met and held lengthy conversations. All of this came to an abrupt end the day of my nomination. To begin with, the word "port" has a double meaning in the Russian language; in the parlance of the village it stands for "pants." The columnists said that "Grand Duke Alexander Michailovich has taken away Witte's pants." Incredible as it may appear, that brilliant man fell a victim to his fear of ridicule. Another effort by the newspapers aided by the vaudevillians, and Witte commenced to hate me. If at least he had been able to attack me, he would have felt better, but the necessity of treating me with the respect due a grand duke caused him immeasurable sufferings. He never contradicted me when I spoke at the meetings of the ministers. He sat and glared at me, his artificial smile failing to disguise his animosity. He fought me with all secret means at the disposal of the Minister of Finance. Report after report was sent by him to the Czar complaining of the "heavy burden put on the budget of the empire by the costly undertakings of the Minister of Merchant Marine." The newspapers began to publish articles, obviously inspired by Witte and vehement in their criticism of my ministry. The members of the cabinet, with the notable exception of the ministers of War and Navy, rallied around their powerful colleague and shared his hatred for the intruding grand duke. A hard struggle lay ahead of me. I would have had to conduct it on my own had it not been for the enthusiastic support extended to me by all men sincerely interested in the growth of our foreign trade. I succeeded in forcing the unwilling Government to establish a new steamship line connecting Russia with the Persian Gulf and to grant an important subsidy to the four existing steamship companies which deserved to be helped in their competition with the Germans and the British.

This initial victory gave me courage to proceed with my "ten-year plan" that established the budget of our commercial ports for ten years in advance, thus insuring Russian merchants against the changing moods of the cabinet.

The problem of developing our oil resources came next. I proposed to the Imperial Council that the Government organize a company for the exploitation of the immense oil fields situated in the Baku district and belonging to the Ministry of the Navy. I had no difficulty in proving that the profits derived from the marketing of our oil products would easily cover the costs of a large naval program and would leave a sufficient surplus to be used for all sorts of improvements. This clear and logical proposition was greeted by a storm of vociferous shouts. I was accused of trying to make "wildcat promoters" out of the Imperial Government. I was a "socialist," a "dangerous person striking at the very foundations of the régime"; I was an "enemy of the sacred prerogatives of private initiative," etc., etc.

My project was voted down by an overwhelming majority of the cabinet. The oil lands of the navy were sold for a ridiculous price to a group of enterprising Armenians. Anyone familiar with the pre-war value of those "Armenian holdings" in Baku would realize that a sum well over a billion dollars was thrown out of our Treasury. Reading the accounts of the Teapot Dome scandal in the United States in 1923 I had a feeling of living once more through the days of my unsuccessful fight for governmental decency. The scope of dishonesty and stupidity is international, to be sure.

4

On January 22, 1903, "all" St. Petersburg danced in the Winter Palace. I remember the date as it was to be the last spectacular ball in the history of the empire.

Almost a quarter of a century had passed since the night Nicky and I watched the Czar-Liberator appear with Princess Yourievskaya on his arm in these high-ceilinged halls that reflected in their mirrors seven generations of the Romanoffs.

DRIFTING

The uniforms of the Chevalier Guards remained the same but the rest of the empire had undergone a terrific change. A new and a hostile Russia glared through the large windows of the palace. I smiled sadly on reading the text of the invitation which demanded that all guests wear the costumes of the seventeenth century: for at least one night Nicky wanted to be back in the glorious past of our family.

Xenia wore a very becoming costume of a "boyarina," richly embroidered and covered with glittering jewels. For myself I had chosen the costume of a court falconer, consisting of a white-and-gold long coat,—with golden eagles embroidered on the breast and on the back,—a pink silk shirt, blue silk trousers and yellow leather boots. All other guests followed their fancy, always remaining within the limits of the seventeenth century. Nicky and Alix appeared dressed as the first Czar and the first Czarina of the house of the Romanoffs. Alix looked stunning, but Nicky was obviously not sufficiently tall to do justice to his magnificent garb. The chief honors of the night were disputed between Ella (Grand Duchess Elizabeth) and Princess Zinaida Yousoupoff. My heart ached a bit at the sight of these two "mad devotions" of my early youth. I danced every dance with Princess Yousoupoff, until it came to the famous "Russkaya." She did it better than any ballerina but I limited my participation to hand-clapping and silent admiration.

The ball was pronounced a huge success. It was repeated in all its details a week later in the house of Russia's multimillionaire Count Alexander Sheremeteff.

This magnificent pageant of the seventeenth century must have made a strange impression on the foreign ambassadors: while we danced, the workers were striking and the clouds in the Far East were hanging dangerously low. Even our myopic Government came to the conclusion that "something" had to be done to alleviate the universal fears. General Kouropatkin, then Minister of War, decided to make a "tour of personal inspection" in our Asiatic possessions. Naturally he returned with an "all's well" report. To believe him, nothing could have been sounder or safer than our position in the Far East. The Japanese Army was a colossal joke, a product of the fertile imagination of its British press agents. Port Arthur could withstand a ten-year siege, our fleet was certain to give "the licking of his life" to the Mikado, and our fortifications in the Isthmus of Kinjou (dividing the Port Arthur peninsula from the mainland) were positively impregnable.

There was no point in arguing with a blind person. I listened to his report quietly, counting the minutes that it would take him to finish it and let me free to rush to Czarskoie-Selo. "Politeness be d——d," I thought on my way to Nicky, "the Czar of Russia must know the truth."

I commenced by asking Nicky to treat the matter with all due seriousness, not in the way of our perennial "Nicky-Sandro disputes."

"Kouropatkin is either a blundering idiot or a madman, or both. No sane person can doubt the fighting qualities of the Japanese Army. Port Arthur may have been all right as a fortress in the days of the old-fashioned artillery, but it has no chance whatsoever against the modern heavy guns. The same goes for our Kinjou positions. The Japanese will break them like a house of cards. There remains the navy. Let me tell you, Nicky, that last year in the course of our naval game in the College I had the Japanese side of the board and although I do not possess the experience of the Mikado's admirals, I destroyed the Russian Fleet and made a victorious landing against the forts of Port Arthur."

"What makes you believe, Sandro, that you are better qualified to judge the Japanese army and navy than one of our most illustrious strategists?" asked Nicky with a tinge of sarcasm.

GRAND DUKE ALEXANDER INSPECTING A NEW AERODROME IN
ST. PETERSBURG, 1912.

CZAR NICHOLAS II IN HIS SUMMER RESIDENCE IN PETERHOF IN
1912. GENERAL VOYIEKOFF IS BESIDE HIM. GRAND DUKE DIM-
ITRY IS BEHIND, WITH TWO FOREIGN MILITARY ATTACHES.

CZAR NICHOLAS II LEAVING THE IVERSKAIA CHAPEL IN MOSCOW.

"My knowledge of the Japanese, Nicky. I studied their army not from the window of a salon car nor from behind a desk in the War Office in St. Petersburg. I lived there for two years. I saw them every day. I mixed with all classes of the population. Laugh as much as you will, but the Japanese are a nation of wonderful fighters."

Nicky shrugged his shoulders:

"The Czar of Russia has no right to prefer the opinionated judgment of his brother-in-law to that of his recognized experts."

I went back to my office swearing never again to volunteer advice.

In the early spring we moved to Gatchino, in June to Peterhof, following the well-established routine and pretending that everything was perfectly all right.

One morning in July a telephone call came from Michailovosky Palace: my father had a paralytic stroke and was found lying unconscious on the floor of his bedroom.

For three weeks he hovered between life and death, watched by us day and night. It was heartbreaking to see that giant helpless and unable to speak. At seventy-one, having outlived three Emperors, he suffered excruciatingly from the thought that he could die at the darkest hour of Russia. His superhuman will to live pulled him through; in the middle of August he recovered his speech and showed signs of improvement in the right side of his body. Escorted by two physicians and three aides-de-camp he left in a special train for Cannes. Fate decreed that he should live six years more and witness the debacle of the Russian Army.

5

Ay-Todor in September. Back in St. Petersburg in October. Long hours at the office. The meetings of the Imperial Council, so strange in the absence of father. My

213

own growing children. The necessity of hiring the pack of my old enemies, the tutors and the teachers. The forced gayety of the social season. New Year's Eve. "Many happy returns in 1904"—hackneyed phrase of demoniac sarcasm under the circumstances.

I decided to spend the month of January in Cannes, so as to see with my own eyes the reported improvement in father's health. On the day of my departure I saw Nicky. Officially we—the grand dukes—were obliged to ask his permission to leave Russia; unofficially those farewell visits meant a friendly reunion around his luncheon table.

The Empress was pregnant and Nicky hoped that it was going to be a boy this time. After lunch we sat in his study, smoking and talking of this and that. He made no reference to the situation in the Far East. He seemed quite cheerful: his favorite manner of avoiding a conversation on a loathsome subject. It naturally awakened my suspicions.

"People claim, Nicky, that the war is at hand."

He continued to smoke.

"Are you still of the same determination to avoid war at no matter what cost?"

"There is no question of war," he replied dryly.

"But how can you prevent the Japanese declaring war unless you yield to their demands?"

"The Japanese are not going to declare war on Russia."

"Who will stop them?"

"They won't dare to."

"Are you or are you not going to yield to the Japanese demands?"

"That's annoying, Sandro. I am telling you that there will be no war with Japan nor with anyone else."

"I wish it were true."

"It is true."

A maddening dialogue and a senseless one. I left for Cannes. Three weeks later, on my way back to Russia, getting off my train at the Gare de Lyon in Paris I saw the seven-column headlines:

"Japanese torpedo boats made an unexpected attack on the Russian squadron of cruisers in Port Arthur."

True to the old Oriental custom, they delivered their blow first and afterward declared their intention of doing so.

CHAPTER FOURTEEN

NINETEEN HUNDRED FIVE

I

I MET Nicky the morning of my return to St. Petersburg from Cannes. He was standing in his study in the Anichkoff Palace, haggard and upset, his eyes fixed on the large windows with a vacant stare, probably watching the drizzling rain.

My entrance startled him. His face twitched. He anticipated a dreary talk, an avalanche of reproaches, a long cry over the snows of yesteryear. I at once waved his fears aside.

"I came to you, Nicky," I said in a casual tone, "to ask your permission to go to Port Arthur. You must sympathize with my natural desire to join my friends of the navy."

He was obviously relieved.

"Of course I do, Sandro, but I cannot let you go. We need you here in St. Petersburg. We could use your experience. I wish you would see Uncle Alexis and the Minister of the Navy at once."

I fought with him for an hour, explaining that I could be of greater value in Port Arthur but he would not have it. I suspected he acted under the influence of his mother and Xenia who did not want me to risk my life.

That same afternoon I saw Avelan, my former captain of the *Rynda,* an excellent seafaring man but grossly miscast in the administrative post of Minister of the Navy. Neither he nor his chief of staff, Admiral Rojdestvensky, was in a position to tell me what was going to happen and how we expected to score a victory over the British-built battleships of the Mikado with the old-fashioned forty-five units constituting our Pacific Fleet.

The apoplectic eyes of Avelan threatened to jump out with anguish, while Rojdestvensky simply said he was ready to sail for Port Arthur and face the Japanese in an uneven battle. His quasi-Nelsonic speech sounded ludicrous coming from a man entrusted with the operations of our navy. I reminded him that the nation had a right to expect from its military leaders something besides willingness to go down to the bottom of the sea.

"What can I do?" he exclaimed. "Public opinion has to be satisfied. I know it. But I likewise know that we haven't a chance against the Japanese."

"You should have thought of it, admiral, years ago when you were laughing at the Mikado's sailors."

"I was not laughing," said Rojdestvensky stubbornly. "I am willing to make a supreme sacrifice. That is the maximum you can expect of anyone."

And that man with the psychology of a suicide wanted to lead our navy! I shuddered, and forgetting for a second the well-known characteristics of our handsome grand admiral, made for his office. It was laughable. All the Mikado's men, horses and ships could not have changed Uncle Alexis. With him it was the same magnificent "je me fiche de tout." Somehow and in some way he expected our "eagles" to give a "sound beating to the yellow-faced monkeys." This question settled, he preferred to discuss the latest news of the Côte d'Azure. What wouldn't he give to be now in Monte Carlo! Had I seen Mrs. X and how did I find Mrs. Y? Would I not come for dinner and have a long chat about the good old days? His chef had secured a new recipe for cooking sturgeon, bringing out its natural flavor in a way that not even the gods of Greece in all their glory ever knew or tasted.

General Kouropatkin had just been appointed commander-in-chief of our army. Unlike the men of the navy, he bristled with enthusiasm and had the Japanese beaten on all the fronts long before his train pulled out of St. Petersburg. A typical theoretician of the War College he relied unreservedly on his plans, dispositions and calculations. No matter what the enemy was going to do, he knew how to parry their moves. He made a great hit with the St. Petersburg journalists. He was always "good copy."

Endless trains packed with soldiers were crawling across the Ural Mountains. Seventy per cent of these people who were supposed to do the actual fighting had discovered the existence of Japan on the day of their mobilization. It seemed queer to them that they should leave their villages and risk their lives in a war with a nation that never did them any harm.

"How far is the front?" they all asked their officers.

"About seven thousand miles."

Seven thousand miles! Even their very eloquent commander-in-chief could not have explained to them why anyone should quarrel with a country situated seven thousand miles away from the spot where one was struggling with the soil for a meager living.

As a distinct innovation, the departing regiments were blessed by the ikon of St. Seraphim Sarovsky, a saint recently canonized by the Holy Synod. His unfamiliar features affected the soldiers most depressingly. If God and the saints had to be involved at all in the Far Eastern crime, Nicky and his bishops should have stuck to the old reliable St. Nicholas, who saw the empire through three hundred years of fighting. It came to a point toward the end of the Japanese War that I began to loathe the very name of Seraphim Sarovsky. He may have led an exemplary life but as an inspiration for the troops he had proved a total failure.

2

There would be little sense in my retelling the history of the Russo-Japanese War. We marched from debacle to debacle, for eighteen successive months. When all was over, and Witte succeeded in bluffing the Japanese into accepting surprisingly moderate terms of peace at Portsmouth, New Hampshire, our great strategists said they would have won the war if given more time. I thought they should have been given twenty years of "time" to ponder over their criminal negligence.

No nation ever could or did win a war fighting an enemy seven thousand miles distant, being knifed in the back at the same time by a revolution at home.

My own experience in 1904-1905 proved most disheartening. In February, 1904, I was entrusted by Nicky with the task of organizing the so-called "cruiser war"—in order to stop military contraband from reaching Japan. Acting on the strength of the information provided by our Intelligence Service, I worked out a plan approved by the Imperial Council, whereby a squadron of armed passenger vessels was going to patrol the main ocean routes leading to Japan. Through my agents in Hamburg I bought four steamers, of 12,000 tons each, from the Hamburg-American Line, which combined with several steamers given to me by our Volunteer Merchant Marine Company constituted the bulk of the squadron, well equipped with modern long range guns and commanded by officers of courage and initiative.

Camouflaging its movements by choosing an innocent-looking itinerary, the squadron made its appearance in the Red Sea just in time to seize an armada of twelve contrabandists, loaded with ammunition and raw materials shipped from Germany and England and making their way toward Japan. The results obtained were well worth the efforts and money spent in executing my plan. I was prepared to receive congratulations. All of a sudden, our Minister of Foreign Affairs rushed to Czarskoie-Selo with a bunch of telegrams: there was the devil to pay in Berlin and London. The British Foreign Office sent in a "strenuous protest"; Kaiser Wilhelm went London one better and referred to the actions of our squadron as an "act of unprecedented piracy on the high seas, liable to cause the gravest international complications."

Coming to the palace in answer to a telephone summons I found Nicky and the Minister of Foreign Affairs in a state of despair. Uncle Alexis and Avelan were crouching in their chairs looking like children caught by their governess while stealing jam. Grand Duke Alexander was the naughty boy who had taught them all those awful things and they wanted Nicky to understand distinctly that he and only he should be punished for the mischief done. Nicky himself seemed to have forgotten that the original idea of the "cruiser war" was conceived in his presence and with his whole-hearted approval. He demanded explanations.

"What explanations?" I asked in sincere bewilderment. "Since when does a great power apologize for preventing military contraband from reaching its enemy? What did we send our cruisers to the Red Sea for if not for the sole purpose of catching the contrabandists? What is it anyway, a war or an exchange of niceties between diplomatic chancelleries?"

"But don't you understand, Your Imperial Highness?" shrieked the Minister of Foreign Affairs who had gone completely gaga by that time. "We are running a risk of having a war with Great Britain and Germany. Don't you realize what the Kaiser means in his frightful telegram?"

"No, I do not, and what is more, I doubt whether the Kaiser himself realizes what he means in his wire, besides the fact that he runs true to his habit of double-dealing. Is he a friend of ours or an enemy? What happened to that philosophy of his—loyalty of White Men in the face of the Yellow Peril and all that sort of rot?"

"You see, you see, Your Majesty," cried the Minister of

Foreign Affairs. "His Imperial Highness does not understand the seriousness of the situation. He is even trying to defend the actions of his squadron."

"My" squadron? I glanced at Avelan and Uncle Alexis. Surely, they would be manly enough to stop this nonsense, but they remained silent. I was the ringleader, they were just misguided kids.

"My decision is taken, Sandro," said Nicky firmly. "You will immediately dispatch an order to your squadron to release the twelve captured steamers and to refrain from further activities."

I choked with humiliation. I thought of my officers and men so proud of their achievement and expecting to be praised. I visualized the hateful face of the Kaiser triumphant in his treachery. And my former friends in Tokio! What a gorgeous laugh was coming to shrewd old Count Ito!

In normal times I would have handed in my resignation from all posts, including the Ministry of Merchant Marine, but a grand duke cannot desert his sovereign at a moment of national disgrace. So I had to execute his orders and keep my sorrow to myself.

3

The episode with the "cruiser war" made me weary of the whole mess. I hoped Nicky would leave me in peace and stop soliciting my advice and assistance. I was mistaken. My opinion was sought again. Once more—it was getting to be a nightmare—I sat with Nicky, Uncle Alexis and Avelan in the Czarskoie-Selo Palace debating a question of vital importance. We were to decide whether we should acquiesce in Admiral Rojdestvensky's plan of taking our remaining battleships to the Far East where certain defeat was being prepared for them by the Japanese.

The admiral himself entertained no hopes for victory. He merely thought that "something should be done to satisfy the public demands." Our fleet and the lives of thousands of sailors had to be sacrificed to please the ignorant "naval experts" of the newspapers. The latter had recently discovered the existence of the technical terms like "fighting coefficient," "aggregate tonnage," etc., and were daily proving in their columns that the Japanese could be wiped off the face of the ocean by the combined forces of our Pacific and Baltic fleets.

Nicky explained the purpose of our meeting and asked us to state our opinions frankly. Uncle Alexis had nothing to say and had the courage to admit it. Avelan talked at great length without saying anything. It was "yes" and "no," "of course" and "on the other hand." Rojdestvensky gave another proof of his knowledge of Nelson's biography. I spoke last and spared nobody's feelings. To my extreme stupefaction it was unanimously decided to follow my advice and not to send our Baltic Fleet to its grave in the Pacific.

All remained quiet for two weeks, at the end of which period Nicky changed his mind. The fleet was to leave for the Far East, after all, and I was to escort my sovereign to Kronstadt for a farewell review of the ships. Going to Kronstadt aboard his yacht I renewed the dispute, ably seconded by the experienced captain of H.I.M.S. *Standard*. Nicky wavered again. Inside his heart he knew I was right all the time.

"Let me talk once more to Uncle Alexis and Avelan," he said when we boarded the Admiral's ship. "Only let me talk to them alone. I do not want them to be influenced by your arguments."

Their conference lasted several hours, with the "bad boy" of the navy waiting outside.

"You win," announced Avelan, appearing on deck. "We have taken an irrevocable decision not to send the Fleet."

The irrevocability of Nicky's decision lasted ten days. Then he changed his mind for the third and last time. Ships and officers and men were to be delivered on the altar of Public Opinion.

On May 14, 1905,—the ninth anniversary of Nicky's coronation,—our picnic party at Gatchino was interrupted by the arrival of a messenger from Avelan: our fleet had been annihilated by the Japanese at Tsushima and Rojdestvensky taken prisoner. In Nicky's place I would have abdicated then and there. He had nobody to blame for the Tsushima debacle but his own wavering self. He should have recognized that he lacked determination to face the unavoidable consequences of this most humiliating defeat in the history of Russia. He said nothing. As usual. Went deathly pale and lighted a cigarette.

His only son Alexis was nine and a half months old, and but slightly over three months had passed since the day of Uncle Sergei's assassination in Moscow.

4

Russia was on fire. All summer long gigantic clouds of smoke crept over the continent signifying that the Great God Arson assumed command over the peasants in their assault on the landlords. The students and the workers were striking. A mutiny broke out in the Black Sea Fleet and would have taken catastrophic proportions had it not been for the loyalty of my former flagship *Rostislaff*. The new Minister of the Interior Prince Sviatopolk-Mirsky, who replaced the assassinated Pleve, spoke of his "boundless confidence in the wisdom of public opinion," while the high government executives were murdered in the close neighborhood of the place where he delivered his orations. The Latvian and the Esthonian farmers of our Baltic provinces were engaged in a methodic extermination of their perennial oppressors, the German barons, and a crack regiment of the Imperial Guard had to act in the distasteful rôle of their bodyguards. The provincial police went panicky. North, East, South and

West clamored for the protection of the Imperial Guard and the Cossacks. So many governors were killed by the revolutionaries that an appointment to the post of governor acquired the meaning of a death sentence. The signing of the peace with Japan, made possible through the friendly intervention of President Roosevelt, gave birth to another terrifying problem, which had to do with the difficulties of bringing our army back to Russia over the Trans-Siberian Railway paralyzed by the strikes of the engineers and the station personnel.

On August 6, 1905, the Czar signed a manifesto convoking a sort of parliament invested with advisory powers only, a half-measure that increased the boldness of the revolutionaries.

The war brought to an end, there was no use in hurrying with the organization of a squadron of new torpedo boats (still another task wished on me by Nicky and financed by popular subscription). I left for Ay-Todor. A hospital for the convalescent officers built by me the previous summer on the grounds of my estate was doing fine work, but the revolution had already reached even that blessed spot of the Crimean Peninsula. A company of soldiers arrived from Sebastopol to protect us. The grown-ups walked with sour faces. The children felt subdued. The telephonic communication with Sebastopol was interrupted by a strike. Something happened likewise to the mail. Cut off from all news, I spent my evenings sitting on the bench next to the Ay-Todor lighthouse endeavoring to think up a solution. The more I thought the clearer it became that the choice lay between satisfying all the demands of the revolutionaries or answering their challenge with a merciless fight to the end. The former decision would have foreshadowed the formation of a semi-socialistic republic. The latter would have restored the prestige of the throne. In both cases we would have known where we stood. If Nicky was willing to be demoted to a mere Colonel Nicholas Romanoff, the necessary procedure spelled extreme simplicity. But if he wished to keep his oath and remain sovereign, not an inch of ground should be ceded by him to the chatterboxes of the St. Petersburg intelligentsia. The white flag of unconditional surrender or the flying colors of the imperial standard! As the Czar of all the Russias he had no right to display any other emblem at the top of the mast of Czarskoie-Selo.

Fifteen hundred miles separate St. Petersburg from Ay-Todor. A still greater distance divided the ideas of Grand Duke Alexander from the wavering opinions of Emperor Nicholas II. On October 17, 1905, after an endless conference attended by Witte, Grand Duke Nicholas Nicholaevich Jr., and the Minister of the Imperial Court Baron Fredericks, Nicky attached his name to a Manifesto built on a series of equivokes. He refused to appease the fighting forces of the revolution—the peasants and the workers—but he ceased to be the sovereign who had sworn in the Ouspensky Cathedral in Moscow to uphold the institutions of our ancestors. The intelligentsia received its parliament. The Czar of Russia became a mere parody on the King of England in a country that was kneeling before the Tartars in the days of Magna Charta. A son of Emperor Alexander III consented to divide his authority with a band of plotters, political assassins and undercover agents of the Department of Police.

That was the end. The end of the dynasty and the end of the empire. A brave jump from the precipice would have spared us the agony of the remaining twelve years.

The moment telegraphic communication with St. Petersburg was restored, I wired Nicky my resignation as Minister of Merchant Marine. I wanted to have nothing in common with a Government of cowardly compromise, least of all with a combination of individuals headed by Witte, the newly appointed Prime Minister of Russia.

5

The orgies of the year of damnation 1905 continued in ever-increasing tempo.

The end of October witnessed a series of Jewish pogroms which the very liberal Mr. Witte cared not to stop. A self-made Macchiavelli, he imagined he would acquire the support of the extreme chauvinistic elements by letting a drunken mob of hoodlums destroy the shops and the houses of the Hebrew population. The man was both despicable and pitiful in his involvements.

The climax of bloodshed was reached in December, when the Semenovsky Regiment of the Imperial Guard had to be dispatched from St. Petersburg in all haste to supplement the helpless Moscow police in a three-day battle with the revolting workers.

The elections to the Parliament ("First Duma") passed in an atmosphere of political assassinations, strikes, banditry and burning estates of the nobility. The Bolsheviks had advised their followers to boycott the Duma, leaving the field free for the triumph of the "constitutional-democrats," a party of professors, journalists, doctors, lawyers, etc., headed by the worshipers of the English Constitution.

On April 27, 1906, the Dowager-Empress, Grand Duke Michael Alexandrovich, Xenia and myself escorted the Czar and the Czarina from Peterhof to the Winter Palace for the opening of the Duma.

The ceremony took place in the same decorous hall where eleven years before Nicky advised the representatives of the intelligentsia to "forget their senseless dreams"—an awkward phrase that had since become the battle-cry of the revolution.

We all wore our full-dress uniforms, the ladies of the court displaying their jewelry. Deep mourning would have been more appropriate.

After the inevitable Te Deum, Nicky read a short speech,

outlining the problems facing the gentlemen of the Duma and of the reorganized Imperial Council. We stood and listened. I was told by my friends that they noticed tears in the eyes of the Dowager-Empress and of Grand Duke Vladimir. I myself would have cried had it not been for a peculiar feeling that came over me when I saw burning hatred in the faces of some of the parliamentarians. I thought they were a queer lot and that I should watch Nicky carefully lest one of them should attempt to come too close to him.

"I sincerely hope that you will commence your work in an atmosphere of pious diligence, inspired by a sincere desire to justify the confidence of your sovereign and of our great nation. May God's blessing be with me and you."

Such was the concluding sentence of Nicky's speech. He read it well, in a clear resounding voice, controlling his emotions and concealing his sorrow.

The shouts of "hurrah," vociferous on the side of the Imperial Council and perfunctory in the section reserved for the Duma,—and the funeral of the régime was over. We changed our clothes and returned to Peterhof. Witte was dismissed on the eve of the Duma's opening and the crowd of frightened bureaucrats was now headed by Goremykin, an old courtier with carefully washed wrinkles who looked like an upright corpse supported by a pair of invisible hands.

6

The palace reeked with gloom. The courtiers were at the point of firing at their own shadows. I could not breathe. I wanted to get back to the sea. Admiral Birileff, the new Minister of the Navy, suggested my taking command over the Baltic divisions of torpedo boats. I accepted his offer immediately. In the mood I was in, I would have consented to scrub the decks of a freighter. I trembled with joy at the sight of my admiral-flag hoisted on the mast of H.I.M.S.

Almaz, thinking that for at least three summer months I could stay away from the symphony of post-mortems.

Xenia and the children were spending the summer in Gatchino. Once a week they came to visit me. It was agreed that not a word of politics should be mentioned in my presence. I knew that the young and energetic governor of the province of Saratoff, Peter Stolypin, had replaced Goremykin but that was as much as I cared to know. We cruised in the Finnish waters on my brother-in-law Misha's yacht and we talked of things far removed from our "constitutional government."

One morning a message came from Gatchino. My son Feodor had fallen ill of scarlet fever and was in a dangerous state. I had to leave at once.

"I shall be back as soon as possible," I promised my second-in-command, "possibly next week."

"Next week" never arrived. Three days later I received word from my servant, who had stayed aboard the *Almaz*, that the crew were about to mutiny and were awaiting my return to seize me as a hostage.

"I am very sorry, Sandro, but under the circumstances you will have to quit," decided Nicky. "The Government cannot take the chance of delivering a member of the imperial family into the hands of the revolutionaries."

I sat across the table from him with my head bowed. I had no strength left to put up an argument. The military debacle, the failure of my efforts, the disgraceful Duma, the rivers of blood, and now on top of it all, my sailors wanting to seize me as a hostage. . . . A hostage! What a reward for twenty-four years given to the navy! My youth, my ambitions, my energy—I had sacrificed everything I possessed to the glory of our fleet. I had never so much as raised my voice in dealing with the sailors. I had fought their cause with the admirals, with the ministers, with the Czar. I cherished my popularity with my men. I felt so proud of being considered their friend and their confidant. A hostage!

I feared I was going to collapse. What was I to do? Suddenly a thought crossed my mind. It came in a flash. Could I not use the illness in my family as an alibi for leaving Russia?

"Nicky," I commenced, gasping for air and searching for persuasive expressions, "you know, of course, that both Irene and Feodor are ill of scarlet fever. The doctors tell me that a change of climate would benefit them greatly. Do you think it would be all right if I went with them abroad for a couple of months?"

"Certainly, Sandro."

We embraced. Nicky acted nobly that day. Not an inkling did he give of his understanding of the real reasons which prompted my flight. I was ashamed of myself but I could not help it. "I must run away! I must run away!", these words pounded in my head making me forget my duty to the throne, to the state and to the nation. Nothing mattered any more. I hated Russia.

CHAPTER FIFTEEN

THE REBOUND

I

I AM approaching the eight years which intervened between my flight from Russia in September, 1906, and the outbreak of the World War with an odd sensation of being able to look back at that ominous period of my life as a departed soul would view the empty shell of its former incarnation. I do not recognize myself. I despise the stranger who had usurped my name. I blush. And yet, I regret nothing. Were I to live once more through 1906-1914, I would answer again readily and recklessly the irresistible call of that infatuation.

My confession is voluntary. I could, no doubt, succeed in hiding the unpleasant truth under a smoke-screen of pompous platitudes. But then, why write this book at all if it must contain lies? I am not seeking sympathy. There are no extenuating circumstances in my case. I am presenting facts just as they occurred, which is both joyful and painful. Joyful, because I keep faith with myself; painful, because going over those eight years I realize that I have missed a great deal of what so easily could have been achieved by me.

We were staying in Biarritz at the Villa Espoir just above the grounds occupied by the present Hotel Miramar. Our party resembled a migration of nomads: Xenia, myself, six children, three nurses, English and French teachers, Irene's governess, Xenia's lady-in-waiting, my aide-de-camp, five maids, four butlers. Grand Duchess Olga (Xenia's sister) came ahead of us and was living at the Hotel du Palais. The first morning after our arrival, suffering from the depressing September heat, with our faces swollen from an all-night battle with the mosquitoes, we ran to the Grande Plage and buried our bodies in the sand. Our hearts sang: we had escaped from Russia. I thought we would never go back. Irene and Feodor had recovered from their illness and I thanked the Lord for giving me such a convenient opportunity for getting out of the inferno.

The golf links—the fifteenth hole—lay opposite our villa. I had never played the Scotsmen's game before but now I gave myself to it unreservedly, possibly because neither its terms nor its rules reminded me of Russia. Overnight I became acquainted with the majority of the local smart set. Invitations followed. We went out and asked people to come to our house. I caught myself watching women with interest. It came in the nature of a distinct revelation. For the whole twelve years of my marriage I never looked at any woman's face but that of Xenia. Social contacts which formerly came as a matter of routine began to attract my attention. I spoke to my neighbors at the table with a greater amount of animation than was prescribed by the code of etiquette. I proposed toasts and suggested parties.

I knew my new attitude toward life was bound to disturb my happiness but I did not care. Nothing made any difference so long as Russia and ourselves seemed to be going to the devil. Our original intentions called for a stay of three months but at the end of that period I persuaded Xenia to remain longer. Christmas came. Our gayest Christmas in twelve years. No obligation to attend the court receptions. No necessity to exchange visits with exalted bores. No restrictions. Just a real human holiday spent with our children and friends. The hunting season followed, bringing a series of luncheons in the country and dinners in Biarritz in an atmosphere of intimacy, happy fatigue and pleasant excitement. Our friends had led that kind of life since the day they were old enough to drink, but for us it was fascinatingly new. Each morning I rushed to the window to see whether it was true that we were still in Biarritz, separated by miles and miles from the palace, the Imperial Council, the ministers and our relatives.

I began to like a woman who often visited our villa. She was clever in a charming, unaggressive way, free from the fireworks of cocktail-bred brilliance. Her Spanish-Italian ancestry accounted for her solid culture and had taught her that real refinement is an arch-foe of self-consciousness. People called her a "good sport." In an Anglo-Saxon it would have frightened me. In a Latin it was adorable. We went out together a lot. She never said: "I don't want this, I'd much rather have that." She despised the kittenish type of a female. She realized I had barely escaped a total collapse. I could not have found a better companion. If anyone would have asked me the first month I met her: "Do you love her?" I would have answered: "Decidedly not. I am extremely fond of her. I admire her but I cannot call it love. Love comes as a 'coup de foudre' and often departs the same way. Fondness remains and given sufficient time achieves much more than love." The truth was, I could have exercised complete control over myself if I had wished to do so. I preferred not to. Perhaps a hysterical curiosity guided my actions. In any event, instead of pulling back I let go. I was prepared to taste bitter poison at the bottom of that cup and I welcomed it. I compared my feelings toward Xenia with those I experienced toward this new woman: the parallel baffled me. I did not know which one of the two I needed more. One stood for all that was best in my character, another promised a possibility of tearing away from the strain and terror of the past. The French say: "Il faut choisir." A man must choose. But the very thought of making the choice horrified me. I was the father of six children and expected the birth of the seventh in the nearest future.

2

Uncle Bertie—King Edward VII of England—arrived in the spring. Xenia was the favorite niece of his wife and the personal relations between the two reigning families had always been marked by cordiality, even in the years of bad feeling created in Russia by the British support of Japan. He stayed at the Hotel du Palais, surrounded by the touching devotion of the local population who realized that Biarritz owed most of its glamour to the continuous visits of the British sovereign.

We met often. Not a second of boredom could one experience in the presence of King Edward. Whether we played bridge, or sat at the dinner table, or walked on the golf links, his personality made everything look different. Of all the emperors, kings, presidents, and prime ministers I encountered in my life, none could have surpassed him in clearness of thought or in quality of statesmanship. I am not surprised that Kaiser Wilhelm hated him. It could not have been otherwise because with all his insane conceit the jumping Billy must have felt a miserable dwarf next to that natural-born ruler of overwhelming greatness.

It was a genuine pleasure to watch Uncle Bertie enjoy the freedom afforded by his incognito. His simplicity of manner and his kind way of chatting with the humblest employees of his hotel lacked even the tiniest trace of effort so often disclosed by the vacationing multimillionaires and the candidates for the exalted offices of the democracies. He needed not to force himself: "Now I must give a thrill to the assistant porter; he shall remember my graciousness till his dying day." He actually did sympathize with the poor fellow as he sympathized with every honest toiler of the world.

I never envied the British Empire its strength, its wealth and its position under the sun, but I always envied the caliber of its rulers. Queen Victoria, King Edward VII, King

George V, and the present Prince of Wales—what other country can boast of having produced such able sovereigns in four successive generations?

The visit of King Edward naturally increased our determination to prolong our stay in Biarritz. We advised the Dowager-Empress, who was complaining of lonesomeness, to join us in the hospitable country of the Basques. She arrived in her luxurious train, crowded with Russian conductors, servants, bodyguards, etc., causing a great stir by the impressiveness of her retinue. Our friends wondered whether she would deign to accept their company but I do not think even King Edward could have outdone my mother-in-law in willingness to participate in a bit of fun. Although I called her "mother" and was well aware of her age, I considered her as my pal and associate when it came to going out to a party or to arranging a party. I bought a mammoth Delaunay-Belleville, built in accordance with the size of my family, and the Southwest of France soon grew accustomed to the sight of a Russian grand duke driving around with his colony of women and children. June came. I could no longer postpone our return to Russia. We went back in mother's train, shining in her reflected glory and meeting en route innumerable welcoming officials headed by Monsieur Fallières, then President of France.

My youngest son Vassily was born at the end of that month in Gatchino. The doctors thought he could not live and a hastily summoned priest baptized him in his nursery, thus sparing the ordeal of military parade and shouting crowds. Vassily cheated the doctors: he recently married Princess Golitzin in New York.

3

For the sake of appearances I had to remain in Russia until early fall. I went around, paid my visits and performed my duties. Nicky and his ministers talked to me of the seriousness of the political situation. The Second Duma consisted

✦✦

of unmitigated scoundrels inviting by their actions the reading of the riot-act. Nicky was obliged to send them home, ordering new elections for the second time within eleven months. People praised Stolypin's firmness. "Don't you think he is wonderful?" I was asked at every turn. "He is," I answered perfunctorily. I did not care a snap about their Prime Minister nor about the rest of the mess. My thoughts were in Biarritz. By now I loved her. I walked through the gardens of Ay-Todor figuring out whether she would have liked the climate and the coloring of the Crimea.

"Going back abroad so soon?" wondered my friends. So soon! If I had full say, they would not have seen me at all.

We went first to Baden-Baden to visit my father. We found him considerably better, able to walk and possessing all his mental faculties. He was returning for the winter to the French Riviera, so we all motored there by way of Switzerland. My sister Anastasia (Grand Duchess of Mecklenburg-Schwerin) and my "exiled" brother Michael Michailovich met us in Cannes. Anastasia, as beautiful as ever, was greatly admired and fêted by the Riviera society. Michael stayed with his morganatic wife and his two daughters (the present Lady Milford-Haven and Lady Zia Wehrner) in his villa "Kasbek" used as headquarters by their innumerable friends. Only two years before their systematized wasting of time would have incensed me. Now I joined their ranks. The anticipation of meeting the woman I loved worked wonders with my temper. I accepted everything, including Michael's tea-parties and Anastasia's gambling in Monte Carlo.

Rome was our next stop. We invaded the Grand Hotel, the manager refusing to believe that all those men, women, children, uniformed and non-uniformed nurses, servants, and governesses belonged to the selfsame party of Grand Duke Alexander of Russia. Another grand duke like that and they could have started building an annex.

My friend had kept her word. She arrived in Rome on

the day agreed upon months in advance. Our program called for a trip to Venice, the classical city of all lovers. Unless one is in love, one is certain to suffer in Venice and should go to Florence instead where lonesomeness harmonizes well with an ever-present drizzling rain and the sorrowful remnants of a perfidious past. I felt safe—I was in love. We both knew Venice well, my first recollections of the Capital of Romance going back to 1872. We wandered through the palaces of the amorous medieval dukes with a feeling of having met and lost each other many centuries ago.

"I shall see you in Biarritz, very soon."

I returned to Rome to fetch my army of emigrants. Our trunks were packed and bills settled, when my son Dimitry complained of a headache. "Scarlet fever" was the diagnosis. All plans had to be changed. Xenia and six children left for Biarritz, I stayed with Dimitry. Yesterday's lover became a nurse. The complications so frequently accompanying scarlet fever had set in in Dimitry's ear. The doctors shook their heads and anticipated the necessity of a dangerous operation. For four weeks I sat by my boy's side, grieving and brooding. I should have seen a timely warning in his illness; instead of it I dreamed of Biarritz. If Dimitry had not recovered anything could have happened to me. Almost everything had.

Nothing changed in Biarritz since last year. Same parties, same faces, same spells of joy followed by storms of remorse. I was getting madder and madder. I could not keep Xenia in the dark any longer. I told her all. She sat very quiet; then she commenced to cry. I cried too. She behaved like an angel. Her heart was broken, but awful as truth was she preferred it to lies. We viewed the situation from all angles and decided to go on as usual for the sake of the children. We remained friends for the years to come, even closer friends than before because our friendship withstood the shock of calamity. All glory lay on her side, all blame on mine. She showed herself a great woman and a wonderful mother.

THE REBOUND

✦✦

4

Glancing at the paper one morning—we were still in Biarritz—I saw the big headlines announcing the success of the epochal flight of Blériot over the English Channel. This news brought back to life the former Grand Duke Alexander. An enthusiast of aviation in its early days of Santos-Dumont's performances around the Eiffel Tower, I understood that Blériot's achievement was ushering in not only a new means of transportation but an additional weapon of warfare as well. I decided to act at once and introduce the heavier-than-air flying machines in Russia. There were two million roubles remaining in my possession, which were contributed by the nation toward the building of torpedo boats in the closing months of the Japanese War. I drafted a letter to the editors of the newspapers, asking the contributors whether they would approve of their money being spent for the purchasing of airplanes rather than the building of additional torpedo boats. A week later I received thousands of answers containing unanimous approval of my proposition. I went to Paris and entered a working arrangement with Blériot and Voisin: they were to supply the machines and the instructors, I was to provide airdromes, pupils, all facilities and naturally the money. Then I proceeded to Russia. Gatchino, Peterhof, Czarskoie-Selo and St. Petersburg were to see me again in the rôle of "troublemaker."

Nicky smiled. The Minister of the Navy thought I was crazy. The Minister of the War, General Soukhomlinoff, shook with laughter.

"Do I understand you clearly, Your Imperial Highness?" he asked me between two paroxysms of laughter. "You propose to use the Blériot playthings in our army? May I ask you whether you expect our officers to drop their duties and fly across the English Channel, or is it all going to be staged right here, in St. Petersburg?"

"Never mind that, general. All I am asking of you is to give leave to the officers picked out by me for a short stay in Paris where they are to be instructed in flying by Blériot and Voisin. As for the rest, rira bien qui rira le dernier."

Another trip to Nicky and I received the authorization to choose my officers, although he said that even Grand Duke Nicholas Nicholaevich had failed to see any sense in my undertaking.

The first shift of officers left for Paris while I went to Sebastopol to choose a place for the future airdrome. I worked with my old enthusiasm, overruling the objections of the military authorities, ignoring ridicule and going straight to my goal. By late fall of 1908 I had my first airdrome and barracks ready. In the spring 1909 my officers graduated from Blériot's school. In the early summer St. Petersburg witnessed its first sensational "Aviation Week." People gasped and cheered. Soukhomlinoff found the show "stupendously entertaining, though of no use whatsoever for the army."

Three months later, in the fall of 1909, I bought large grounds, ten miles west of Sebastopol, and laid the cornerstone of the first aviation school in Russia, which was to supply the Russian Army in 1914 with the bulk of its aviators and observers.

In December, 1909, while holding a conference with my architects in the Crimea, I received news of father's death in Cannes. He was seventy-seven and had been a partial invalid for the last six years of his life. I felt terribly wretched. The world seemed empty without father. He was one of the very few men I had known who never wavered in his duty and lived up to the standards of Emperor Nicholas I.

A Russian man-of-war brought his body to Sebastopol and from there we took it to St. Petersburg to be buried in the Fortress of Peter and Paul. The route was sadly familiar, the procedure unbearable. Three times before I had traveled aboard a train carrying the remains of a man I cherished.

THE REBOUND

Six tombs glared at me in the Fortress of Peter and Paul: Emperor Alexander II, Emperor Alexander III, Georgie, my brother Alexis, and my parents.

At forty-three one cannot expect to acquire new attachments of everlasting quality.

5

I went ahead with my aviation work, making frequent trips abroad and paying as little attention to political matters as it was possible in surroundings where every second human plotted and schemed.

Jealousy of Stolypin's successful administration and hatred for the rapidly growing influence of Rasputin preyed on the minds of all courtiers. Stolypin was a builder, a genius, a man who had choked anarchy. Rasputin was a mere tool in the hands of international adventurers. Sooner or later, the Czar had to decide whether he intended to permit Stolypin to accomplish his constructive reforms or let the Rasputin crowd prompt the choice of the ministers. On one occasion I felt duty bound to have a serious talk with Nicky and warn him not to trust the enemies of Stolypin. Apart from that single occurrence, my relations with the imperial couple, although extremely friendly on the surface, were handicapped by mutual reservations. We continued to meet several times a week and invite each other for dinners but we could not revive the cordiality of the old days. There was too much malicious talk about the "party of the old Czarina" being opposed to the "party of the young Czarina." My mother-in-law treated these rumors with thorough contempt. Alix, to the contrary, lent a more or less willing ear to her new and dangerous advisers.

Discontent and lack of discipline marked the actions of the other members of the imperial family. During the reign of Alexander III my poor brother Michael had been pitilessly expelled for marrying a morganatic daughter of the Duke of

Nassau, whilst now every one of the grand dukes was usurping the right to follow his own fancies. The Czar's brother Misha married a twice divorced commoner. The Czar's uncle Paul demanded for his morganatic consort the privileges accorded only to persons of royal blood. The Czar's cousin Grand Duke Cyril married his first cousin "Ducky" (daughter of his aunt, and the Duchess of Edinburgh), a thing unheard-of in the annals of the imperial court and the Greek Orthodox Church. All three grand dukes displayed a complete disrespect for the wishes of the Emperor and showed an extremely bad example to Russian society. If Nicky was not able to bring his own relatives to their senses, he could hardly count on a greater success with his ministers, generals and chamberlains. Obviously, we stood on the threshold of moral decadence. Myself more than anyone else. Not satisfied with meeting my friend in Biarritz and Paris, I wanted to be with her forever. In the spring of 1910 I asked her to leave Europe and accompany me to Australia. I was ready to surrender my title and buy a farm near Sydney! Had she said "yes," I would have announced my decision at once. Fortunately, she kept her mental balance intact. It was "no," a firm and spontaneous "no." She reminded me of my duty and told me she would not see me again unless I persevered in my aviation work and stuck to the place where I belonged. Her noble decision saved me from ultimate disgrace. And yet, the twenty years that passed since the day she said "no" failed completely to cure me of my "Australian dreams." Sometimes I think she lacked imagination. Often I believe I missed the greatest opportunity of my life. In the light of the following events it seems as though my adventurous streak acted as a safety valve in 1910.

Life crawled along, embittered by disappointment and doubling up madness with work.

My aviation school grew every year. My pupils participated in the army maneuvers of 1912, spreading air-consciousness among the moth-eaten bureaucrats of the War Office and earning the generous praise of the Czar.

"You were right and I was wrong," Nicky said to me during his visit to my aviation school. "I am sorry for having treated your idea skeptically. You win, Sandro. I am exceedingly glad you do. Are you satisfied?"

I was and I was not. My aviation triumph failed to atone for the tragedy that had befallen me in the navy. Nothing could have healed that wound. Nothing could have made me forget the nightmare of 1904-1906.

Up to 1906 it had always been—"Russia comes first." In 1906-1914 I possessed a different motto: "I have but one life to live."

My spiritual ignorance reigned supreme.

6

Our travels continued, taking us all over Europe.

The traditional spring reunion with Queen Alexandra of England in Denmark; early summer season in London; Xenia's cure in Kissingen or Vittel and after-cure in Biarritz; children's excursions to Switzerland; late winter season in Cannes . . . We covered plenty of ground.

In the summer of 1913 I became bored with our annual program. I had had enough of it. Xenia and the children stayed at an immense hotel in Tréport, while I myself sailed for America. The success of Curtiss and the Wright brothers made my trip imperative, aside from my desire to spend several weeks with my friends in Philadelphia and Newport.

It took me exactly twenty years to fulfill my intention of coming back in a few months.

The shadow of the approaching war had not as yet crossed the Atlantic, although the depression was on and the bankers were shaking their heads knowingly. I was having a hard time with reporters who wanted to know what I had to say about the phenomenal changes that had occurred in New

York since 1893. I was supposed to compliment them on the new skyline, to comment upon the progress of the suffragist movement, to shed a tear or two over the passing of historical landmarks, and to wax enthusiastic about the future of the automobile.

As a matter of fact, there was one startling change which seemed to have escaped the attention of native observers. The building of the Panama Canal and the stupendous development of the Pacific Coast had created a new form of American pioneering; their industries had grown to the point where a foreign outlet had become a sheer necessity. Their financiers who used to borrow money in London, Paris, and Amsterdam had suddenly found themselves in the position of creditors. The rustic republic of Jefferson was rapidly giving way to the empire of Rockefellers, but the average mentality of the man-in-the-street had not yet entirely caught up with this new order of things, and the bulk of the nation was still thinking in terms of the nineteenth century.

How many times, during that second visit of mine, while going through a giant factory or listening to the explanation concerning a new piece of remarkable machinery, my mind went back to the ominous report sent in shortly before by my brother, Grand Duke Sergei, who in Vienna had the opportunity of getting thoroughly acquainted with the feverish work being carried on in the munition plants of the Central Empires.

The difference between America and Europe stood out in stark bitterness!

Late fall of 1913 found me back in St. Petersburg orating on the subject of the approaching European War.

"Are you able to predict the exact date of its outbreak?" queried the very clever and remarkably sarcastic people.

"Yes, I am. Not later than nineteen-fifteen."

"How perfectly dreadful!"

The winter of 1913-1914 came, my very last "social season" in St. Petersburg. The tricentennial celebration of the house of the Romanoffs, which had taken place the preceding spring, provided the main topic of discussion. All went well and in an orderly way. The Government claimed it had the country running more smoothly than ever since the days of Alexander III.

My daughter Irene married Prince Felix Yousoupoff in February. The newlyweds left for a honeymoon in Italy and Egypt, making an appointment to meet us in London in June.

****

CHAPTER SIXTEEN

THE EVE

I

A STRANGER visiting St. Petersburg during the last year of the lull that preceded the suicide committed by Europe on August 1, 1914, felt an irrepressible desire to settle down permanently in the brilliant capital which combined the classical beauty of arrow-like avenues with a passionate undertone of life, cosmopolitan in its leanings but thoroughly Russian in its recklessness. The colored barman of the Hotel d'Europe hailed from Kentucky; the actresses of the Theatre Michel rattled off their lines in French; the majestic columns of the imperial palaces bore witness to the genius of Italian architects; but important Government officials spent from three to four hours over a luncheon table, and in the month of June the pale rays of the midnight sun penetrating into the shady corners of the parks found long-haired students heatedly discussing with pink-cheeked girls the transcendental values of German philosophy. No mistake could have been made as to the ultimate nationality of the city that ordered its champagne by the magnum, never by the quart.

And then, there was Peter the Great. Molded in bronze by the deft hands of Falconet, the Emperor stood in the center of the Plaza of the Senate, observing from his rearing mount the stern blocks formed by clearly-cut streets. He succeeded in building this miracle-town of the North on the treacherous foundation of the Finnish marshes at the cost of one hundred twenty-five thousand lives sacrificed to yellow fever for the sake of a Greater Russia, and an arrogant smile was now lighting his demoniac face. Two hundred

244

GRAND DUKE MICHAEL ALEXANDROVICH ("MISHA"), YOUNGER
BROTHER OF THE LAST CZAR AND BROTHER-IN-LAW OF GRAND
DUKE ALEXANDER, IN 1910.

THE CZAR AND THE CZARINA REVIEWING THE REGIMENT OF
HER IMPERIAL MAJESTY'S GUARD LANCERS IN 1903.

GRAND DUKE ALEXANDER DISTRIBUTING DIPLOMAS TO THE
GRADUATES OF HIS AVIATION SCHOOL, IN 1913.

years had passed since the day when standing on the shore of the Gulf of Finland and looking at the decrepit log cabins of the fishermen, he decided to move his capital from Asiatic Moscow to the border of Western Europe. His hands were strained from pulling the reins of his horse, which he made rear on the brink of a precipice, and it was not an accidental idea of the imaginative sculptor that created this striking pose: he did save Russia from plunging into the depths of Asia, in the wake of its former Mongolian conquerors; he did pull his indolent subjects out of the trap of medieval superstitions, forcing them by a liberal application of his cane to join the cultural family of Occidental nations.

A fiery disciple of the cruel seventeenth century, Peter the Great may not have been particularly ceremonious in his methods. He believed a bit too implicitly that, unlike pepper, human life could be found everywhere in sufficient quantities, and he spared nobody. He even killed his own son for an attempt to interfere with the march of progress. "Peter the Antichrist" he was nicknamed by his terrified contemporaries, but there, right at the foot of the monument, lay the most voluminous proof of his genius: glorious St. Petersburg, the home of the mightiest rulers of the world. He had reached his goal, indeed, and the magnitude of his achievements had become more convincing, if anything, after the passing of two centuries. It was the task of these modern Romanoffs, who were about to celebrate the tricentennial of the reign of their family, to continue the efforts of their superhuman ancestor.

An impressionable stranger visiting St. Petersburg in the year of grace 1913, would have been almost sure to experience the feeling of alarming restlessness transmitted by the monument on the Plaza of the Senate to all persons capable of hearing the tumults of the future. He would also have noticed that the fifteen hundred thousand men and women inhabiting the capital of the Russian Empire merely lived from thrill to thrill, letting a statue of bronze ponder over the hideous expression of an ominous tomorrow reflected in the shining surface of a beautiful today.

2

Everything was beautiful. Everything suggested an imperial town.

The golden needle of the building of the admiralty stood visible for miles around; the immense windows of the grand ducal palaces were burning with the flames of the sunset; a clear echo repeated the hoofbeats of the trotters against the wooden pavement of the wide thoroughfares; the yellow and blue Cuirassiers Guards going for an afternoon stroll glared into the oddly shaped eyes of the stately women piercing through a thin net of laced veils; the decorous footmen seated behind the costly carriages waited in front of the show-windows, which were crowded with rows of pink pearls and green emeralds; the red-bricked chimneys of mammoth factories towered over a shining river chained by numerous bridges; and the human swans of the imperial ballet glided each night to the accompaniment of the best orchestra in the world.

The first decade of the twentieth century filled with terror and assassinations, racked the nerves of the nation. People in all walks of life welcomed the arrival of a new epoch which had the earmarks of normalcy. The leaders of the revolution defeated in 1905-1907 returned to the safety of small Parisian cafés, where they stayed for the next ten years watching the developments in far-away Russia and repeating philosophically the words of the famous warrior: "Il faut reculer pour mieux sauter" (One has to step back in order to take a better jump).

In the meanwhile, both friends and enemies of the revolution suddenly rushed headlong into various money-making schemes. The rural Russia of yesterday, accustomed to borrow its modest roubles from the State Treasury on notes secured by sound property, beheld with a pleasant surprise the unheralded appearance of powerful private banks. The prominent operators of the St. Petersburg Stock Exchange recognized the significant change of the popular mood, and the order to buy was passed along the line.

In the beginning of 1913, the owners of various mills, factories, plants and mines received visits from suave gentlemen speaking with an imposing St. Petersburg accent and displaying lavish generosity.

"Why," asked these refined tempters, flashing the credentials of a well-known bank into the face of their shy host, "should the life of a worthy man be wasted in one continuous grind? The fact that our fathers and grandfathers used to slave and sweat does not necessarily mean that we, the contemporaries of new methods, must follow their example. Now take, for instance, this factory of yours. You are making cigarettes and are marketing them in the same old-fashioned way your ancestors did. That's what we call—bad business! How much money are you able to make anyway? Two hundred thousand roubles per year? Is that all? Struggling as hard as you do? What a pity! Now suppose we would guarantee you the same two hundred thousand roubles per year and would relieve you of all your present troubles. In fact, we would be willing to buy you out completely for a sum of four million roubles payable in five per cent long term obligations issued by the new corporation against your own factory. You will have your two hundred thousand roubles per year plus complete freedom of action. Could anything be fairer than that? Yes, of course, there is going to be a corporation formed and stock issued, for we intend to let the public participate in the benefits derived from the growth of Russia."

Such was the commencement of the famous Russian Tobacco Trust, one of the biggest financial combines in Europe at that time, although created on short notice. Iron, coal, cotton, copper, steel, were "cornered" by the same group of

St. Petersburg bankers. The former owners of the individual enterprises moved to the capital to enjoy their newly obtained wealth and freedom. The "boss" who knew each of his workers by his first name was replaced by an efficient specialist sent from the north. The patriarchal Russia that withstood the attack of the revolution in 1905 thanks only to the fealty of the small owners was giving way to a system imported from abroad and unsuitable to the national character.

This rapid "trustification" of the country, marching far ahead of the real industrial development, gave birth to a veritable fever of speculation in stocks. During the course of the city census taken in St. Petersburg in the spring of 1913, some forty thousand persons of both sexes registered as "stock exchange speculators."

Lawyers, doctors, school-teachers, journalists and engineers were irritated by the dullness of their professions. It seemed to be a shame to continue fighting for pennies, when there existed a glorious opportunity of making fifty thousand sweatless roubles through the simple medium of buying a few hundred shares of "Nichopol-Mariupolsky Metallurgical Common," on margin.

The haughty leaders of society included stock brokers in their visiting lists. The aristocratic officers of the Imperial Guard though unable to distinguish stocks from bonds, began to discuss the imminent rise in the prices on "broad" steel. Smart men-about-town nearly petrified unsuspecting book-dealers by demanding a supply of all the available manuals dedicated to the mysteries of high finance and to the art of understanding the annual corporation reports. Fashionable hostesses acquired a habit of featuring the promised presence of "that marvelous genius from Odessa who has made a terrific killing in tobacco." The holy men of the church subscribed to the financial publications, and the velvet-upholstered carriages of the archbishops were often observed in the neighborhood of the Stock Exchange.

The provinces joined in the gambling orgies of the capital,

and by the fall of 1913 the Russia of idle landlords and under-nourished peasants was seemingly ready for a long jump over the obstacles of the economic laws into the domain of its own Wall Street.

The future of the empire depended on the caliber of the mysterious newcomers who directed its financial destinies. A Morgan, a Baker, a Schwab would have realized that no lasting results could be obtained until the general illiteracy of the peasants was conquered and a decided improvement brought into the frightful living conditions of the workers, but the near-sighted Russian pool operators of 1913 cared little about the distant future. They expected to cash in their chips long before the lightning struck the house.

3

A nephew of a cardinal, a Russian peasant, and an international banker claimed the ownership of Russia on the eve of the war. No dictator ever enjoyed a position similar to theirs. No minister of the crown ever dared to resort to such ruthless means.

Yaroshinsky, Batolin, Pootiloff—these three names were on everybody's lips.

"The Unholy Three of the Empire."

"The Big Three of St. Petersburg."

"The Three Horsemen of the Apocalypse."

The right of choosing an appropriate melodramatic nickname for the combine stayed with the population, but the power belonged to the three gentlemen as their properties included banks, public utilities, gold mines, iron and steel plants, factories, plantations, mills, railroads, agricultural lands, sugar refineries, lumber camps, steamship companies, office buildings, hotels, resorts, newspapers, magazines, news agencies.

A son of a serf liberated in 1861, Batolin started his career as a messenger boy for a firm of wheat merchants; he was so poor that he tasted meat for the first time at the age of nine.

Pootiloff belonged to a well-to-do St. Petersburg family. A man of brilliant education, he spent a considerable part of his time abroad. He felt quite at home in the Place de la Bourse, Paris, and in Lombard Street, London.

The initial steps of Yaroshinsky were wrapped in mystery. Nobody knew his exact nationality. He spoke Polish but his uncle was reputed to be an Italian cardinal occupying a post of importance in the Vatican. He came to St. Petersburg already in possession of a considerable fortune amassed in his prosperous sugar business somewhere in the southwest of Russia.

The biographies of the three "rulers," so different in their essential elements, added a fantastic touch to an epoch overcharged with tension, while the similarity of their methods proved that P. T. Barnum had included Russia in the field of his philosophical observations.

They practiced a system, registered in Russia as "American" but referred to by another name in the financial circles of the United States. They performed no miracles. They disclosed no exceptional genius. The accumulation of their wealth was made possible by the extreme leniency of the Russian banking laws, which even permitted the directors of saving institutions to exercise unrestricted authority over the choice of securities purchased with the funds of the depositors.

They made a specialty of acquiring the so-called "working control" of the banks, which amounted to not more than fifteen per cent of the capital, the enormous distances of the country keeping the small stockholders from attending the annual meetings and the national negligence causing them to forget to mail their proxies.

Once firmly entrenched in a bank, the Big Three elected their own board of directors and passed a resolution recommending the use of all the available surplus for the purpose of securing the "working control" of another bank. The same operation was repeated several times. Mergers followed each other in rapid succession. At the end of a short period, the virtual guardianship over the bulk of Russian capital passed into the hands of these three individuals. The consequences can be well imagined. A factory owner refusing to sell his business to the "trust," ran the risk of seeing his credit cut. Commercial competition was becoming a thing of the past. The wages of labor fluctuated, depending on the requirements of the stock market: whenever a "better statement" of earnings could have helped the further rise of a stock, down went the wages of the workmen engaged in that particular industry.

The Minister of Finance stood on the sidelines watching the performances of this self-styled triumvirate of Russian dictators with an air of sympathetic admiration. The talk of so much money made him dizzy, and he was considering his post but a stepping-stone to the chairmanship of a bank.

The radical newspapers, indefatigable in their denunciations of the Government, kept an unbroken silence on the subject of the trusts, which was quite natural considering that Batolin owned four of the most influential publications in St. Petersburg and Moscow.

A flirtation with the members of the opposition must have entered the plans of the whole group of new multimillionaires, because the well-known Russian novelist and future vice-president of the Leningrad Soviet, Maxim Gorky, was given several million roubles by the Siberian Bank to establish in St. Petersburg a daily newspaper *The New Life* and a monthly magazine *The Annals*. Both publications counted Lenin among their chief collaborators, and openly advocated the overthrow of the existing régime. The famous "school of revolutionary agitators" created by Gorky on the Island of Capri in Italy was financed for a number of years by Savva Morozoff—the recognized king of the Moscow textile industry—and counted Joseph Stalin, the present head of the

Soviet Government, among its successful graduates. Leonid Krassin, the soviet ambassador in London in 1921-1924, served in 1913 as managing director of one of Pootiloff's large factories in St. Petersburg; he was appointed member of the Board of War Industries on the strength of his chief's enthusiastic recommendation.

Nothing could have been stranger than this desire on the part of the "trust" to keep the fires of the revolution burning. The Government at first refused to believe the informers of the Secret Police but there was no sense in arguing with facts. A raid on the residence of Nicholas Paramonoff, one of the richest men in Russia, produced documents establishing his participation in the group of multimillionaires who financed the printing and the distribution of Bolshevik pamphlets throughout the country. Paramonoff was tried and condemned to serve two years in jail, this sentence, however, being suspended in recognition of his large subscription to the fund collected for the building of a monument commemorating the tricentennial of the House of Romanoff. From the Bolsheviks to the Romanoffs—all within a year!

"A desire to protect themselves and their interests against all possible political upheavals characterizes the actions of our capitalists," reported the Under-Secretary of Police sent to Moscow to investigate the case of Lenin's wealthy friend Morozoff. "So sure are they of their ability to use the revolutionaries as their tools in a rather childish feud with the Government, that Morozoff deems it advisable to finance the publication of Lenin's magazine *The Spark,* printed in Switzerland and brought into Russia in double-bottomed trunks. Each and every issue of *The Spark* advocates strikes at the textile factories owned by Morozoff! The latter tells his friends that he is sufficiently rich to afford the luxury of supporting his enemies."

The suicide of Morozoff occurred shortly before the war and spared him the shock of seeing his estates confiscated by the order of Lenin and his heirs arrested by the former graduates of his own school of agitators on the Island of Capri.

Batolin, Yaroshinsky, Pootiloff, Paramonoff, and the rest of the "far-sighted" millionaires escaped the soviet firing squad only by running away from Russia.

4

The eccentricity displayed by the bankers was influenced to a large degree by the plain insanity of the period.

All signs of the threatening war were ignored. All warnings of our military agents abroad were ridiculed and dismissed with a shrug of the shoulders.

On his return from Austria in the fall of 1913, my brother, Grand Duke Sergei Michailovich, notified the Government of the feverish preparations observed by him in the munition plants of the Central European powers. The ministers laughed. The idea of a grand duke giving sound advice seemed blasphemous. It had been always conceded that a grand duke should play the part of a glorified ne'er-do-well.

The Minister of War summoned the editor of an evening paper with a large circulation and dictated to him an article full of ill-disguised threats against Germany and entitled "We Are Ready."

At that moment we were not only short of cannons and rifles, but our stock of boots and overcoats would not have sufficed to clothe even a fraction of the millions of men to be mobilized in case of war.

On the evening of the appearance of this unwarranted provocation, the Under-Secretary of the Treasury was dining in a popular St. Petersburg hostelry patronized by men of wealth and society.

"What is going to happen now? What will the Market say tomorrow?" he was asked by a prominent newspaperman.

"The Market?" The wise statesman laughed deprecatingly. "Why, my dear fellow, blood always makes the Market rise."

The Market did go up next morning, and the whole episode was forgotten by everybody, with the possible exception of the German ambassador.

The remaining three hundred days of peace were filled with gambling, sensational crimes and a rather significant epidemic of suicides.

That year they danced the tango. The languorous tempo of its exotic music sounded from one end of Russia to another. The gypsies cried, the glasses clinked, and the Rumanian violinists, clad in red, hypnotized inebriated men and women into a daring attempt to explore the depths of vice. Hysteria reigned supreme.

At five o'clock in the morning—the endless winter night was still glaring through the high Venetian windows covered with frost—a young man with drunken gait crossed the polished dancing floor of the night club "Yar" in Moscow and stopped in front of a table occupied by a beautiful woman seated in company with several elderly gentlemen.

"Listen, you," shouted the young man, leaning against a column, "I will not stand for it. You have no business remaining in a place like this at such an hour of the night."

The woman sneered. They had been divorced for eight months. She saw no reason for taking his orders.

"So, it's like this," said the young man somewhat more quietly and fired at her six times through the pocket of his tuxedo.

The notorious "Prasoloff Case" began.

The trial lasted twenty-eight days.

The jury acquitted Prasoloff, having taken a great fancy to the quotation from Goethe made by the defense: "I have never heard of a crime, no matter how gruesome, which I could not have committed myself."

The District Attorney appealed and demanded a change of venue. "The people of Moscow," he explained to the

254

Supreme Court, "have reached a state of mind when they no longer understand the value of human life. I would ask your honors to transfer this case to one of the provinces."

The second trial took place in a small town in the Northeast of Russia. It lasted four weeks, and Prasoloff was acquitted again.

This time the District Attorney threatened to make a "pilgrimage to the grave of Mrs. Prasoloff" and tell her that "Russia refuses to defend the honor of a woman."

Had it not been for the war, the nation would have been treated once more to the nauseating details of the Prasoloff Case, and the very talkative witnesses would have narrated for the third time the unbelievable stories of the revolting orgies taking place in the millionaire set of Moscow.

Every conceivable variety of vice was paraded before the juries in both trials and broadcast by the newspapers for the edification of the youth of Russia.

The lives of the murderer and his victim were analyzed from the moment they had met on the premises of an organization known as "The Suicide Club" to their wedding feast staged in the "Villa Black Swan" built by a famous millionaire in quest of thrills.

The names of the witnesses read like a page out of the Social Register of Moscow. Their deeds were sufficient to warrant a new series of trials. Two of them committed suicide while waiting for their turn to testify. Many others hurriedly went abroad challenging extradition proceedings.

St. Petersburg refused to be "outsinned" by Moscow, and while the Prasoloff Case was still pending, two titled students of the most exclusive college in Russia killed and robbed a well-known actress.

Promptly caught by the police, they confessed the crime and explained its motives. A day before they had issued invitations for a champagne supper to be given in an exclusive restaurant. They needed cash. They approached their parents. They were turned down. They knew that the actress possessed valuable jewelry. They went to her apartment armed with kitchen knives.

"A real gentleman," commented a sarcastic columnist, "is obliged to keep his social engagements at no matter what price."

The coroner, the detectives, and the insurance companies bore the brunt of the next sensation of that crowded year.

A mutilated body was found in a rooming house in the center of the capital. The passport and several other documents identifying the prosperous engineer Ghilevich were lying on the table a bit too conspicuously to satisfy the experienced detectives, but a surviving relative dispelled their doubts. He recognized his brother at once by a "birthmark on the right shoulder." A month went by. The insurance companies—engineer Ghilevich carried four separate policies for an aggregate sum of three hundred thousand roubles—forwarded their checks to the beneficiary of the policies and ordered their investigators to close the case. The criminals thought their battle won. Engineer Ghilevich became tired of hiding in Paris and decided to visit Monte Carlo. The luck of the wheel turned against him. He sent a telegram to his brother asking to transfer some money. The clerk of the St. Petersburg bank, a diligent reader of newspapers, wanted to learn the identity of the party in Monte Carlo who was about to receive five thousand roubles from the grieving brother of the "famous" Ghilevich. He notified the authorities. A set of photographs and a detailed description of the "murdered" bewhiskered engineer were mailed to the Paris police, and the Monte Carlo plunger, although smoothly shaven by now, failed to deceive their sharp eyes. As he was about to leave the bank, a firm hand tapped him on the shoulder. In one glance Ghilevich appraised the situation and swallowed a pill which he carried in his waistcoat pocket. The next moment he fell dead into the arms of the French detectives.

THE EVE

5

The future historian will be justified in writing a treatise on the part played by criminal sensationalism in clogging the minds of the Europeans on the eve of the war.

Soldiers were already posting the mobilization order in the streets of Paris, while the crowds of thrill-seekers continued to watch the proceedings of the trial of Mme. Henriette Caillaux, the wife of a former French Prime Minister, who killed Gaston Calmette, the editor of the newspaper *Figaro,* accusing him of trying to blackmail her husband. Up to July 28, 1914, the front pages of the European newspapers "played" the Caillaux case much stronger than they did the Austrian ultimatum to Serbia.

Passing through Paris on my way back to Russia from London, I was inclined to doubt my own ears: statesmen of importance and diplomats of responsibility stood in animated groups debating whether "she" would be acquitted or condemned.

"Who is she?" I asked quite innocently. "Do you refer to the coming appearance of Austria before the Tribunal of Peace in The Hague?"

They thought I was trying to be humorous. Naturally they meant Henriette Caillaux.

"Your Imperial Highness, why are you in such a hurry to return to St. Petersburg?" asked our ambassador to France, Isvolsky. "What is the attraction of running into the dead summer season . . ."

The War? He waved his hands. Never. Never. It was just "one of those things" that visit Europe now and then. Austria will make a few more threats. St. Petersburg will get excited. Kaiser Wilhelm will show his teeth. And everything will be forgotten by the fifteenth of the next month!

Now, Mr. Isvolsky had spent thirty years in the diplomatic service of Russia. For a while he occupied the post of Minister of Foreign Affairs. One had to be quite presumptuous to dispute with this man of experience. I decided to be presumptuous for once in my life and left for St. Petersburg.

I did not like the array of "coincidences" that featured the month of July of the year 1914.

Kaiser Wilhelm "happened" to go on a cruise on the eve of the presentation of the Austrian ultimatum to Serbia.

The President of France "happened" to be on a visit in St. Petersburg.

Winston Churchill, then First Lord of the British Admiralty, "happened" to give an order to the British Navy to remain in complete battle order after the termination of the summer maneuvers.

The Serbian Minister of Foreign Affairs "happened" to show the text of the Austrian ultimatum to the French ambassador Berthelot, and Monsieur Berthelot "happened" to write an answer, thus relieving the Serbian Government of the necessity of doing their own thinking.

The workers of the munition plants in St. Petersburg "happened" to declare a strike the week preceding the mobilization, and several agitators speaking Russian with a strong German accent "happened" to be caught at their meetings.

The chief of the Russian General Staff "happened" to dispatch the order of mobilization with such promptitude that he felt "frightfully sorry but unable to do anything whatsoever," when the Czar telephoned him a few hours afterwards countermanding the order.

The worst thing of all was that the common sense of the nations "happened" to be on leave.

Individually none of the hundreds of millions of Europeans wanted war; collectively they all would have lynched the man who would have dared to advise moderation. They killed Jaurès in Paris, and they imprisoned Liebknecht in Berlin for an attempt to describe the calamities of a war.

Germans and French, English and Austrians, Russians and

Belgians were driven by that same instinct of destruction which evidenced itself in the crimes, the suicides, and the orgies of the preceding year, and which reached its logical climax on August 1, 1914.

Margot Asquith, the wife of the then Prime Minister of Great Britain, remembered the "shining eyes" and the "bright smile" of Winston Churchill as he walked into 10 Downing Street, on that fatal night.

"What is it, Winston?" asked the Prime Minister. "Is it peace?"

"It is war," answered Mr. Churchill.

At the same hour and minute, German officers were congratulating each other in Unter den Linden, Berlin, on "this glorious chance to execute the plan of Moltke," and the same Mr. Isvolsky, who but three days earlier had predicted that everything would be all right by the fifteenth of the next month, said now triumphantly on leaving the building of the Foreign Office in Paris: "C'est ma guerre! (It's my own war!)."

Kaiser Wilhelm making a speech in Berlin and Czar Nicholas II addressing the people in St. Petersburg used the same expressions to describe their feelings. They both asked their God to punish the initiators of the coming fratricidal war.

Everybody was right. Nobody was wrong. Not a sane man could have been found that day in the countries spread between the Gulf of Biscay and the Pacific Ocean.

On my way back to Russia I saw the suicide of a continent!

CHAPTER SEVENTEEN

ARMAGEDDON

Nous sommes incapable du vrai et du bien, nous sommes tous condamnés.—PASCAL.

I

Not unlike the excited eye-witnesses of a murder, the historians of July, 1914, disagree both in their testimony and in their conclusions. The British and the French talk too much of the part played by the German determination to violate the neutrality of Belgium, a detail thoroughly irrelevant to the origin and the issues of the conflict. The Germans disclose a desire to "rewrite" Russian history in the spirit of the present claims of innocence made by Wilhelmstrasse. The readers of Emil Ludwig's *July 1914* would be disappointed to learn that some of the Russian "discoveries" of their favorite author are based on his failure to distinguish between two brothers Maklakoff in his fantastic description of the war conference in Czarskoie-Selo. He introduces the Russian Minister of the Interior Nicholas Maklakoff as a "forceful orator," a "panther," and a "former leader of the liberals" who, according to him, practically "forced" the Czar of Russia to sign the order of general mobilization.

It happens that Nicholas Maklakoff, a man of extremely conservative leanings and bitterly opposed to the war, had a brother by the name of Vassily Maklakoff, who although not quite a "panther" was nevertheless a forceful orator, a lawyer of distinction and a leader of the opposition up to the very moment of the revolution of 1917. Neither of the brothers exercised the slightest influence on the Czar's de-

THE SEVEN CHILDREN OF GRAND DUKE ALEXANDER IN 1914. LEFT TO RIGHT: IRENE (THE PRESENT PRINCESS YOUSOUPOFF), ANDREW, FEODOR, NIKITA, DIMITRY, ROSTISLAV, VASSILY.

GRAND DUKE ALEXANDER, WHEN COMMANDER-IN-CHIEF OF
THE RUSSIAN AIR FORCES, WITH MEMBERS OF HIS STAFF, 1916.

cisions: Nicholas Maklakoff was never asked to express his opinion on military matters, Vassily Maklakoff was naturally never admitted to the palace. The famous "Maklakoff war speech" quoted by Ludwig belongs to the realm of pure imagination, the author being too lazy to check up on names and data.

Nobody has yet written an unbiased account of the last week of the Old World. I doubt that anyone ever will. The information possessed by me and gathered both before and during the war, leads me to believe in the conclusiveness of three facts only:

1. The conflict was caused by the Anglo-German rivalry for the economic supremacy of the world and by the combined efforts of the military cliques of Berlin, Vienna, Paris, London and St. Petersburg. Had it not been for the assassination of the Archduke Franz-Ferdinand, another pretext of equally abysmal cynicism would have been chosen by the international champions of war. Kaiser Wilhelm naturally wanted to "have it over with" before the completion of the Russian Military Program in 1917.

2. Nicholas II did all in his power to prevent the outbreak of hostilities, finding but little, if any, support for his conciliatory efforts among his advisers of the Russian Foreign Office and the Russian General Staff.

3. Up to the stroke of midnight, July 31, 1914, the British Government could have averted the catastrophe, had it declared its readiness to stand by France and Russia. A simple declaration made to that effect by Herbert Asquith or Sir Edward Grey would have pacified even the most belligerent Junkers in Berlin. The "Belgian alibi," advanced by the British Government three days later, made up in human appeal what it lacked in cool logic. The British Empire went to war not because of its holy respect for the inviolability of international treaties but on account of its bitter feelings toward Germany. Were Herbert Asquith less of a lawyer

✠✠✠

and more of an outspoken humanitarian, no war would have been declared by Germany on August 1, 1914.

All other "ifs" exploited by the historians of 1914 are fanciful and meaningless. We might just as well go back to 1912 and ask ourselves what would have happened to the world if the Republican National Convention in Chicago had nominated Roosevelt instead of Taft. Possibly, the United States would have joined the Allies on May 8, 1915, the morning after the sinking of the *Lusitania;* more likely, however, Mr. Roosevelt would have recalled the American ambassador to the Court of St. James's long before that date, as a protest against British interference with the eastbound movements of American merchant ships.

2

My mother-in-law and my wife were spending the summer of 1914 in London, staying in Marlborough House with the former's sister Dowager-Queen Alexandra of England. They refused to join me aboard the Oriental Express. They said there was going to be no war: they had it from the "most reliable source." I left alone on July 26, having wired the commander-in-chief of our Black Sea Fleet to be met by a cruiser in the Rumanian port of Constanza.

On my way through Austria I saw crowds of recruits storming the stations and was ordered to pull down the shades in my compartment. By the time we reached Vienna, a doubt arose whether the Oriental Express would be allowed to proceed. After hours of waiting and negotiating, it was decided that we should be taken as far as the Rumanian border. From there on, I went afoot several miles to reach the special train prepared for me by the Rumanian Government. Approaching Constanza I recognized from the distance the mast of my former flagship *Almaz*, a name ominous in 1906 but a delightful one in July, 1914.

"We are leaving at once, not a moment to be wasted!"

I told the captain, and we landed in the Crimea eight hours later to find Russia gripped by the nervous enthusiasm of the general mobilization.

It was war. "A popular war this time," said the people in the cathedral of Yalta, where I was asked to make a short address after the solemn Te Deum. The expression struck me forcefully. "Why is this war popular?" I asked myself while listening to the chatter of the officers and the civilians. "Is it because bands are playing and newspapers are raving about little heroic Belgium? What do these people know about the hardships, the calamities and the long years of fighting that are facing us in a war with an adversary as powerful as Germany? Since when had our villagers commenced to hate the Germans, a nation for which they had always experienced feelings of respect and admiration? How many of them even know of the existence of Belgium? Is there anyone in Russia willing to leave his home and family for the sake of returning Alsace and Lorraine to France? How can our Government account to the nation for the fact of our fighting on the side of Great Britain, the traditional arch-foe of the Russian Empire? And what are we going to fight with, considering that our War Office made no preparations at all for an emergency of this caliber? How long will this surprising enthusiasm of our intelligentsia last, intelligentsia that had suddenly exchanged their pacifistic philosophy of yesterday for their present idiotic animosity towards all things German, including Wagner's operas and Wiener schnitzel?"

Forty-eight hours spent in the train between the Crimea and St. Petersburg failed to alleviate my fears. The Russia of the editors, soap-box orators and profiteering industrialists shrieked in the blazing headlines of supreme optimism. The Russia of deserted wives and fatherless children cried along every mile of my way, the order of the general mobilization having affected all able-bodied males from between twenty-one and forty-eight. The bemedaled officials meeting my

train in the large cities unanimously stated that the call to
arms was answered "readily and enthusiastically." The
horror-stricken faces, the disheveled hair, and the bloodshot
eyes that glared in the windows of my salon-car for forty-
eight hours were not mentioned in their reports. I thought
of the old peasant expression: "It's all right, St. Nicholas
the Miracle Worker shall see us through." Now was the
time for the venerable saint to exercise his magic power.

I found the Czar hard at work and doing his utmost to
justify the popular acclaim given to him the day of the
declaration of the war. Never in all Nicky's twenty years
of luckless reign had he heard so many spontaneous hurrahs.
National solidarity, coming at this late day, pleased him
enormously. He spoke plainly and modestly. He admitted
to me that he could have avoided the war had he been willing
to commit an act of treachery against Serbia and France,
but that was not in his character. One-sided and fatal as
the Russo-French alliance was, Russia's signature had to
be honored.

"I shall not sheathe my sword while one single German
soldier remains on our soil!"—It seemed rather ironic that
Nicky should repeat on the occasion of a war with Germany
the famous words used by Emperor Alexander I on the night
of Napoleon's invasion in 1812.

For no immediate reason my heart sunk. I could not suppress the tragic premonition that he had invariably conveyed
to me by his appearance. There is no way of tracing the
origin of an intuition: whenever I saw Nicky officiating at
the head of a procession or talking solemnly, I felt pangs of
fear. I questioned his ability to use this gigantic war as a
pivot in his career, and I was certain that should it continue
for more than one year we would be doomed. We, the
Romanoffs, and they, the Russia of fifteen million mobiliz-
able men and one hundred forty-five million inhabitants of
a continent paralyzed in its activities by the insatiable demands of the military authorities.

My mother-in-law and my wife arrived safely. Kaiser Wilhelm refused to let them pass through Germany and they traveled via the Scandinavian countries. My children had their mother back, so I was able to leave for the front assigned by Grand Duke Nicholas Nicholaevich to be stationed in the headquarters of the fourth army as a collaborator of its commander Baron Saltza—a former aide-de-camp of my father in the days of my childhood.

3

A long talk with Baron Saltza and his staff demonstrated to me the existence of a situation which I thought abnormal and which was to continue throughout the twenty-six months of Russia's actual fighting. I learned that the army of the Russian Empire was to be used by Great Britain and France as their mammoth shock-absorber and that our commanders were to be guided in their strategy by the order to save Paris "at no matter what cost." In terms of human lives it meant that we should sacrifice some five hundred thousand officers and soldiers in our ill-timed offensive on the eastern front for the sake of "easing up the German pressure against Paris," a far-away alien city whose name had no sentimental sound for our men and whose ultimate fate meant nothing to the future of our country.

While our fourth army fought the onrush of the Austrians, our first and second armies invaded Eastern Prussia, heading with their eyes open straight for the trap prepared by Hindenburg. The bulk of the second army consisted of the Imperial Guard Corps, the best trained troops of Russia and the chief mainstay of the imperial régime for the past fifty years, now thrown into an inevitable slaughter for the Greater Glory of Paris.

We cursed and raved. All diplomats should have been put in the ranks if they wanted to participate in this war. But orders were orders. Our soldiers died without a murmur.

The second army ceased to exist, its commander, General Samsonoff, using his last bullet to avoid the humiliation of being taken prisoner. Paris was saved by a hecatomb of Russians killed on the Masurian Marshes in East Prussia. Humanity at large preferred to remember that battle as "Joffre's victory of the Marne."

At the end of my sixth day with the fourth army Baron Saltza asked me to make a flying trip to the Stavka (Russian for G.H.Q.) and explain to Grand Duke Nicholas Nicholaevich that he needed reserves: we were badly outnumbered by the Austrians who continued their attack notwithstanding terrific losses. They in turn tried to "relieve the Russian pressure against Eastern Prussia" and were treated by the Germans in the same cannon-fodder manner the Allies had used with Russia. I saw their wounded, lying side by side with our own soldiers. They were terribly frightened but nice-looking lads, endeavoring to straighten up in their beds at the sight of my imperial shoulder monograms and the golden cords of a General A.D.C. They looked at me with anguish, expecting to be comforted by a person of such voluminous importance. The chief surgeon, walking by my side, provided explanations of each case in a hoarse indifferent whisper:

"This one is hopeless."

"As good as dead."

"Both lungs shot through."

"May recover unless general blood poisoning sets in."

The war was ten days old but already all had adapted themselves to its merciless conditions. The soldiers expected to die, the chief surgeon counted the beds that were certain to be vacant by midnight.

I left for the Stavka, situated at the junction of four important railway lines in the small town of Baranovichi. The place could not house the countless departments of General Headquarters, and Grand Duke Nicholas Nicholaevich, his brother Peter, and his immediate assistants lived aboard their special train.

Grand Duke Nicholas Nicholaevich paced the floor with long strides, towering, immense, stupendously domineering in his brand-new immaculate uniform. He talked and listened, listened more than he talked, it being his traditional habit to leave a visitor impressed by his ability to keep his own counsel. The telephones rang, the numerous aides came in with mysterious faces, the generals bent over their maps. All was as it should have been in the G.H.Q. of a modern commander-in-chief, who at best could coördinate only approximately the actions of several millions of soldiers spread over a front of three thousand miles.

I watched the grand duke perform his duties and wished I could chase away my feeling of mistrust. Chances were, it was just another prejudice of mine, too well rooted by forty years of acquaintance to be dispelled by the Stavka's paraphernalia. Our mutual antipathy increased our politeness toward each other. We made desperate efforts to be friendly. He suggested my taking command of the air forces of the front and gave me carte blanche. I took this appointment in the spirit it was proposed, as a flattering though somewhat belated compliment to my pioneering aviation work. We both knew that no one else in the army could have fitted the post. A salon car, to serve as my temporary headquarters, was provided by the Stavka; the rest, including airplanes, machine guns, repeating rifles, flyers, observers, technical staff, motor cars, even the typewriters, had to be gotten through my own ingenuity. As a sinecure the post of commander-in-chief of the Imperial Air Forces fared rather moderately. I did not complain, however, because everything else pertaining to warfare had to be improvised by our commanders. After the first month of continuous battles we ran short of munitions and equipment, while all deliveries from abroad had to travel by way of the Far North arriving either at the freezing port of Archangel or at the ice-free port of Mourmansk, the latter not connected by railway with the interior of the country.

Many a time during that month of August, 1914, I thought of our Minister of War General Soukhomlinoff and his "We Are Ready" proclamation written two years before. At the headquarters of our southwestern army group I met my critical brother, Grand Duke Nicholas Michailovich, the very last man for me to see if I wanted to preserve an iota of optimism. A prize-graduate of the War College and a student of strategy, he found formulas and scientific expressions for my irrational fears. He bitterly criticized the whole lot of our commanding generals, beginning with our exalted cousin and finishing with the "chancellery rats" supervising the preparations in the rear. He spoke cynically, crudely, and in nine cases out of ten justly. He explained to me that our losses had wiped out our regular army and had put us in the tragic position where we had to rely upon badly trained reservists. He said that unless Grand Duke Nicholas Nicholaevich stopped at once his quasi-victorious march through Galicia and pulled the troops back to a line of fortified positions in the rear, we were bound to bump headlong into a disastrous defeat not later than the spring of 1915. He talked for three hours, quoting figures, substantiating his conclusions and getting gloomier every moment. My head ached. I appreciated the patriotic inspiration of his pessimism, but I trembled at the thought that I would have to take my meals with him twice a day.

4

The gods of war must have overheard my brother's prophetic speech. Our best soldiers and our meager stock of munitions spent in the reckless "Save the Allies" offensive of 1914-1915, we had no strength left to parry the famous Mackensen Carpathian move in May, 1915. According to official sources, the enemy fired one hundred rounds of shrapnel against a single one of ours. In truth, the proportion was even more formidable, our officers estimating it at three hundred to one. At a given moment our artillery became silent and our bearded reservists faced the Mackensen phalanx armed with rifles "model 1878," with orders "not to fire unnecessarily (!) and take the ammunition of the killed and wounded." Weeks in advance of the debacle my aviators brought reports warning the Stavka against the massing of German-Austrian artillery and troops on the other side of the river Dounaitza. A nineteen-year-old sub-lieutenant understood that the quicker we would commence our retreat the smaller would be the casualties. But the Stavka persisted in its determination to remain in Galicia till the very last moment, declaring that our retreat would affect unfavorably the Allied démarches in Greece and Rumania, the two states sitting on the fence comparing German bids with Anglo-French promises.

Early fall of 1915 found our army hundreds of miles from the positions occupied by it in the spring. For six consecutive times I was obliged to change my headquarters, the hopes of stopping our retreat on this or that fortified line failing one after the other. The news of the dismissal of Grand Duke Nicholas Nicholaevich was the only bit of cheer coming from the Stavka for four disastrous months. We evacuated Galicia, we lost Poland and we surrendered a considerable part of the northwest and the southwest of Russia, as well as a series of fortresses considered impregnable by the text-books of our General Staff. The appearance of the Czar in the rôle of commander-in-chief created in me a double reaction. The political consequences of his prolonged absence from the capital were dubious, but his decision was correct in so far as the army was concerned. Nothing short of the Emperor himself assuming nominal command could have inspired new courage in the army and given an opportunity of cleaning the Stavka of its inept generals and diplomat-strategists. General Alexeieff, the new chief of staff, impressed me as a cautious sort of leader, mindful of our handicaps and prepared to bid for time. As strategists go, he rated well. Not a Napoleon and not even a Ludendorff, but an experienced old general realizing that in modern warfare there were no "commanders of genius," except maybe in the dispatches of the war correspondents or in their own memoirs. The combination of the Czar and Alexeieff would have been perfect, subject to two conditions: a continuous watch over the St. Petersburg schemers on the part of Nicky, and a sacred promise to abstain from interference with the political affairs on the part of Alexeieff.

The exact opposite happened. Nicky remained for too long periods away from Czarskoie-Selo, where the Rasputin crowd reached new heights of influence during the Czar's absence, while Alexeieff became involved in the plots of the enemies of the régime, who were hiding at that time under the innocent attire of the representatives of the various "auxiliary organizations," such as the Red Cross, the Union of the Russian Municipalities, the Union of the Russian Zemstvo, etc. The initial enthusiasm of our intelligentsia gave place to their original hatred for the régime simultaneously with our defeat of 1915. They visited the front regularly, supposedly to inspect the fighting lines and ascertain the needs of the army, in fact for the sole purpose of gaining the sympathy of the commanding generals. The members of our Duma, who swore to support the Government in the beginning of the war, worked day and night for the disintegration of the army. They claimed they were opposed to the régime because of the "German sympathies of the young Czarina," and the typewritten sheets of their speeches, "killed" by the military censors in the newspapers, were distributed in the trenches among the officers and soldiers. Of all the accusations thrown against the imperial couple, that particular one made my sympathies go back to the Empress. I knew her mistakes. I loathed Rasputin. I wished Alix would not take her synthetic palace-born picture of a Russian peasant for a reality, but I must admit that she was far above all her contemporaries in fervent Russian patriotism. Raised by her father, the Duke of Hesse-Darmstadt, to hate the Kaiser, she dreamed all her life to see the day of Prussia's debacle, and next to Russia her admiration lay on the side of Great Britain. For me, for my uncles and cousins, for anyone who ever met or talked to Alix, the very suggestion of her "German sympathies" sounded monstrous and ridiculous. Our efforts to trace these incomprehensible libels to a definite source led us to the Duma. Its members, when shamed and questioned, blamed Rasputin: "If the young Czarina is such a great Russian patriot, why does she tolerate the presence of that drunken beast, who is openly seen around the capital in the company of German spies and sympathizers?" Their argument was good, if true, and we were breaking our heads trying to find some superhuman words to persuade the Czar to have Rasputin put out of the capital. "You are his brother-in-law and his closest friend," said many people visiting me on the front, "why don't you talk about it to him?" Why didn't I talk to him! I had fought with Nicky over that damnable Rasputin matter many times long before the war; were I to try my luck again, I knew he would listen to me attentively, would say, "Thanks, Sandro, I appreciate your interest," would embrace me, and would do nothing whatsoever to follow my advice. I could not have moved him an inch, as long as his wife thought that the presence of Rasputin guaranteed her against a fatal turn in their son's illness. I was helpless and I recognized it to the point of desperation. I wanted to forget everybody and everything not included in the circle of my duties as commander-in-chief of Russian aviation.

5

Nineteen-sixteen came. I moved my headquarters to Kieff and was preparing to assist General Brussiloff in his projected summer offensive.

My mother-in-law arrived for a visit with me and her younger daughter Grand Duchess Olga, who had been at the head of her own hospital in Kieff since 1915. After the whispering mud-slinging St. Petersburg the war-like atmosphere of Kieff pleased the old Empress. She decided to remain with us for the duration of the war. Each Sunday we three met in her Kieff palace, an old-fashioned dwelling built on the right bank of the wide Dnieper. After lunch, when all strangers left, we would sit in her boudoir discussing the events of the past week. We presented a pathetic group; there we were, mother, sister and brother-in-law of the Emperor, the three of us loving him not only as relatives but as faithful subjects, willing to do everything he could ask of us, well aware of his virtues and shortcomings, cognizant of the approaching upheaval, and yet wholly incapable of opening his eyes! My mother-in-law kept in close touch with the goings-on in St. Petersburg. She knew of the ministers being appointed on the strength of Rasputin's recommendation, and she grieved. During fifty years of her life in Russia she exchanged weekly letters with her sister Alexandra (first Princess of Wales, then Queen of England, and finally Dowager-Queen of England) and the impossibility of receiving news from England regularly during the war years of 1914-1917 increased her worries. Immensely popular with the Kieff population, she went every day for a ride in her open car, smiling cheerfully, acknowledging the greetings of the passers-by, and thinking all the time of her son Nicky, her daughter-in-law Alix and her poor sick grandson Alexis. The rest of her family caused her no concern. Her eldest daughter, my wife, Grand Duchess Xenia, stayed with the children in St. Petersburg, supervising a large hospital for wounded and convalescent soldiers. Her grandson, my son, Prince Andrew, was about to be promoted officer in the Chevalier Guards and join the army. Her youngest son "Misha," Grand Duke Michael Alexandrovich, was a particular favorite of the front, the "wild" cavalry division of Caucasian highlanders, led by him through innumerable battles, being recognized by G.H.Q. as our best fighting unit. As to Olga, her younger daughter and my sister-in-law, even the rabid foes of the Romanoffs waxed enthusiastic in describing her totally unassuming work for the wounded. One does not meet many women of Grand Duchess Olga's qualities. Somberly clad in the traditional Red Cross uniform and sharing a small bedroom with another nurse, she commenced her day at 7 a.m. and the early hours of next morning found her still dressing the wounds of the newly arrived men. Sometimes the soldiers refused to believe that the young woman tending patiently and cheerfully to their sufferings was really the Czar's sister and a daughter of the great Emperor Alexander III. Sorrow had marred Olga's personal life. Married to the Prince of Oldenburg, a man of vastly different character, she was deeply in love with a simple Russian officer by the name of Koulikovsky. We all hoped the Czar would countenance her divorce and a second marriage. I felt highly elated when on a clear winter evening in 1916, with the soft snow falling thickly, we escorted Olga and Koulikovsky to a miniature chapel somewhere on the outskirts of Kieff. It was an exceedingly modest, almost a secret ceremony: the bride, the bridegroom, the old Empress, myself, two Red Cross sisters, and four officers of Olga's own Akhtyrsky Hussar Regiment. An elderly priest officiated in a thin voice, which seemed to be coming from far beyond the half-lighted chapel. Our faces beamed. I never thought of Olga merely as a sister-in-law of mine; she was a dear friend, a staunch companion, a dependable counselor in moments of spiritual distress.

Had it not been for her and a young nurse by the name of Vassilieva, I would have been the loneliest man in the world during the crucial years of the World War. Miss Vassilieva is now married to Mr. Tchirikoff and lives in Cannes. I visit her often and we talk again and again of the sad and eventful winter of 1916-1917.

6

With the advent of summer, 1916, the enthusiastic mood prevailing in our by then well-equipped fighting lines presented a striking contrast with the ugly disposition of the rear. The army thought of defeating the enemy and saw its wish realized in the lightning offensive of Brussiloff. The politicians dreamed of a revolution and "viewed with alarm" the continued success of our troops. My tours of inspection took me frquently to St. Petersburg. Each time I came back to Kieff with my strength sapped and my mind poisoned.

"Is it true that the Emperor has taken to drinking?"

"Have you heard that the Emperor is in the care of a Buriat medicine-man, who prescribes for him strange Mongolian remedies liable to clog his brain?"

"Are you aware that Mr. Stürmer, our new Prime Minister, is in constant communication with the German agents in Stockholm?"

"Have you heard that latest story of Rasputin's behavior in Moscow?"

Never a question about our army! Not an inkling of satisfaction with Brussiloff's victory!

Nothing except lies, libels and calumnies, served to an average inhabitant of the capital with his morning coffee and given the semblance of truth by the important position of their originators, titled ladies-in-waiting to the Empress and authoritative chamberlains of the imperial court.

It seemed certain that we were going to have a revolt in the rear just at the moment when the army would be ready to deal the enemy a decisive blow. I was in a rage. An itching desire possessed me to go straight to the Stavka, shake Nicky by the shoulder and ask him to wake up. If he himself felt incapable of restoring order in the rear, he should entrust some man of proven integrity with dictatorial powers. Go to the Stavka I did. Five times. Nicky grew more worried and less willing to accept advice from me or anyone else with each consecutive visit. The thrill of Brussiloff's triumph wore out and assumed insignificant proportions in comparison with the bad news coming from the capital. The commander-in-chief of 15,000,000 soldiers sat pale and silent in his headquarters (moved in early fall 1915 to Mogileff). Reporting to him on the progress of our aviation and the certainty of our ability to cope with the German air raids, I saw that he just wished I would cut short my presentation of important facts and leave him alone to his thoughts. When I changed the subject and tried to discuss the political life of St. Petersburg, mistrust and coldness appeared in his eyes, an expression never before seen by me during our forty-one years of friendship.

"You do not seem to trust your friends any more, Nicky," I said half-jokingly.

"I believe no one but my wife," he answered icily, looking past me toward the window; and then as though frightened at his own frankness he added in the familiar tone of friendliness, "You are staying with me for luncheon, Sandro, aren't you? I want to hear all about mother and Olga."

I stayed for luncheon, served in the garden adjoining the buildings of G.H.Q. The conversation was made up, everybody being chiefly interested in the bright repartees of the twelve-year-old heir apparent, who arrived for a few days' visit with his father in Mogileff. After the meal I went to the quarters of my brother Grand Duke Sergei Michailovich, then Inspector-General of Artillery, and listened to his prognostications. Compared with Sergei, my brother Nicholas Michailovich could have been accused of optimism. The

275

latter at least suggested remedies and believed in reforms, but Sergei saw no hope at all. Living side by side with the Czar, he watched his fatal drifting at close range.

"Just as he told you himself, Nicky believes nobody but his wife, which means that he is going to stand by all her prejudices and errors. Do not waste your time, Sandro, trying to open his eyes. Go back to your work and pray that we be spared a revolution for another year. The army is in the pink of condition. Artillery, munitions, technical equipment, everything is ready for a decisive offensive in the spring of nineteen-seventeen. This time we are going to smash both the Germans and the Austrians, provided we are given a chance to start. The only salvation for the Germans lies in their ability to provoke a revolution in our rear. They know it well and are doing all they can. With Nicky acting the way he does, I do not believe we can postpone a revolution much longer."

I trusted Sergei implicitly. His meticulous mathematical mind was never engaged in guesswork. His statements were based on first-hand information and a careful analysis of the secret reports.

Our conversation took place in a small vegetable garden planted by him back of his quarters.

"Something to divert my mind," Sergei explained shyly. I understood and envied him. In a world gone mad with slaughter and smelling of corpses, the growing of potatoes and cabbages gave him a welcome taste of constructive life-preserving work. My own rare minutes of recreation were spent in thinking of the bankruptcy of official Christianity.

7

On the morning of December 17, 1916, my aide-de-camp entered the dining-room with his face lit up by a broad smile.

"Your Imperial Highness," he said in a tone of triumph,

GRAND DUKE ALEXANDER AND HIS WIFE GRAND DUCHESS XENIA
DURING THE WAR.

GRAND DUKE ALEXANDER AND HIS SISTER-IN-LAW GRAND DUCH-
ESS OLGA IN 1915 IN THE GRAND DUKE'S PRIVATE CAR ON THE
FRONT.

CZAR NICHOLAS II AT HIS HEADQUARTERS IN MOGILEV, 1916, WITH MILITARY AT-
TACHES OF THE ALLIED POWERS. 1. COLONEL MERENGO, 2. GENERAL BARON DE
RYCKEL, 3. GENERAL WILLIAMS, 4. GENERAL MARQUIS DE LA GICHE, 5. COLONEL
APALKERITCH.

"Rasputin was assassinated last night in St. Petersburg in the house of your son-in-law, Prince Felix Yousoupoff."

"In Felix's house? Are you certain of that?"

"Quite certain, Your Imperial Highness. You must feel exceedingly happy as it is rumored that Prince Yousoupoff killed Rasputin with his own hands, assisted by Grand Duke Dimitry Pavlovich."

My mind flew to my darling daughter Irene, who was staying in the Crimea with her parents-in-law. My aide-de-camp was puzzled by my lack of enthusiasm. He said the people of Kieff were congratulating each other in the streets and were praising the patriotic courage of Felix. I expected they would do that as I myself felt glad to be rid of Rasputin, but there were two other points of greater importance to be considered. The effect this sensational news would have on the young Czarina and the responsibility of the imperial family for a murder committed in the presence and with the participation of two of its members. I knew Alix would see in Rasputin's assassination a thrust at herself and at her policies. Suspicious and hysterical, she would crave revenge and would fight harder than ever for the ministers put in their positions by the alleged "savior" of her son. Felix and Grand Duke Dimitry showed themselves poor tacticians. Too young to understand the soul of an offended woman, they had played straight into the hands of the Rasputin crowd. Rasputin alive was just a man, known to everybody as a drunken peasant reaching for money. Rasputin dead stood a chance of becoming a slaughtered prophet. He had always threatened that the imperial family and Russia would follow him to his grave, should anyone make an attempt against his life. I laughed at his blackmailing prophecies but I visualized the despair of superstitious Alix who took his words for Gospel-truth.

I found my mother-in-law still in her bedroom and was the first to tell her of the latest sensation.

She jumped up: "No! No!"

Whenever she heard something alarming she expressed her anguish and stupefaction in that half-interrogating, half-exclamatory "No!"

Her reaction was similar to mine: the Lord be praised for taking away Rasputin, but we were in for a much greater trouble. The idea of her granddaughter's husband Felix and her nephew Dimitry stooping to murder caused her pain. As an Empress she was horrified; as a Christian she was opposed to the shedding of blood, no matter what noble considerations had prompted the culprits. We agreed I should wire Nicky for permission to go to St. Petersburg. The affirmative answer arrived from Czarskoie-Selo: Nicky had left the Stavka in the early morning, rushing to the side of his wife.

On my arrival at the capital I was immediately submerged in the tense atmosphere of its usual disgusting rumors and foul libels coupled this time with universal rejoicing, malicious satisfaction and a tendency to glorify Felix and Dimitry. The two "national heroes" confirmed to me that they had taken part in the assassination, refusing, however, to disclose the name of the actual murderer. Later on I understood that they were trying to shield Mr. Pourishkevich, an unbalanced member of the Duma who had fired the last fatal shot.

The members of the imperial family asked me to defend Dimitry and Felix before the Emperor. I was going to do so anyway, although their ravings and cruelty nauseated me. They ran around, they conferred, they gossiped, and they wrote a silly letter to Nicky. It almost seemed that they expected the Czar of Russia to decorate his two relatives for having committed a murder.

"You are strange, Sandro, you do not realize that Felix and Dimitry have saved Russia."

They called me strange because I could not forget that Nicky in his quality of Supreme Protector of Justice was duty bound to punish the assassins, particularly as they happened to be members of his family.

I wished to God Nicky would greet me with severity!

Disappointment awaited me. He embraced me and talked to me with overemphasized kindness. He knew me too well not to understand that my real sympathies were entirely on his side and that only my fatherly devotion to Irene brought me to Czarskoie-Selo.

I delivered my speech for the defense, faking a tone of conviction. I begged him not to treat Dimitry and Felix as common murderers but as misguided patriots inspired by a desire to help their country.

"A very nice speech, Sandro," he said after a silence. "Are you aware, however, that nobody has the right to kill, be it a grand duke or a peasant?"

Straight to the point! Nicky may not have been as much of an orator as some of his relatives but he certainly knew his A.B.C. of justice.

When I was leaving, he promised to be "moderate" in the choice of a punishment for the two youngsters. As it happened, they were not punished at all. Dimitry was sent to the Persian front, Felix exiled to his comfortable country estate in the province of Kursk. Next day I left for Kieff traveling with Felix and Irene who had rushed from the Crimea to meet us on our way. While in their car, I learned the full and gruesome details of the crime. I wished then and I do now that Felix would some day repent and realize that no decorous explanations and no acclaim of the masses could justify a murder in the eyes of a true Christian.

Back in Kieff I drafted a long letter to Nicky, stating my estimate of the measures to be taken, if the army and the empire were to be saved from a rapidly approaching upheaval. My six-day stay in the capital left no doubts in my mind as to the fact that the outbreak of the revolution was to be expected not later than early spring. The worst of what I saw and learned dealt with the odd encouragement given to the plotters by the British ambassador, Sir George Buchanan. He imagined he was protecting the interests of the Allies and that a liberal government would be better capable of scoring victories. He discovered his mistake twenty-four hours after the triumph of the revolution and wrote a dignified post-morten several years later. Czar Alexander III would have thrown an ambassador of that species out of Russia without even the ceremony of handing him back his credentials. Czar Nicholas II stood for anything.

8

The new year of 1917 ushered in changes in the cabinet and more gloom. Prince Golitzin, appointed Prime Minister, was a living illustration of the French word "ramolli." He understood nothing, knew nothing, and only Nicky or Alix could have explained what made them think of that old courtier of no administrative experience whatsoever. Together with the Minister of the Interior Protopopoff—a hysterical coward and a former liberal turned into an orthodox conservative by Rasputin's magic—they presented a pair extraordinarily fit for the last act of the Death of a Nation.

In the beginning of February I received orders from the Stavka to attend a conference in St. Petersburg with the representatives of the Allied Governments to ascertain our needs of munitions for the following twelve months. I was glad of this opportunity to see Alix. I did not care to increase her distress in December but this time I felt sufficiently enraged to confide my thoughts to her. Any day now I expected to hear of a revolt in the capital. Some "experts" claimed it would arrive in the guise of a Palace Revolution, meaning that the Czar would be forced to abdicate in favor of his son Alexis with the regency powers invested in a special council of persons who "understood the Russian people." This project amazed me. I have never met anyone who understood the Russian people. The idea sounded foreign, traceable as it was to the British embassy. A handsome lad of wealth, formerly known as a ballet enthusiast only, paid me a visit in Kieff and talked vaguely and nonsensically of something resembling that British plan. I told him he had chosen a wrong man for his confession, coming to a grand duke believing in the inviolability of his oath of allegiance to the Emperor. His stupidity saved him from being chastised by me in a much harsher manner. With the advent of the revolution he became a glorified valet to Mr. Kerensky and occupied the posts of Minister of Finance and Minister of Foreign Affairs.

Once more I was in St. Petersburg, fortunately for the last time in my life. On the day fixed for my talk with Alix a message came from Czarskoie-Selo informing me she did not feel well and could not receive me. I wrote her a strong letter imploring her to give me a chance to see her as I was staying in the capital for but a few days. Awaiting her answer I interviewed numerous persons. My brother-in-law Misha was in town. He proposed that we both should talk to his imperial brother, one after the other, as soon as I succeeded in seeing Alix. The President of the Duma, Mr. Rodzianko, an insipid fat man at best, called on me with a handful of humors, theories and anti-dynastic plans. His arrogance knew no bounds. Combined with his mental deficiencies it created the impression of that famous "bluff character" in medieval comedies. A month later he pinned a Cross of St. George on the soldier of the Volinsky Regiment who was the first man to kill his commanding officer in 1917. Nine months later Rodzianko was obliged to run away from St. Petersburg pursued by Bolshevik police.

Then I received an invitation from Alix to be present at a luncheon in Czarskoie-Selo. Oh, those luncheons! It seems that forty years of my life were wasted in going to luncheons in Czarskoie-Selo.

Alix was in bed and promised to see me the moment I had

finished the meal. We were eight at table: Nicky, myself, the heir apparent, the four imperial daughters, and the aide-de-camp Linevich. The girls wore Red Cross uniforms and spoke of their work in their own hospital. I had not seen them since the first week of the war and I found them grown matured and very attractive. The eldest—Olga—resembled her aunt and namesake, Grand Duchess Olga Alexandrovna, in her spiritual inclinations. The second—Tatiana—was the leading beauty of the family. All were in a happy mood, totally ignorant of political events, joking with their brother and praising the achievements of their Aunt Olga. It was the last time I was to sit at the table in the Czarskoie-Selo palace, likewise the last time I was to see the Czar's children.

We took our coffee in the "mauve salon," while Nicky went into the adjoining bedroom to announce my visit to Alix.

I walked in cheerfully. Alix lay in bed, dressed in a white negligee embroidered with lace, her beautiful face set in a serious expression which augured trouble for the determined intruder. An attack was forthcoming! It saddened me. I came to help, not to hurt. The sight of Nicky, sitting on the side of their large double bed displeased me as well. In my letter to Alix I underlined the words: "I want to see you in strict privacy so as to talk with you face to face." It was embarrassing to reproach her for dragging her husband into an abyss in that husband's presence.

I kissed her hand, and her lips just skimmed my cheek, the coldest greeting given me by her since the first day we met in 1893. I took a chair and moved it close to her bed, facing a wall covered with innumerable ikons lighted by two blue-and-pink church lamps.

I began by pointing toward the ikons and saying that I would talk to her as to my father-confessor. I gave a general outline of the political situation, dwelling upon the fact that the revolutionary propaganda had penetrated into the masses of the population and that the libels and calumnies were taken by them for truth.

She interrupted me sharply:

"It is not true. The nation is still loyal to him"—she turned toward Nicky—"only the treacherous Duma and St. Petersburg society are my and his enemies."

I admitted she was partially correct in her statement.

"There is nothing more dangerous, Alix, than a half-truth," I said, looking straight at her. "The nation is loyal to its Czar but the nation is likewise indignant over the influence which has been exercised by that man Rasputin. Nobody knows better than I your love and devotion for Nicky, and yet I must confess that your interference with affairs of state is causing harm both to Nicky's prestige and to the popular conception of a sovereign. I have been your faithful friend, Alix, for twenty-four years. I am still your faithful friend, and as a friend I point out to you that all classes of the population are opposed to your policies. You have a beautiful family of children, why can you not concentrate on matters promising peace and harmony? Please, Alix, leave the cares of state to your husband."

She blushed. She looked at Nicky. He said nothing and continued to smoke. It is annoying that when talking of the last Czar's behavior in moments of distress, I am obliged to repeat that same silly phrase: "he said nothing and continued to smoke." But what can I do if any other description of his attitude would be likely to distort the truth?

I went on. I explained that opposed as I was to all parliamentary forms in Russia, I believed that the granting of a government acceptable to the Duma and coming at this dangerous moment would lift the responsibilities from Nicky's shoulders and would make his task easier.

"Please, Alix, do not let your thirst for revenge dominate your better judgment. A radical change of our policies would provide an outlet for the nation's wrath. Do not let that wrath reach the explosion point."

She sneered: "All this talk of yours is ridiculous. Nicky is an autocrat. How could he share his divine rights with a parliament?"

"You are very much mistaken, Alix. Your husband ceased to be an autocrat on October seventeenth, nineteen-five. That was the moment to think of his divine rights. It is too late now. Perhaps in two months there will be nothing left in this country of ours to remind us that we ever had autocrats sitting on the throne of our ancestors."

She answered something incoherent and raised her voice. I raised mine too. I decided to change the tenor of my conversation.

"Remember, Alix, I remained silent for thirty months!" I shouted at her in a wild rage. "For thirty months I never said as much as a word to you about the disgraceful goings-on in our government, better to say in *your* government! I realize that you are willing to perish and that your husband feels the same way, but what about us? Must we all suffer for your blind stubbornness? No, Alix, you have no right to drag your relatives with you down a precipice! You are incredibly selfish!"

"I refuse to continue this dispute," she said coldly. "You are exaggerating the danger. Some day, when you are less excited, you will admit that I knew better."

I got up, kissed her hand, received no kiss at all in return, and left. I never saw Alix again.

Passing through the "mauve salon" I saw the Czar's aide-de-camp Linevich talking to Olga and Tatiana. His presence next to the Czarina's bedroom surprised me. Madame Virouboff, the chief confidante of Alix in the latter years of the régime and an admirer of Rasputin, tells in her memoirs that "the Czarina feared lest Grand Duke Alexander should lose his temper and try something desperate." If it is true, then Alix must have been bereft of her senses, which would explain her stubbornness and her actions.

Next day Misha and I talked to the Czar, wasting his time

and ours. At the end of my turn I was hardly able to speak, nerves and emotion choking me. "Thanks, Sandro, for the letter you have sent me from Kieff." That was the only reference he made to my many pages of written advice.

The bread-lines in St. Petersburg grew longer, although wheat and corn were rotting along the Trans-Siberian railway and in the Southwest. The garrison of the capital, consisting of recruits and reservists, could not have been of any value in case of serious disorder. I naturally asked the generals-in-charge whether they thought of bringing reliable fighting units from the front. They answered they expected the arrival of the thirteen cavalry regiments of the Imperial Guard. Much later I learned that the exalted traitors of the Stavka had obeyed the instructions of the Duma's leaders and had countermanded the order of the Czar.

9

I wish I could forget the damnable month of February, 1917! Every day I met some one of my relatives and friends whom I was never to see again: my brother Nicholas Michailovich, my brother George Michailovich, my brother-in-law Misha, my cousins Paul Alexandrovich and Dimitry Constantinovich and many, many others.

George Michailovich passed through Kieff on his way to Stavka. Since the beginning of the war he had served as the Czar's special investigator, going from army to army and compiling data on the general situation. His view of things confirmed my worst fears. The army was ready but so were the plotters; the former to go over the top, the latter to destroy the empire.

I dived into my work and ignored the rest. If our future could have been judged by the growth of my department, we were riding on the crest of the wave. Hundreds of airplanes manned by courageous officers and armed with the latest type of machine guns awaited the signal. Flying over the lengthy line of our front they discovered signs of preparations for a retreat made by the enemy, and they hoped, sincerely though naïvely, that the Emperor would "score a victory in his own capital." They were a splendid lot, those young men of culture, loyalty and genuine patriotism. I was proud of them. Thirty months before I had started with a single salon car which housed both my clerical and my fighting forces. By now a score of aviation schools worked at full speed, and three brand-new Russian factories were turning out a daily output of airplanes in addition to the continuous deliveries from England and France.

The end came in the least expected manner. The morning papers spoke of the increasing strikes among munition workers in St. Petersburg. It was bad, occurring on the eve of our offensive; it had, however, happened before. The night telegrams mentioned "hunger" as the main reason for the strikes. That was a lie. St. Petersburg experienced a certain shortage of bread owing to the disorganization of the transport but that shortage never reached the proportions of a famine. Coming an hour later, the news of the first clash between the hesitating reservists and the crowds provided the necessary explanation: shortage of bread was to be used by the Duma as a pretext for a revolt.

The following morning I wired Nicky suggesting I join him in the Stavka and put myself at his disposal. Simultaneously I called my brother Sergei on the telephone. His voice sounded alarmed.

"Things are going from bad to worse in St. Petersburg," he said nervously. "There has been more fighting in the streets and it looks like the garrison is going over to the rioters."

"But what happened to the cavalry of the Imperial Guard? You mean to say they too are unreliable?"

"That order has been countermanded in a strange and mysterious fashion. The cavalry of the Guard has never left the front."

✦✦

Nicky's answer arrived: "Thanks. When you will be needed here, shall communicate with you. Love: Nicky."

He was alone in the Stavka, with nobody but my brother Sergei to give him sane advice. I thought of the treacherous generals surrounding him and I felt it in my bones I should go to the Stavka without his permission. The general telegraph office, from which I talked with Sergei, buzzed like a beehive. The faces of the clerks, all of them secret enemies of the régime, told me the story not transmitted by the Stavka and the newspapers. That day I remained till midnight in the palace of the old Empress. I need not describe her worry and despair. Trusted friends were dropping in on us relating rumors and various "unconfirmed versions" of the latest events in the capital.

At six a.m. I was called again to the general telegraph office to talk with Sergei over the "direct wire."

"Nicky left last night for St. Petersburg but the railway officials, obeying the orders of the Duma, have stopped his train at the station Dno and turned it in the direction of Pskoff. He is practically alone aboard his train. A delegation of the members of the Duma are to see him in Pskoff, submitting their ultimatum. The St. Petersburg troops have joined the mob."

Nothing else. He was in a frightful hurry.

Another day of wild rumors passed. The Dowager-Empress, Olga, and myself ran out of words. We glared at each other in silence. I thought of the empire, they of their son and brother.

My aide-de-camp woke me at dawn. His lips were blue. He handed me a single sheet of printed paper. The Manifesto of the Abdication. Nicky refused to part with Alexis, turning the throne over to Misha. I sat in my bed and read it again. Nicky must have lost his mind: since when does a sovereign abdicate because of shortage of bread and partial disorders in his capital? The treason of the St. Petersburg reservists? But he had an army of fifteen million men at his disposal! The whole thing, including his reckless trip to St. Petersburg, seemed ludicrous in 1917. It still remains so in 1931.

I dressed and went to break the heart of a mother. We ordered the train and left for the Stavka in the afternoon, as in the meanwhile we learned that Nicky had received "permission" (!) to pay a farewell visit to G.H.Q.

Upon arrival in Mogileff our train was brought to the "Imperial Platform," where the Czar usually started on his trips to the capital. Nicky's motor car drew up to the station a minute later. He walked slowly along the platform, said good morning to the two Cossacks standing at the entrance to his mother's car, and went inside. He was pale, but nothing otherwise disclosed his authorship of the horrible Manifesto. He remained closeted with the old Empress for two hours. She never told me of the subject of their conversation. When I was invited to join them, she sat in a chair sobbing aloud, while he stood motionless, looking at his feet and, of course, smoking. We embraced. I did not know what to say. The calmness of his demeanor showed his firm belief in the righteousness of his decision, although he did criticize his brother Misha for refusing to accept the throne and for leaving Russia without a ruler.

"Misha should not have done a thing like that," he concluded sententiously. "I wonder who could have given him such strange advice."

This remark, coming from a man who had surrendered one-sixth of the earth's surface to a mob of drunken reservists and rioting workers left me speechless. After a painful pause he volunteered a casual explanation of the reasons that prompted his decision. He mentioned three principal ones: 1, his unwillingness to plunge Russia into a civil war; 2, his desire to keep the army out of politics and in a condition to help the Allies; 3, his belief that the Provisional Government would rule Russia better than he had.

None of the three arguments impressed me. Even then,

on the second day of the New Era of Freedom, it was obvious that we were going to have a fratricidal slaughter and witness the disintegration of our army. A twenty-four-hour battle in the suburbs of St. Petersburg would have restored order.

He produced a pack of telegrams received from the different commanders in answer to his wire asking for suggestions. With the exception of General Gourko, every one of them showed a yellow streak—Brussiloff, Alexeieff and Rouzsky among the others—and advised the immediate abdication of their sovereign. He never thought much of them anyway and would have ignored the whole bunch of traitors but there was one more telegram, at the very bottom of the pack, urging his abdication and signed by Grand Duke Nicholas Nicholaevich.

"Even he," said Nicky and his voice broke for the first time.

Luncheon was announced. I believe Baron Fredericks and several members of the Czar's personal staff sat with us at table. I say "I believe" because complete darkness clouded my eyes. I would much rather be burned at the stake than go through that luncheon again. Banalities, soothing lies, exaggerated politeness of the attendants, the tear-stained face of my mother-in-law, a glimpse of Nicky's hand putting another cigarette in the holder, my excruciating thoughts of having, perhaps, not done all I could to avert the debacle, the memories of Alix in bed with her beautiful face expressing cold hatred!—my head ached, my ears rang. I ate automatically, trying to dodge Nicky's glances.

In the afternoon I saw my brother Sergei engaged in reading the first act of the Provisional Government. The soldiers of all companies, battalions, regiments, etc., were invited by the new rulers to form their own administrative committees—Soviets—and to decide which officers they wanted to retain. The selfsame Order No. 1 proclaimed the abolition of military discipline, such as the necessity of saluting the officers, etc.

"That is the end of the Russian Army," said Sergei. "Hindenburg himself could not have improved upon this order. The garrison of Vyborg has already assassinated its officers. The others will follow."

We remained in the Stavka for three days more, each minute of that time burned into my memory.

First Day

General Alexeieff invites us to assemble in the main hall of G.H.Q. Nicky is to address the members of his former staff. By eleven a.m. the hall is packed. Generals, officers, and persons in attendance on the Emperor are present. Nicky enters—calm, reserved, bearing the semblance of a smile on his lips. He thanks the staff and begs them to continue their work "with the same loyalty and in a spirit of self-sacrifice." He invites them to forget all feuds, to serve Russia and lead our army to victory. Then he says his adieus, in curt soldier-like sentences, avoiding words that could suggest pathos. His modesty makes a tremendous impression. We shout "hurrah," as we never had in the last twenty-three years. Elderly generals cry. A moment more, and someone is bound to step forward and implore Nicky to reconsider his decision. Such a move would be useless: the Czar of Russia does not go back on his word. Nicky bows and walks out. We lunch. We dine. Our conversation drags. We talk of the days of our childhood in the Crimean palace of Livadia.

I pass the night watching the illuminated town and listening to the shouts of the celebrating crowds. The windows of the old Empress' car are lighted. The Provincial Government delays its decision as to whether the Czar should be permitted to join his family in Czarskoie-Selo, and Nicky is worried about Alix. She is alone in the North and her four daughters have measles.

Second Day

General Alexeieff invites us to take our oath of allegiance to the Provisional Government. He seems elated; the new rulers promised to appoint him commander-in-chief of the army in recognition of his coöperation with the revolution.

Troops are lined in front of the house occupied by the Czar. I recognize the uniforms of his personal escort. The St. George Battalion (composed of the knights of that high order), a section of the Railway Battalion, my Aviation Group and all the officers of the staff are likewise present.

We stand behind General Alexeieff. I wonder how the others feel, but I myself fail to understand how anyone could take an oath of allegiance to a combination of schemers who had just broken their own oath. The priest is chanting the words which I do not want to hear. A Te Deum follows. For the first time in three hundred and four years of the existence of the régime the name of the Emperor is not mentioned in the prayer. My thoughts go to Nicky, who remains in his room until the end of this show. What tortures he must suffer at this moment! The Provisional Government deigned to acknowledge his petition, and his departure is fixed for tomorrow. At four o'clock in the afternoon he and Sergei are to leave for St. Petersburg, the old Empress and myself for Kieff.

The absence of all other members of the imperial family causes me deep humiliation. Were they afraid that their coming to the Stavka might jeopardize their standing with the Provisional Government or were they forbidden to make the trip? The answer to this question is unknown to me.

Third Day

We lunch together. Nicky is trying to cheer up his mother. He expects to see her "soon." There is some talk of his going to England, although he would much rather stay in Russia. Quarter to four. His train is stationed opposite ours. We get up. He covers his mother's face with kisses. He turns to me and we embrace. He goes out, crosses the platform and enters his salon car. The gentlemen of the Duma, who came to the Stavka to escort Nicky to St. Petersburg and incidentally to spy on his aides, shake hands with General Alexeieff. They exchange cordial bows. No doubt, they have reasons to be grateful to the general.

Nicky's train whistles and commences to move slowly. He stands in the large mirrored window of his car. He smiles and waves his hand. His expression is infinitely sad. He is wearing a simple khaki blouse, with the cross of St. George in its buttonhole. The old Empress cries unrestrainedly now that the Czar's train has become a stream of smoke on the horizon. My brother Sergei comes in. He is leaving for St. Petersburg in ten minutes. "Good luck, Sergei." "Good-by, Sandro." We both know we shall never meet again. Our train moves. Back in my compartment I take off my coat and notice the disappearance of the imperial monograms which I had worn for thirty years on my shoulder straps. I recall—the provisional Government has issued some order to that effect.

GRAND DUCHESS OLGA, YOUNGEST SISTER OF THE LAST CZAR
AND SISTER-IN-LAW OF GRAND DUKE ALEXANDER, DURING THE
WAR WHEN IN CHARGE OF HER HOSPITAL IN KIEFF.

IN EXILE: GRAND DUCHESS XENIA, PRINCESS IRENE YOUSOUPOFF AND PRINCES ANDREW, FEODOR, NIKITA, DIMITRY, ROSTISLAV AND VASSILY, IN LONDON.

CHAPTER EIGHTEEN

ESCAPE

I

On my return from G.H.Q. I had to think of my family which consisted at that moment of my mother-in-law (the Dowager-Empress Marie), my wife (Grand Duchess Xenia), my sister-in-law (Grand Duchess Olga), my six sons and Olga's husband Koulikovsky. My daughter Irene and her husband, Prince Yousoupoff, exiled for the part he had taken in the assassination of Rasputin to his estate near Kursk, joined us in the Crimea a few weeks later.

I personally would have liked to stay in Kieff on account of its proximity to the front. Feeling no bitterness against the nation I hoped to be of service to the army. I had given ten years of my life to the development of military aviation and I hated the idea of parting with my favorite work.

Nothing happened during the first two weeks to cause us any discomfort. We walked in the streets mingling with the joyful crowds, and stood on the sidewalks watching the gigantic demonstrations staged in the honor of newly acquired liberties.

Countless meetings took place every minute of the day, and the popular orators promised peace, prosperity and happiness for everybody. It was slightly difficult to comprehend how all of this could have been accomplished while there remained the war to be fought, but then one had to make necessary allowances for the natural exaggerations of Russian eloquence.

People appeared to be very friendly with me. They stopped me in the street and shaking my hand said they knew my liberal views. Officers and soldiers continued to stand at attention on meeting me, although the military discipline had been abolished by the famous "Order No. 1" of the St. Petersburg Soviet.

All this seemed too good to be true. Bloodless revolutions are being made on the screen only, and there was the German General Staff to be reckoned with. General Ludendorff would not have deserved his stars were he to let slip the marvelous opportunities offered by our internal troubles. In fact, it was his very last chance to prevent the launching of the Russian offensive of 1917. No deus ex machina could have rendered a greater service to Germany than this unexpected turn of events.

By the end of March, German agents had the situation well in hand, both in St. Petersburg and in the provinces. It would be idle to speculate as to whether the Bolshevik leaders took money from Ludendorff, or merely accepted his kind offer to let them pass through Germany in a sealed car. To quote Lenin himself: "I'd take money from the Devil if it could but promote the cause of the revolution."

Strange accomplices, Lenin and Ludendorff had no illusions about each other. They were willing to travel part of the road together, as long as it brought them nearer to their respective goals. The general tried to keep his face straight, thinking of the foolishness of this theoretician, Lenin. The Communist had a good laugh some twenty months later, when the mob of his followers in Berlin attempted to hang the hero of Tannenberg in Unter den Linden.

A series of new slogans appeared in boldface type on the standards carried by the enthusiastic processions in Kieff:

"We demand immediate peace."

"We want our husbands and sons home."

"Down with the capitalistic government."

"To hell with the Dardanelles. Who wants Constantinople?"

"Fight for an immediate Ukrainization of the Ukraine."

The last one—a master stroke of German strategy—needs to be explained. The word "Ukraine" referred to the immense Southwestern district of Russia, bordered by Austria in the west, the Central provinces in the north and the Don district in the east, with Kieff considered as its capital, and Odessa on the Black Sea its principal port exporting wheat, grain, sugar, etc. Four centuries before it served as a battleground for the continuous skirmishes between the Poles and the bands of free Cossacks who called themselves "Ukrainians." Czar Alexei Michailovich took it under his scepter in 1649, and in the course of years it became stupendously prosperous, Catherine the Great being the first to foresee its agricultural and industrial future. Ninety-nine per cent of its population spoke, read and wrote Russian, but a small coterie of fanatics insisted on equal rights for the Ukrainian language. They were ridiculed in numerous cartoons; in fact, the Kentucky mountaineers demanding the usage of their slang by the Louisville school-teachers would have been much less ridiculous.

Kaiser Wilhelm frequently teased his Russian cousins on this subject, but what had been a joke before the revolution suddenly acquired the dimensions of a nightmare in March, 1917.

The leaders of the Ukrainian Separatist Movement were quickly summoned to German Headquarters and promised the status of a free state, should they succeed in paralyzing the rear of the Russian armies.

Millions of leaflets flooded Kieff and the adjoining towns. "Russians must get out of the Ukraine," demanded their authors. "If they want to continue this war, let them fight it on their own soil."

A delegation of irate nationalists left for St. Petersburg and demanded of the new Government permission to organize a Ukrainian Army consisting of soldiers then serving in the different corps of the Russian Army. Even the most radical members of the Provisional Government under-stood that the whole thing smacked of treason and threat-ened to explode the army from within, but the Bolshevik leaders of the soviet rallied to a man to this insane project. The Ukrainian demand was satisfied. Almost simultaneously the German General Staff commenced taking divisions off the eastern front and sending them to France. The Russian steam-roller had been shot to pieces.

2

Greatly encouraged by this first triumph, the combine of German agents, slackers and Ukrainian nationalists increased their efforts. The attack against the old institutions was reinforced by an appeal to beware of the Enemies of the Revolution. A moment arrived when the pulling down of the monuments erected to former Emperors failed to satisfy the crowds. Overnight the Kieff newspapers changed their attitude toward our family.

"The whole dynasty must be drowned in mud," pro-claimed a popular columnist, and the mud-slinging began. No more reference was made to the liberalism of my brother, Grand Duke Nicholas, nor to the supreme unselfishness of Grand Duke Michael. All of us became just "Romanoffs, the Enemies of the Revolution and the Russian people."

My poor mother-in-law, greatly grieved over the uncer-tainty surrounding the fate of her imperial son, could not stand this new sobriquet added to our former titles. I tried in vain to explain to her the pitiless course of all revolutions. A woman in her late seventies, she could not comprehend why the family that had given Russia Peter the Great, Alex-ander I, and her own beloved husband, Alexander III, should be accused of being hostile to the Russian people.

"My unfortunate Nicky may have made some mistakes, but to say that he is an enemy of his people— Ah, never, never. . . ."

She trembled with indignation. She looked at me with eyes which seemed to say: "You know it is not true. You know it is an unmitigated lie. Why then don't you do something to stop it?"

My heart bled. My own sense of humiliation was drowned in the realization of what life had done to her. The fascinating Princess Dagmar of Denmark of fifty years ago, she had sacrificed her youth, her beauty and her happiness to the service of this strange country. She saw her kind-hearted father-in-law, Emperor Alexander II, brought home to the palace with his limbs torn by the bomb of a terrorist. Unable to interfere and helpless to protest, she watched her husband work himself into a premature grave, and now fate brought her here, hundreds of miles away from her boys, to this provincial town where people wanted to talk Ukrainian. She could not believe that Nicky had ceased to be the Emperor, and if he had, was not her grandson Alexis the heir apparent to the throne? Oh, had Nicky abdicated for both of them? Very well, what about her favorite son, Michael? Couldn't the new Emperor bring his mother back where she belonged?

My former subordinates came each morning begging me to leave while there was still a possibility of getting the permission of the Government to go to our Crimean estates. The rumors had it that Nicholas II and all the grand dukes would be deported to Siberia, although it had been agreed on March 2 that the Emperor could choose between England and Crimea. Mr. Kerensky, then the only Socialist in the first revolutionary cabinet, informed some friends that Lloyd George had refused to admit the former Czar to England. The British ambassador to Russia, Sir George Buchanan, issued an immediate denial but the time had been lost, and the real masters of the situation, the heads of the St. Petersburg Soviet, insisted on a Siberian exile.

I asked my sister-in-law to see what she could do to persuade the old Empress to go to the Crimea. At first she met with a flat "no." Never would the old Empress consent to be still farther away from Nicky. If this new barbarian Government wouldn't let Nicky come to Kieff—we had finally succeeded in making her realize the actual state of affairs—why could she not join him in his northern imprisonment? His wife, Alix, was too young to stand the suffering alone. She felt certain Nicky needed his mother.

Her daughter had to surrender, so beautiful was mother's sentiment in its sincerity. After all, Olga said, one has to respect the decisions of the Almighty. If the worst was to come, they would much rather face it together.

No doubt a few sympathetic friends, touched by our predicament, endeavored to exercise whatever political pull they could muster, for a representative of the Government called at our house and transmitted an order to leave immediately for the Crimea. The local soviet approved wholeheartedly considering that "it presented a grave danger for revolutionary Russia to keep enemies of the people so close to the German front."

We almost had to carry my mother-in-law to the station. She fought till the very last moment, declaring herself ready to be arrested and put in prison.

3

Upon our arrival in Ay-Todor—the voyage had been made under a heavy guard of sailors—we received a long list of "don'ts" from a gentleman who bore the resounding title of Special Commissioner of the Provisional Government.

We were to consider ourselves prisoners, our movements limited to the borders of our estate—175 acres of Ay-Todor's park, right on the water front, made this restriction rather enjoyable but the other regulations created a great deal of misery.

A patrol of armed sailors, picked for their radical views, had the right to enter our rooms at any time of the day or night. No correspondence could be received or sent by us without special permission of the commissioner, who was to be present at all meals. An interpreter followed on his heels, in case we should attempt to double-cross the revolution in a foreign language. Friends desirous of paying us a visit had to be searched, both on entering and on leaving the estate.

The amount of candles and kerosene was to be checked every other day. The purpose of the last measure being somewhat vague to my old-fashioned mind, I assured the commissioner that we possessed no formula of making bombs out of candles and kerosene.

"It is not that," he said, blushing. "It is to keep the soviet quiet. They think you may signal to the Turkish Navy."

It would have taken quite a candle to signal to the fleet that stood in the Bosphorus, some four hundred miles away from the coast of Crimea, but this asinine remark opened my eyes on the precarious position of the commissioner. He represented the Provisional Government, while the sailors safeguarded the interest of the soviets. No love was lost between the two organizations. The sailors distrusted the commissioner, and the commissioner watched with anguish the assortment of hand grenades attached to their belts. A former member of the Russian Parliament, raised and educated in a well-to-do family, he attempted to ride the storm thinking that in a month or two the country would get back to normal life, leaving the power in the hands of his friends. Like all irresponsible Russian liberals he got caught between two fires, and his utter insincerity failed to deceive the cynical sailors. They treated him with open contempt, disregarding his orders and even refusing to stand up in his presence. No matter how hard he tried to show extreme discourtesy toward me and the members of my family, the Bolsheviks continued to accuse him of plotting to arrange the escape of Grand Duke Nicholas, the former commander-in-chief of the Russian armies, who came to the Crimea shortly after our arrival, accompanied by his wife (Grand Duchess Stana) and his brother (Grand Duke Peter).

A worried, frightened expression never left the face of the commissioner. Looking sidewise at his terrifying assistants, he would address us in a manner which tended to imitate their revolutionary harshness. "Former Grand Duke Alexander" in April, I became "Admiral Romanoff" in May. By June 1 I was plain "Citizen Romanoff." One word of protest from me would have made him supremely happy. My indifference brought his designs to naught. He was in despair. He glared with hatred at the old Empress, hoping against hope that she at least would protest. I doubt if she ever noticed him. From morning till night she sat on the veranda, reading her old family Bible that had accompanied her on all voyages since the day she left Denmark in the early sixties of the last century.

The great commissioner of the Government that promised Liberty, Equality and Fraternity for all, wound up by trying his luck with my youngest son. He must have heard somewhere of a similar method practiced during the French Revolution. He addressed the boy in the language of Robespierre, so as to stick to the model in every detail. My son corrected his French phrasing and let it go at that.

My wife laughed but I felt a peculiar presentiment of danger. Alarming news coming from the north indicated an imminent seizure of power by the Bolsheviks. In order to be in the good graces of the soviets this guardian of ours would have to qualify at no matter what price.

4

I woke up with a start. Something cold was touching my forehead. I raised my hand to ascertain its nature but a gruff voice said in threatening tones:

"Not a move or I'll shoot you on the spot."

ESCAPE

I opened my eyes and saw two silhouettes standing over our bedside. It must have been around four o'clock judging by the grayish light creeping through the windows.

"What do you want from us?" asked my wife. "If you are after my jewels, you will find them on the little table in the corner."

"No such luck," answered the same voice. "We are after you aristocrats. Your game's up. The whole house is surrounded. We are the representatives of the Sebastopol Soviet. I would advise you to obey my orders."

So the inevitable had come. Trying to keep cool and reserved I assured the half-visible speaker that we would like nothing better than to obey his orders, but would he mind switching on the lights and showing his warrant?

"Hey, you," he instructed someone, "give us some light. Citizen Romanoff wants to see the signature of the triumphant proletariat."

This brought a hearty laugh and several more figures stepped out of the darkness of the adjoining corridor.

The lights went up. The room was full of sailors armed in a fashion never before observed outside the comic strips.

The warrant authorized a "thorough search of the place known as Ay-Todor and occupied by the imprisoned citizen Alexander Romanoff, his wife, Xenia Romanoff, and their children."

"Suppose you remove your guns from our foreheads and give us a chance to dress," I proposed, thinking that should he consent to my demand, it would indicate that we were to be removed to jail.

He guessed my thoughts and smiled sarcastically:

"You don't need to dress, Citizen Romanoff. We are not taking you out yet. Just get up quietly and show us around the house."

He motioned to his comrade, and removed his gun a couple of inches from my forehead.

I had to laugh: "Are you so terrified of two disarmed people?"

"We are not permitted to take any chances with the enemies of the people," he said gravely, "in case you have secret panels or buttons or something around."

"May I smoke?"

"Go ahead. Only, say, don't you try stalling for time. We've got to attend to our job. First of all, we want to see that big desk in your library. Hand me the keys. No good smashing up the furniture, it belongs to the people."

This remark supplied the explanation for the raid. The sneaky face of the Commissioner of the Provisional Government crossed my mind. Each time I started rearranging some of my documents and letters, he would enter the library for no particular purpose and cast a lingering look at the open drawers of the desk.

I took the keys from under the pillow.

"Here they are, but where is the Commissioner of the Provisional Government?"

"Not necessary. We'll get along without him. Now, show us the way."

Surrounded by sailors, their guns still trained on my head, I led the procession down the corridor. There must have been not less than fifty sailors in the house. We met groups of them stationed at every door.

"Fine job," I complimented the chief. "Even the old Empress and the children are overpowered by at least six to one."

He ignored my irony and pointed toward the window: three heavy trucks filled with men were parked on the lawn, with machine guns mounted on special platforms.

I helped him open the desk. He picked up a bundle of letters with foreign stamps.

"Correspondence with the enemies? Not bad for a beginning."

"I am sorry to disappoint you. All these happen to be letters written by my English relatives."

"How about this one?"

"It comes from France."

"France or Germany, it's all alike to us. Capitalistic enemies of the working class."

After ten minutes of search he succeeded in reaching the drawer containing the letters written in a language he could understand. He read them slowly.

"Exchanging messages with the former Czar," he pronounced his verdict, "plotting against the revolution."

"Why don't you look at the date? It was written before the war."

"That's so! Well, I guess I'll leave it for the comrades in Sebastopol to decide."

"You mean to say you will take away my personal correspondence?"

"You bet. We have specialists for this kind of stuff. What I am after is the ammunition. Where do you keep those machine guns?"

"Are you trying to be funny?"

"I am dead serious. I promise to you before these comrades not to cause you any harm if you'll surrender your machine guns peacefully. We'll find them, sooner or later, only it will be much harder on you and your family."

It was useless to continue the discussion. I lit a cigarette and settled down in a chair.

"One, two, three,"—he got up menacingly—"do we search or don't we?"

"You know better."

"Suits me. Come on, comrades, let's do some work."

They started back for Sebastopol at six in the afternoon, leaving the house in a state of complete destruction and carrying away my personal correspondence and the Bible belonging to my mother-in-law. The old Empress begged them not to deprive her of this precious souvenir of her youth, proposing her jewels in exchange.

"We are not thieves," said the chief, completely disgusted

at the failure of the raid. "This is an anti-revolutionary book, and an old woman like you should know better than to poison her brains with such trash."

Ten years later, while in Copenhagen, my mother-in-law received a package containing her Bible: a Danish diplomat visiting Moscow bought it from a dealer in rare books. She died holding it in her hands.

5

By early fall the process of dissolution had reached its peak. The divisions, brigades and regiments of yesteryear ceased to exist, and the crowds of pillaging deserters were invading the rear.

The commander-in-chief of the Black Sea Fleet in Sebastopol, Admiral Kolchak, left for St. Petersburg on his way to the United States to volunteer in the American Navy. Until the last moment he strove to maintain discipline but the soviets presented a more attractive line of goods to his subordinates. He could not outbid their offer to the sailors to take all the money to be found in the Crimean banks, so he broke the gold sword, given to him for extraordinary bravery, threw it into the sea in a spectacular gesture and quit.

During my daily walks in the park I often saw Grand Duke Nicholas. Political differences had strained our relations in the past, and the depth of our mutual grief would have made all arguments superfluous, but I think the former commander-in-chief of the Russian Armies began to understand at this late date the truth of my unheeded warnings.

Every day we expected to hear the news of the fall of the Provisional Government and our thoughts went to our relatives. With the exception of the Czar and his family, who were transferred to Tobolsk in Siberia, all of them stayed in St. Petersburg. My brothers, Nicholas, Sergei and George, would have been alive today had they joined us in Ay-Todor. Beginning with October, 1917, I received no news from the north and only learned of their tragic fate in Paris, in 1919.

A morning came when the commissioner failed to make his usual appearance. It could have meant but one thing. We started to prepare for the ordeal of meeting the new rulers of Russia. Around noon, a dust-covered automobile stopped at our gate and a heavily armed giant in sailor's uniform stepped out. After a brief talk with the guard he came in unannounced.

"I have been given orders by the Soviet Government," he said with a certain pride, "to take charge of this place."

I asked him to be seated.

"I know you," he continued, "you are former Grand Duke Alexander. Don't you remember me? I served in your aviation school in Sebastopol in 1916."

I had two thousand aviators serving under my orders there, so naturally I could not have recalled his face but it made our acquaintance with this new warden much easier.

He explained that "strategical considerations" necessitated our immediate removal to the adjoining estate of "Dulber," belonging to my cousin, Grand Duke Peter.

It had been quite a while since I had heard this military expression. What had "strategical considerations" to do with the imprisonment of our family? Were they preparing for the landing of the Turks?

He grinned:

"Much worse than that. The comrades of the Yalta Soviet insist on your immediate execution, but the Sebastopol Soviet told me to protect your lives till we receive orders from Comrade Lenin. No doubt, the Yalta crowd will try to take you away by force, so I have to be ready for their attack. Dulber with its high walls is much easier to defend than Ay-Todor. Your place here is open on all sides."

He produced a carefully drawn map of Dulber covered with crosses in red ink indicating the spots convenient for the mounting of machine guns. Never did I think that the beautiful villa of Grand Duke Peter would present such advan-

tages from a strictly military point of view. When he started
to build it, years ago, we ridiculed the exaggerated height of
the solid walls and asked him whether he intended to engage
in the profession of a Blue Beard. Our jokes failed to shake
his determination. He used to say that one could never fore-
tell what circumstances might arise in the distant future.
Thanks to this extreme vision the Sebastopol Soviet possessed
a well-fortified jail in November, 1917.

6

The events of the following five months justified the wise
measures of precaution taken by our new warden. Every
second week the Yalta Soviet sent its representatives to Dulber to carry on negotiations with our involuntary defenders.

Heavy trucks loaded with men and machine guns would
stop before the walls and demand an interview with comrade
Zadorojny, the commissioner of the Sebastopol Soviet. The
stalwart comrade Zadorojny—he stood six-feet-four in his
stockinged feet—would approach the gates and inquire the
purpose of this friendly visit. The prisoners, who were ordered on such occasions to remain inside of the house listening through the open windows, learned by heart the ensuing
dialogue.

"Zadorojny, we are sick and tired of your line of talk. The
Yalta Soviet claims its rights on the Romanoffs unlawfully
held by the Sebastopol Soviet. We give you five minutes
to make up your mind."

"You tell the Yalta Soviet to go to hell. You guys are
beginning to get my goat. I've a good mind to let you have a
taste of Sebastopol lead."

"How much did you get from the aristocrats, Comrade
Zadorojny?"

"I've got enough to pay for your funeral."

"The president of the Yalta Soviet will report your counter-revolutionary activities to Comrade Lenin. We'll teach

you not to monkey with the Government of the Working Class."

"Get the order of Comrade Lenin and the prisoners are yours. And don't you talk to me of the working class. I am an old Bolshevik. I belonged to the party in the days you were serving a jail sentence for theft."

"You'll regret these words, Comrade Zadorojny."

"Oh, shut up, and get off this highway."

The speaker of the Yalta Soviet, a young man wearing a leather coat and leather breeches, frequently attempted to harangue the Sebastopol machine gunners, whose faces he could not see but whose presence he felt somewhere on the top of the walls covered with ivy. He spoke to them of the historical necessity of beheading the counter-revolution, he appealed to their spirit of "proletarian fairness," and he mentioned the inevitability of gallows for all traitors. They remained silent. Once in a while they would hit him with a small stone or throw a butt of a cigarette at him.

As Zadorojny expressed it in his colorful way, every one of his boys would have liked to shoot a grand duke but not before the order was given by the Sebastopol Soviet. Zadorojny's idea of revolutionary discipline had been built on the supposition that the Bolshevik Government ruled over the Crimean Peninsula through the medium of the Sebastopol Soviet only, and that the Yalta Soviet consisted of chameleons who were passing as Communists.

Grand Duke Nicholas refused to understand why I permitted Zadorojny to engage me in lengthy conversations.

"Do not imagine," he said, "that you can bring this man to your way of thinking. One word from his masters and he'll shoot you with the greatest of pleasure."

Needless to say, I realized it as well as he did, but there was something singularly attractive about the roughness of our warden's manner and the clearness of his purpose. Anyway, I preferred his outspokenness to the hypocrisy of the Commissioner of the Provisional Government. Each night before going to bed I used to ask Zadorojny half-jokingly: "Well, any chance of our being shot in the next eight hours?" His promise "not to do anything final" unless a telegram arrived during the night from the north, gave me as much reassurance as possible under the circumstances.

He was obviously impressed by my confidence and often solicited my advice in the most secret matters. I helped him to supervise a new set of fortifications added to the line of machine guns, and in the editing of his daily report to the Sebastopol Soviet on the behavior of the imprisoned former grand dukes and their families.

At last he approached me on a subject of extraordinarily delicate nature.

"Say," he commenced awkwardly, "the boys in Sebastopol are afraid that the counter-revolutionary generals will send a submarine after you people."

"Now, Zadorojny, how could you be such a fool? After all the years you have served in the navy, don't you know that a submarine cannot possibly land here? Look at the rocks along the water front. Consider the tide and the depth of the bay. A submarine could land in Yalta or Sebastopol, but never here, in Ay-Todor."

"That's what I said to them, but what in hell do they know about a submarine? They are sending a couple of searchlights tonight, and the trouble is none of my boys can handle one. Would you help us out?"

I readily consented to do whatever I could to interfere with the mythical submarine that was supposed to carry us all to safety. My family was completely baffled by my comings and goings with Zadorojny. When the searchlights were properly installed we invited everybody to watch them in action. My wife thought that eventually Zadorojny would ask me to load the guns of the firing squad.

PRINCESS IRENE YOUSOUPOFF, THE ONLY DAUGHTER OF GRAND
DUKE ALEXANDER, IN 1930 IN PARIS.

GRAND DUKE ALEXANDER AS HE LOOKS TODAY.

✦✦

7

The absence of news constituted the greatest privation imposed upon us by our imprisonment. We grew accustomed to the scarcity of food. We laughed at the hundred per cent vegetarian recipe for preparing a "Wiener schnitzel" out of carrots and cabbage, but with all the sense of humor in the world we could not suppress the gloom spread by the reading of soviet newspapers. Long columns describing vociferous speeches made by Trotzky and Lenin failed to mention whether the Brest-Litovsk treaty was followed by a veritable cessation of hostilities, and the roundabout way used by the writers in their references to the events in the Southwest made us suspect that the soviets had encountered an enemy of mysterious identity in Kieff and Odessa. Zadorojny pleaded complete ignorance but the frequency with which he talked on the phone with Sebastopol suggested anxiety on his part.

The Yalta Soviet found a new argument in their correspondence with the Central Government. We were accused of hiding General Orloff, who had suppressed the revolutionary outburst in Esthonia in 1907, and a warrant arrived from Moscow authorizing a search under the supervision of our regular visitor, enemy of Zadorojny.

The truth was that we did have with us a former aide-de-camp of the Czar by the name of Orloff but he had nothing in common with General Orloff. Even the fiery Yalta speaker, considering our Orloff's age, agreed he couldn't have been a general in 1907. Nevertheless, he wanted to take him away for thorough identification by the Esthonian comrades.

"You'll do nothing of the kind," yelled Zadorojny, irritated by this intrusion. "The Moscow order mentions former General Orloff but it gives you no right to arrest former Prince Orloff. I wouldn't let you pull this trick on me. I know you. You'll shoot him outside and claim afterwards that he was General Orloff and that I tried to hide him. Get out of here!"

The young man in leather coat and breeches turned pale. "Please, Comrade Zadorojny," he begged in a trembling voice, "let me do it or something awful will happen to me. My boys are so sore at these continuous trips to Dulber that unless I produce a prisoner of some description they'll get nasty with me."

"That's your lookout," said Zadorojny sneeringly. "You've tried to ruin me and have dug a grave for yourself. Out you go."

He opened the heavy gates and nearly threw his enemy out.

Around midnight Zadorojny knocked on the door of the bedroom and called me outside. He spoke in harsh whispers:

"We are in a jam. I've got to think fast. These Yalta bandits did shoot him."

"Shoot whom? Orloff?"

"No, Orloff is in his bed. He is all right. They killed the talkative guy. Just as he said, got sore at him for coming back empty-handed and shot him on the way to Yalta. There's hell to pay. Sebastopol just rang up and told me to be prepared for a big attack. They are sending five trucks of men right away, but Yalta is nearer this place than Sebastopol. I am not afraid of machine guns, but suppose Yalta should send artillery? Don't go to bed, better stick around. If worst comes to worst you can reload the guns for the boys."

I could not suppress a smile. My wife was right.

"I know it sounds queer," agreed Zadorojny, "but the point is I've got to keep you alive till morning. If I succeed you'll be saved for keeps."

"What do you mean? Did the Government decide to release us?"

"Don't ask me any questions. Just stick around." He walked away rapidly, leaving me in a state of bewilderment.

I sat on the veranda. The April night was warm and the

strong odor of lilacs permeated the air. I knew that the odds were against us. The walls of Dulber would never be able to withstand an artillery bombardment. At best the Sebastopol reënforcements could arrive around four in the morning, while the slowest truck would cover the distance between Yalta and Dulber in slightly more than one hour.

My wife appeared in the doorway and asked what was the matter.

"Oh, nothing in particular. Zadorojny simply asked me to go and see about the searchlights. They have gone out of order again."

I jumped up thinking I heard the distant noise of a motor.

"Tell me the truth," she said. "I can see you are worried. What is it? Is it something about Nicky? Did you receive bad news from the north?"

I repeated word for word what Zadorojny had explained to me. She breathed a sigh of relief. She did not believe any harm would come to us that night. She sensed the approaching end of our sufferings. I did not contradict her. I admired her faith and her courage.

Time dragged on. The clock in the dining-room struck one. Zadorojny passed by the veranda and said they could be expected now any minute.

"I am sorry," remarked my wife, "they have taken mother's Bible. I would have liked to open its pages at random, as we used to do in our childhood, and read the passage fate would put under our finger."

I went to the library and brought her a pocket edition of the Bible overlooked by last summer's raiders. She opened it and I lit a match. It happened to be verse 28, chapter 2, of Revelation: "And I will give him the morning star."

"You see," my wife said. "Everything will be all right."

Her confidence was transmitted to me. I fell asleep in the chair. When I opened my eyes again I saw Zadorojny. He was shaking me by the shoulder. A broad smile played on his face.

"What time is it, Zadorojny? I must have slept a few minutes."

"A few minutes?" He laughed boisterously. "You mean three hours. It's four o'clock. The Sebastopol trucks just rolled in, guns and everything."

"How about Yalta?"

"I can't make it out. They should have been here long ago. Unless . . ."

"Unless what?"

He shook his head and went back to the gates.

At six o'clock the telephone rang. I heard Zadorojny's loud voice repeating excitedly: "Yes, yes, yes. I shall do just as you want me to."

Once more he came on the veranda. For the first time in all these five months I saw him in a state of panic.

"Your Imperial Highness," said he, lowering his eyes, "the German general will be here in an hour."

"The German general? You are insane, Zadorojny. What has happened to you?"

"Nothing has happened to me as yet," he answered, "but it looks like something may happen, unless you protect me."

"How can I protect you? I am a prisoner."

"Not any more. The Germans occupied Yalta two hours ago. They just telephoned threatening to hang me if any harm should befall you within the next hour."

My wife gave him a sharp glance. She thought the man had lost his mind.

"Now, come, come, Zadorojny. Don't talk such nonsense. The Germans are more than a thousand miles away from the Crimea."

"Well, I succeeded in keeping at least this secret from you, Your Imperial Highness. The Germans occupied Kieff last month and since then have marched from twenty to thirty miles daily. But will you please remember, Your Imperial Highness, that I never caused you any unnecessary suffering. I had to obey orders."

It was too pathetic for words to see this giant tremble at the thought of the approaching Germans and hear him address me by my full title.

"Don't you worry, Zadorojny," I said, patting him on the shoulder, "you were awfully good to us. I have nothing against you."

"But how about Grand Dukes Nicholas and Peter?"

We both laughed and my wife reassured Zadorojny that she would see to it that neither one of the elder grand dukes made a complaint against our former warden.

I shall never forget the stupefaction of the German general, who arrived at seven o'clock sharp, when I asked him to leave the detail of sailors headed by Zadorojny on guard at Ay-Todor and Dulber. For a moment he felt sure that the long imprisonment had affected my brain. "Aber dass ist ganz unmöglich," he exclaimed with all the irritation of a Prussian officer confronted by an illogical proposition. Did I realize that Kaiser Wilhelm, and my nephew, the Crown Prince of Germany, would never forgive him should he permit those "bloody murderers" to remain at large and in close proximity to the relatives of His Imperial Majesty?

I had to swear I would notify his masters in writing of my willingness to assume full responsibility for such a "verrückte Idee." Even then he muttered under his breath something about "diese fantastische Russen."

8

In accordance with the terms of the Armistice the Germans were to evacuate the Crimean Peninsula and all other parts of the former Russian Empire occupied by them during the spring of 1918.

The British Fleet arrived at Sebastopol and its commander-in-chief, Admiral Calthorpe, conveyed to us the offer of His Britannic Majesty to put a ship at our disposal for our voyage to England. My mother-in-law thanked her royal nephew for this kind attention but was unwilling to leave the Crimea, unless permitted to take along several scores of friends who figured in the so-called "black lists" of the Bolsheviks. King George consented to it with his usual thoughtfulness, and everybody began to make preparations for the voyage.

Extremely anxious to see the heads of the Allied Governments, then gathered in Paris, in order to present to them a report on the situation in Russia, I wrote a letter to Admiral Calthorpe and asked him to arrange for my departure ahead of our party, which was to sail in the beginning of March, 1919. He sent a destroyer to Yalta to bring me to Sebastopol, and it had been agreed that I would leave the very same night aboard H.M.S. *Forsythe*.

It was odd to see the city of Sebastopol gayly bedecked with American, English, French and Italian flags. My eyes searched in vain for a Russian flag or a Russian battleship. Looking at the branches of holly decorating my cabin, I suddenly realized that the Russian December 11 corresponds to the European and American Christmas Eve. It would have been of decidedly bad taste to spoil the gayety of my hosts with a display of my sorrow, so I asked to be excused from being present at dinner and went on deck.

We were gathering speed and the lights of the shore were growing dimmer. Turning to the open sea I caught sight of the Ay-Todor lighthouse. It was built on the land cultivated by my parents and myself for the past forty-five years. We planted its gardens and worked in its vineyards. My mother took pride in its flowers and fruits. We boys had to protect our shirts with a napkin when eating its enormous juicy pears. It was strange that, having forgotten so many faces and events, I should have retained the memory of the aroma and sweetness of those pears. It was stranger still that after fifty years spent in unsuccessful efforts to escape from the life of a grand duke, I should win freedom aboard a British battleship.

CHAPTER NINETEEN

THE AFTERMATH

I

PARIS smelled of winter, roast chestnuts and burning charcoal.

A blind musician stood in front of the Café de la Paix singing in a tremolo voice the gay verses of "Madelon of the Victory."

> Oh, Madelon, remplis les verres,
> Et chante avec les poilus,
> Nous avons gagné la guerre,
> Hein, crois-tu qu'on les a eus? *

The last line, imitating in its sharp staccato the footbeats of the marching soldiers, called for an accompaniment of fists hitting the marble tables, but the horizon-blue French and the khaki-clad English and Americans sat motionless. The Armistice was two months old, and they all felt poorer for the realization of the difficulties surrounding the return to the life that had ceased to exist on August 1, 1914. They knew they were cheated out of their youth and wanted to forget everything reminding of the war.

I went to Versailles carrying my report on the situation in Russia, which I had prepared in the course of my voyage to France on board H.M.S. *Forsythe.* I was anxious to talk to Georges Clemenceau before the opening of the Peace Conference, although the ranking representatives of the Allied powers whom I visited in Constantinople and Rome displayed

* Hey, Madelon, refill the glasses
  And with the soldiers sing a song,
  For we have won the war at last,
  We licked them good, come, sing a song.

but mild interest in the actions of Lenin, Trotzky and other possessors of equally strange names.

"Stop worrying, Your Imperial Highness," said a French general, proud of his victories in the Near East, "we are about to land a division or two in Odessa with strict orders to march straight to Moscow. Very soon you shall be living again in your palace in St. Petersburg."

I thanked the honorable gentleman for his kind words, not wishing to undertake single-handed the gigantic task of exterminating the ignorance of official Europe. After all, he could not have had a very high opinion of the leaders of a régime that was Don-Quixotic enough to sacrifice millions of Russians for the sake of assuring the military ascendancy of France.

I did hope for somewhat better results with Clemenceau. The well-known cynicism of the old man seemed to help him considerably in discerning real facts through the thick maze of voluminous eloquence and asinine theories. I could not believe for a second that he would fail to realize the world-wide proportions of the Bolshevist danger.

The Peace Conference was to open in a few days. The corridors of the historical Palace of the French kings were already humming with rumors and intrigues. The Rumanians, the Czechoslovaks, the Portuguese, and the other disputable participants of the victory were tearing apart the dead bodies of the three fallen empires. The famous words of Bismarck came to my mind: "The Rumanians are not a nation, they are a profession."

Nobody cared to remember that the former Russian Empire had fought on the side of the Allies; numerous Russian provinces were being allotted in advance to Rumania, and to the newly created states of Poland, Finland, Esthonia, Latvia, Lithuania, Georgia and Azerbaijan, represented in Versailles by former Russian small-town lawyers now posing as ambassadors extraordinary.

The plenipotentiaries of the twenty-seven nations gathered

in Versailles swore by the name of President Wilson, but in reality the whole show was directed by the so-called Big Four —the French, the British, the Italians and the Japanese. Looking at the familiar faces of their delegates I understood that the cannon of the Armistice signified the revival of the forces of blind selfishness: the conditions of the Eternal Peace were to be worked out by the very same statesmen who had caused the war! The joke seemed too gruesome even for the old school of diplomats, but there, leaning against a column, shaking hands and coining witticisms, stood Arthur Balfour who had dedicated many years of his life to the business of fostering quarrels between Berlin and London.

"Here I am," said his whimsical smile, "ready to plant my feet under the table of the Peace Conference in company with a bunch of old foxes who did their damnedest to promote the slaughter. All great editorial writers to the contrary, the four years of war failed to change the cast of characters of our little drama. Kaiser Wilhelm may be imprisoned in Doorn but his spirit is marching on."

Aside from the American delegation, which consisted of inexperienced men of sufficient innocence and which was largely inspired by that Sphinx Without a Mystery, Colonel House, every other Versailles plenipotentiary could have been easily indicted as an accessory to the Crime of 1914.

None of the omniscient newspaper correspondents saw fit to look up the past records of the peacemakers. It fell to the lot of Colonel T. E. Lawrence to mutter well-chosen curses at the sight of the glorified diplomats. Melodramatic in his flowing white robes of a Bedouin warrior, the youthful hero of Arabia realized from the very first day of the Conference that the Big Four would make it a point to break the promises given by him to the Chiefs of the Desert in 1915-1916, in exchange for their very necessary aid against the Turks. A breathing impersonation of the Eternal Protest, poor Lawrence walked through the dainty gardens of Versailles, viewing with hatred the fine aristocratic features and the baggy clothes of Arthur Balfour. I sympathized with him. We both spoke of the past to people who recognized only the present. We both came to remind of the "services rendered" to statesmen who were never known to keep their obligations. We both tried to appeal to the honor of those for whom "honor" meant just another word to be found in the dictionary under the letter "H."

2

"Monsieur le Président would very much like to see you and to talk to you," said the secretary of Georges Clemenceau, "but he is so crowded with work at the present moment that he is obliged to ask me to receive you on his behalf."

In the original French this short speech sounded perfect. Thinking of it now I appreciate the fine choice of words and the immaculate phrasing. In the month of January, 1919, it meant that the Prime Minister of France and the Chairman of the Peace Conference, Georges Clemenceau, did not want to be bothered with Russia, inasmuch as being fair with the Russians would have interfered with his plans of rewarding the Poles and the Rumanians.

"What are Monsieur Clemenceau's intentions toward the former ally of France?" I asked, trying to control my temper.

The young man smiled pleasantly. He welcomed this opportunity of playing the head of the French Government. He started to talk with great gusto. He talked for quite a while. I never interrupted him. I sat quietly thinking of something else, something that happened in 1902, during the visit to St. Petersburg of Mr. Loubet, then President of the French Republic. Mr. Loubet talked just as well as this young impersonator of Georges Clemenceau, although the subject of his speech delivered in the presence of the Czar of Russia was slightly different. I was now being told why France could not mingle in the affairs of Eastern Europe, while Nicholas II was at that time given a solemn promise that "no adverse winds would ever be able to extinguish the flame of the traditional Franco-Russian friendship." The official spokesman of victorious France suggested my taking a comfortable chair and smoking to my heart's delight, while Mr. Loubet went as far as laying an exquisite sword of gold and ivory on the grave of Emperor Alexander III, with the words "Fœderis Memor" engraved on its bejeweled hilt.

"Fœderis Memor!" "I shall always remember our Alliance."

The passing of seventeen years does things to the best of Latin expressions. In 1902 the President of the French Republic remembered his country's debt of gratitude to the originator of the Franco-Russian Alliance. In 1919 the Prime Minister of France asked his secretary to explain to a cousin of that self-same Emperor Alexander III that he was entirely too busy to reminisce over the treaties signed by his predecessors. But then, of course, in 1902 the Russian Government was still paying the annual interest on the Russian bonds held by French investors, and the Russian Army was still willing to shed blood for the French cause.

"So you see," concluded the secretary of Georges Clemenceau, "circumstances alter cases. Had it not been for the unfortunate events in Russia, we would naturally be only too anxious to live up to the letter of our agreement."

"Naturally," said I.

"But taking things as they are now, France has to think of the future. We owe it to our children to foresee the possibility of Germany seeking revenge. Hence we simply must create a chain of states on the eastern border of Germany that would be strong enough to assume the duties formerly fulfilled by the Russian Empire."

"With all of it, I am still in the dark as to what your Government intends to do against Bolshevism."

"Oh, that is simple," the young diplomat shrugged his shoulders. "Bolshevism, Your Imperial Highness, is the malady of the defeated nations only. Mr. Clemenceau has given

careful thought to the Russian problem. He believes it
would be efficient to declare a blockade against the Soviet
Government."

"To declare a what?"

"A blockade, a sanitary cordon, as Mr. Clemenceau calls
it. Not unlike that which paralyzed Germany in time of
war. The Soviet Government won't be able to buy or sell
goods. A sort of gigantic fence will be erected around Russia. In a few months the Bolsheviks will be obliged to surrender and permit the reëstablishment of a legitimate Government."

"Is your chief ready to assume responsibility for the untold
sufferings his method is bound to cause the innocent Russian
people? Does he realize that millions of children will be facing starvation?"

The young man made a grimace:

"The Russian people, Your Imperial Highness, will be thus
given a powerful impetus for an uprising."

"You are very much mistaken, sir. I am certain that Mr.
Clemenceau's sanitary cordon will provide the Bolsheviks
with a most efficient weapon of propaganda. A year of
blockade will succeed in consolidating the large masses of the
Russian population around the Moscow régime. It could not
happen otherwise. Put yourself in the position of the average Russian, who knows nothing of high politics but who dis-
covers that France is attempting to cause famine in his country. With all due respect to the achievements of Mr.
Clemenceau, I do consider this particular idea of his both
ludicrous and extremely dangerous."

"What would you suggest?"

"The same thing that I suggested to the French high command in the Near East. No bloodshed. No blockade. Do
what the Germans succeeded in doing last summer in Southwest Russia. Send an army that would proclaim in no uncertain terms that it is bringing peace, order and the safe-
guard for a free election."

THE AFTERMATH

"Our Government cannot afford to risk the lives of French soldiers, now that the Armistice has been signed."

I looked at him sharply. I wished Georges Clemenceau were seated in his place. I would have liked to ask him whether he had forgotten the battle of Tannenberg in August, 1914, when 150,000 Russian soldiers were deliberately thrown into the trap prepared for them by Ludendorff in East Prussia, so as to relieve the pressure of the German armies against Paris. I would have likewise recalled to him that the real name of the victor of the Marne was not Joffre but Samsonoff—that hapless martyr of Tannenberg who knew in advance of the doom awaiting him and his troops. But all that would have dealt with the past, whereas nobody had accused the diplomats as yet of letting the past interfere with their future. I got up and left.

So much for Monsieur Clemenceau and the French. There remained the British, the Americans, the Italians and the Japanese.

Signor Orlando, the very amiable Prime Minister of Italy, cheerfully enough confessed his inability to grasp the Russian problem. He would have liked to see his compatriots reinstated in their properties taken away by the Bolsheviks, which did not mean, however, his willingness to send Italian soldiers to accomplish that task. The internal political situation in Italy grew from bad to worse: another six months of war would have brought the future "ideal state" of Mussolini to a revolution patterned after the Russian style.

The Japanese were willing to coöperate at the price of important territorial concessions in Manchuria and Asiatic Russia. Their demands aroused the ire of the American delegation. President Wilson was, no doubt, a great statesman and a farsighted American in his strenuous opposition to the further expansion of the Japanese Empire, but unfortunately he remained just a Princeton theoretician so far as the Russian crisis was concerned. On February 14, 1919, Mr. Winston Churchill made a passionate speech in the secret conference

321

of the Versailles mighty begging the president to decide upon immediate measures against the Bolsheviks. Monsieur Clemenceau sank back in his chair and closed his eyes, as was his habit whenever the conversation turned toward subjects not pertaining to France. Signor Orlando looked at Churchill curiously: not understanding a word of English he just wondered at Winston's excitement. The wise old Japanese smiled noncommittally and gave Wilson a sharp glance.

"I am awfully sorry," said the President, getting up and resting his elbow on Clemenceau's chair, "but I am leaving tonight for America. I must have sufficient time to study Mr. Churchill's proposition. Russia is a problem to which I do not pretend to know the solution."

It is a worthwhile fact to record that at the time of the Peace Conference Mr. Winston Churchill was the only European statesman who realized the great danger of Bolshevism. His old instinct of a "head-hunter" and his ever vigilant imagination of a soldier of fortune made him suggest measures that would have insured swiftness and dispatch. The British Empire of today would have been relieved of worry over the "Five-Year Plan" if the ultimate decision of the Russian question had rested with flamboyant Winston. As it was, the British delegation took its orders from David Lloyd George and Arthur Balfour. The former knew nothing of Russia; the latter possessed all the typical characteristics of a little Englander. Lloyd George spoke at length of the successes presumably scored by the "White Russian General Kharkoff," whereas Kharkoff was and is the name of a large industrial city situated in the south of Russia! He left the whole thing to Arthur Balfour, who summed up the British point of view in the following manner:

"We would certainly refuse," declared that parliamentarian noted for his brilliant talents and a profound understanding of foreign politics, "to see our forces, after more than four years of strenuous fighting, dissipated over the

****

huge expanse of Russia in order to carry the political reforms in a state which is no longer a belligerent ally."

Further efforts of mine would have been decidedly futile. If the greatest thinker of modern England considered the fight against the soviets as an attempt to "carry political re- forms" in an alien country, what could I expect from one of lesser magnitude?

3

The early spring of 1919 saw the launching of a series of costly Allied adventures in Russia that helped install the Bol- sheviks on the pedestal of champions of Russian national in- dependence.

At that time there were three different White armies in Russia, which could have defeated the soviets if given suffi- cient assistance by England and France.

General Denikin—the former commander-in-chief of the Russian armies in 1917—succeeded in gaining a foothold in the Northern Caucasus where he counted on the support of the Cossacks of the provinces of Don, Kuban and Terek.

Admiral Kolchak—the former commander-in-chief of the Black Sea Fleet—had chosen Siberia for his anti-red activities, thinking that the proximity of Japan would assure him an ample supply of munitions.

General Youdenich—the former commander of the Cau- casian Army—stood an excellent chance of capturing St. Petersburg: in fact, in the late summer of 1919 his cavalry patrols approached within ten miles of the national capital.

Thus the Bolsheviks were threatened in the northwest, the southeast and the far east of the empire. The Red Army was still in its infancy, and even Trotzky himself was in- clined to question its fighting abilities. It is safe to assume that the appearance of a thousand heavy guns and several hundreds of tanks on any one of the three fronts would have spared the world all sorts of future troubles. The numerous Allied military experts, who went to inspect the armies of

Denikin, Kolchak and Youdenich, were unanimous in their conclusions. "It is just a question of letting these people have an adequate amount of munitions," they said to Clemenceau and Lloyd George on their return to Paris.

And then a strange thing happened. Instead of following the counsel of their own advisers, the heads of the Allied Powers worked out a policy that turned the sympathies of the majority of the former Russian officers and soldiers toward Trotzky.

The British, coming from Persia, landed in the port of Baku and organized the independent state of Azerbaijan in that fabulously wealthy oil district of Russia. The port of Batum on the Black Sea received the status of "Free City" placed under a British protectorate, with its civil governor, a former Manchester oil broker, supervising the shipping of oil and raw materials to England.

The meek Italians appeared in Tiflis and assisted in the formation of the independent state of Georgia in the southern part of Caucasus famous for its manganese mines.

The French occupied the port of Odessa, the most important center of the Russian export trade, and lent a willing ear to the propositions of the same leaders of the "independent Ukraine" who but a year ago were fulfilling the duties of General Ludendorff's undercover agents. The French forces comprised several battleships manned by their own marines and two divisions of Greek infantry. They treated the Russian civilian population in the manner of conquerors, and there was a general panic when, after the passing of a few weeks, the outbreak of revolt aboard the French battleships and the ignominious defeat dealt to the Greeks by a small band of Bolshevik guerillas, caused the French high command to order the evacuation.

About that time a small contingent of Americans and Japanese landed in Vladivostok on the Pacific Ocean, and the British Fleet dropped anchor in the Baltic port of Reval, proclaiming the birth of the two independent states of Latvia

THE DOWAGER-EMPRESS MARIE OF RUSSIA, MOTHER-IN-LAW OF
GRAND DUKE ALEXANDER, IN 1924 IN DENMARK.

THE FOURTH GENERATION: IRENE, NIKITA AND MICHAEL, THE THREE GRAND-CHILDREN OF GRAND DUKE ALEXANDER, IN PARIS IN 1929.

and Esthonia in the rear of the White Army of General Youdenich.

All in all, nine independent states were organized by the Allied Powers in the spring of 1919 on the territory of the former Russian Empire, while the Rumanians occupied the Russian province of Bessarabia long in advance of the final decision of the Peace Conference.

The Russians were bewildered. The attitude of the Allies impressed them most unfavorably, particularly because the newly organized independent states kept aloof from the White armies, going so far as to forbid the transportation of anti-Bolshevik volunteers across their borders and jailing the agents of Denikin and Youdenich.

"The Allies are obviously anxious to turn Russia into a lucrative domain of the British interests," remarked Trotzky in one of his proclamations to the Red Army, and for once in his life he was not far from the truth. Whether prompted by Sir Henry Deterding, the powerful chairman of the Royal-Dutch-Shell oil combine, or merely obeying the classical dictates of the old Disraeli program, the British Foreign Office displayed a bold desire to deal a death-blow to the Russian Empire through the medium of distributing the wealthiest Russian provinces among the Allies and their hirelings. When the necessary munitions—guns, tanks and airplanes—were finally ready for shipment, they were sent to Poland, and the army of Pilsudsky invaded Russia, taking the ancient Russian cities of Kieff and Smolensk. The great statesmen of Paris and London must have been thrilled by their own cleverness: with one stone they expected to kill both the Bolsheviks and the possibility of Russia staging a comeback.

The position of the anti-Bolshevik leaders had become impossible. There they were, pretending not to understand the tricks of the Allies and preaching the Holy War against the soviets among their barefooted volunteers, while Lenin stood on guard over the Russian national interests, vehemently protesting against the disintegration of the Czar's Empire in his daily radio messages to the Proletarians of the World!

General Brussiloff, the celebrated hero of the Russian offensive in 1916, expressed the thoughts of thousands of Russian officers when, upon joining the Bolsheviks, he proclaimed in tones of unquestionable sincerity: "When our ancient enemies, the Poles, are besieging the Russian fortresses with the help of the nations whom we saved from certain defeat in the beginning of the war, then with all my blood I am wishing victory to the Red Army. So help me God."

The psychological effect of Brussiloff's declaration was worth more than a dozen army corps to the Soviet Government. "What are we fighting for?" asked the tired White officers and soldiers who had waited patiently for munitions and clothes promised by the Allies. "Are we risking our lives just to help England corner the Russian oil? Are we going to be hanged by the Bolsheviks just to assure the triumph of that arrogant Pole Pilsudsky who fought on the side of the Austrians during the war? In the name of what justice are the Allies glorifying their former enemies and neglecting their former friends? Where are those tanks and airplanes we were to get more than a year ago?"

Nothing proves the narrow selfishness of the Allies better than the so-called "conditions on which France would consider assisting the White Armies" that were presented by the head of the French Mission in the South of Russia, Captain Fouquet, to General Krassnoff, then the chief of the anti-red Cossacks of the Don. A former Guardsman and a man of brilliant talents, Krassnoff liberated the Province of the Don from the Bolsheviks and was preparing to launch an anti-red offensive on a large front. Like all the other White generals, he was lacking munitions. He wrote several letters to Marshal Franchet-d'Esprey, the Commander-in-Chief of the Allied Forces in the Near East. Finally, on January 27, 1919, Captain Fouquet arrived at the capital of the Don Province bringing a long document to be signed by General Krassnoff.

THE AFTERMATH

"The Cossacks of the Don," said the most important clause of this remarkable paper, "do hereby pledge all their personal properties, as a guarantee that the claims of the French citizens, who have suffered heavy material losses in consequence of the absence of order in Russia, would be satisfied to the full extent. The Cossacks of the Don do hereby undertake to reimburse the French citizens who have suffered bodily harm at the hands of the Bolsheviks, and to pay an adequate indemnity to the families of those who were killed by the Bolsheviks. The Cossacks of the Don likewise promise to consider the claims of those enterprises, controlled by French capital, which were obliged to shut down their plants on account of the general chaos in the country. The last clause applies not only to the enterprises incapacitated by the revolution but as well to those forced to accept the arbitrarily low Government prices during the war of 1914-1917. It is understood that the French owners and the French stockholders of all such enterprises should receive as indemnity the aggregate amount of the dividends and profits not collected by them since August 1, 1914, the said dividends and profits to be based on the average earnings of the pre-war years. A 5 per cent compound interest is to be added to the said dividends, and profits for the time elapsed between August 1, 1914, and the date of the future settlement. A special commission consisting of the representatives of the French owners and stockholders and presided over by the French consul-general will be formed to consider all possible claims of the French citizens."

In other words, the Cossacks of the Province of the Don, who fought the Germans in 1914-1917 and the Bolsheviks in 1917-1919, were expected to repay the damages caused to the French by the self-same Germans and Bolsheviks!

"Is that all you want?" asked General Krassnoff, hardly able to suppress his indignation.

"That is all we want," confirmed Captain Fouquet, "but, my dear friend, let me tell you something, so as to avoid waste

327

of time. Unless you sign this document without any changes whatsoever ('tel quel'), not a single French soldier will embark for Russia and not a piece of Allied ammunition will be given to the White Armies. Beggars can't be choosers, my dear friend, so let us have it over with at once."

"Shut up," exclaimed General Krassnoff. "I shall deem it my duty to let my Cossacks know of the terms on which their great and noble ally is willing to help them. I have the honor of bidding you good afternoon, Captain Fouquet. You shall not get your pound of flesh, if I am to continue to command the Cossacks of the Don."

4

"France has committed the greatest blunder in its history," wrote in November, 1920, the famous French war correspondent, Charles Rivet who had accompanied the White Armies both during their march toward Moscow and in the course of their retreat. "We did not understand that helping the White Armies would have amounted to taking an insurance policy against a menace which is capable of destroying the whole civilized world. We were asked to pay a rather reasonable premium on that policy, considering the size and the imminence of the danger: just a few thousands of guns, and a shipment or two of military equipment that we had taken away from the Germans and that we ourselves could not possibly have used for any practical purpose. We are so wise and so prudent in all small matters, but we showed ourselves a bunch of fatheads in handling the Russian problem. We insure our lives; we insure our houses; we insure our workers against accidents and unemployment, but we refused to insure our children and grandchildren against the red leprosy! The generations of Frenchmen to come shall condemn the criminal negligence of our present leaders."

This fiery valedictory appeared in the Parisian newspaper *Le Temps*, a few days after the hungry and frozen army of

THE AFTERMATH

General Wrangel had left the Crimean Peninsula and sailed for Constantinople, thus bringing to an end the anti-Bolshevik movement in Russia. Put in concentration camps in Gallipoli, where the war prisoners were kept by the Turks in 1914-1918, the officers and soldiers of Wrangel had been given plenty of time to meditate on the eternal subject of human ingratitude. The Europe that had sent these stern-faced boys, unarmed and unclothed, against the regiments of Trotzky, refused to accept them now when they were defeated. They remained in the filthy Turkish camps for three long years, before the League of Nations extended to them a choice between joining the French Foreign Legion or settling on farms in the Balkan countries. And yet they had to consider themselves lucky, for the Allies had reserved a much harsher treatment for Admiral Kolchak, the commander-in-chief of the White Siberian Armies, who was delivered into the hands of the Bolsheviks by General Janin, the head of the French Military Mission in the Orient.

Kolchak's ordeal constitutes the most tragic page in the history of the Russian Revolution. The former admiral of the Imperial Black Sea Fleet, decorated for bravery and universally recognized as one of the outstanding heroes of the Great War, he had accepted in 1918 the offer of the Allied Governments to organize a regular army out of former Austrian soldiers of Czechoslovakian descent, who were taken prisoners by the Russians and kept in Siberia. Marshal Foch had hoped that Kolchak would succeed in restoring the anti-German front in the Far East of Russia. The Armistice naturally caused the Allies to lose all interest in the fate of their Siberian emissary, although in the meanwhile he commenced a strenuous drive against the Bolsheviks. Receiving no news from Paris and using every device to keep Czechoslovaks from quitting, Kolchak bombarded Winston Churchill with cables. He was guaranteeing to take Moscow if supplied with tanks, airplanes and clothes suitable for the Siberian climate. The matter was taken "under advisement" by Clemenceau, Lloyd George and Balfour, and on May 26, 1919, seven months after the receipt of the first report from Kolchak, the Supreme Council of Versailles drafted a long contract to be signed by the heartbroken admiral in the name of the "future government of Russia." Its text followed closely the contents of the paper presented by Captain Fouquet to General Krassnoff. This time the demand of heavy financial indemnities to be paid by Russia was accompanied by a clause sanctioning the existence of the "independent states" so generously created by the Allies in the four corners of the fallen empire.

Admiral Kolchak thought of his rapidly melting army and decided to sign the Versailles contract. He was immediately recognized by England, France and Japan as the Supreme Ruler of Russia, but the promised tanks and the overcoats never arrived! The Bolshevik cavalry continued to chase his starving Siberian volunteers across the endless Asiatic plains toward the city of Irkutsk.

The Czechoslovaks, some eighty thousand strong, flatly refused to fight. They wanted to go home to Czechoslovakia, and the soviets were willing to let them reach the port of Vladivostok on the Pacific Ocean and embark for Europe peacefully, provided Admiral Kolchak was delivered into the hands of the red sympathizers in Irkutsk. Needless to explain, these negotiations, conducted by the French General Janin, had been kept secret from the unsuspecting Supreme Ruler of Russia. Janin had repeatedly given him "the word of honor of a soldier" that no matter what happened he would be assisted in his flight to Vladivostok and Japan.

On the morning of January 14, 1920, two heavily laden trains crept into the suburbs of Irkutsk: the admiral was traveling in one of them, protected by the "storm battalion" of Czechoslovaks picked by Janin for their bravery; 650 million gold roubles (around 350 million dollars) belonging to the Russian Treasury and captured by the army of Kolchak in the city of Kazan, were being transported in the other.

The commander of the "storm battalion" entered the car occupied by Kolchak unannounced.

"I have received an important telegram from General Janin, admiral," he said dryly.

"What is it?" asked Kolchak, continuing to study the map. "Are you bringing me good news?"

"To the contrary, admiral, I am being ordered by General Janin to arrest you and transmit you to the local powers in Irkutsk."

Kolchak looked at his aide-de-camp Malinovsky, the sole survivor of the tragedy who remembered this gruesome scene in its minutest details. They both understood the sinister meaning of the words—"the local powers in Irkutsk."

"Well," said the admiral quietly, "this constitutes, I suppose, the most appalling act of international treachery. General Janin only yesterday gave me the guarantee of his Government for an unhindered passage to the East. Who is going to get the six hundred fifty million gold roubles?"

The Czechoslovak blushed:

"We shall surrender the money to the Soviet Government. Such are the orders of General Janin."

Kolchak smiled. He knew it was a lie. He shook hands with the officers of his staff and went out to face the waiting soldiers.

General Janin, the gentlemen of the foreign missions, and the courageous Czechoslovaks proceeded on their way east. Admiral Kolchak was put in jail in Irkutsk and shot three weeks later, on February 7, 1920.

The soldiers of the firing squad trembled on seeing his erect figure and Napoleonic profile outlined against the wall of the prison's back yard. Kolchak opened his massive gold cigarette-case decorated with diamonds—the Czar's gift to him in recognition of the naval victories in 1916—and counted the cigarettes.

"Just enough for every one of us," he remarked casually, "but I wish you men were a bit steadier. You have shot many other good Russians, so why tremble? Who wants my cigarette-case? I shall have no pockets in my shroud."

The Allied Governments appointed a special commission to investigate the actions of General Janin. They did not go far, however, as Janin met all queries with the same extremely uncomfortable phrase: "Je suis obligé de repeter, messieurs, que pour Sa Majesté Nicholas II on a fait moins de ceremonies." ("I am obliged to state once more, gentlemen, that much less fuss was made over His Majesty Nicholas II.") This was to the point: the Allied Governments had shown, indeed, still smaller concern over the fate of Czar Nicholas II.

Until this day, the participants of the Siberian epic, the Bolsheviks as well as their adversaries, are trying to ascertain the identity of the persons who helped themselves to a portion of the six hundred fifty million gold roubles of Kolchak. The soviet rulers claim to have been cheated out of some ninety millions. Winston Churchill believes that a mysterious deposit was made in one of the San Francisco banks during the summer of 1920 by a group of individuals who spoke English with a strong foreign accent. Several French experts entertain similar doubts as to the origin of the Russian gold that appeared in Prague, the capital of Czechoslovakia. In any event, all parties agree that the thirty pieces of silver were paid in gold.

5

All of this happened thousands of miles away from Paris, where at the age of fifty-two I had become an immigrant, a man without a country, a "former Grand Duke of Russia." Not only could I not have done anything to help the armies of Denikin and Kolchak, but a public display of my sympathies would have hurt their cause by laying it open to the attacks of the French Socialists alarmed at the presence of "so many Romanoffs" in Paris. In reality, but a minority of the members of the Russian imperial family had succeeded in escaping the Bolsheviks. Outside of our "Crimean party" —consisting of my mother-in-law, the Dowager-Empress Marie, my sister-in-law, Grand Duchess Olga, my wife, Grand Duchess Xenia, my cousin, Grand Duke Nicholas, my cousin, Grand Duke Peter, my six sons and one daughter— only four other grand dukes and two grand duchesses were fortunate enough to count themselves among the living.

Grand Duke Cyril—the legitimate successor to the throne of Russia and eldest son of my cousin Vladimir—had, perhaps, the most exciting story of all to tell: he crossed the frozen Gulf of Finland on foot, carrying his pregnant wife, Grand Duchess Victoria (who is a sister of Queen Marie of Rumania), and being hotly pursued by Bolshevik patrols.

His two brothers, Grand Duke Boris and Grand Duke Andrew, owed their lives to one of those amazing coincidences which, if described by fiction writers, would be sure to cause sophisticated readers to sneer incredulously. The Bolshevik commander entrusted with their execution happened to be a former struggling artist who had spent most of his life in Paris trying in vain to find purchasers for his paintings. A year before the war, Grand Duke Boris ran across an exhibit of very artistically painted cushions, while strolling in the Latin Quarter. He fancied their originality. He bought quite a few of them. That was all. The Bolshevik commander could not see himself shooting the man who had appreciated his art! He put Grand Duke Boris and Grand Duke Andrew in a car bearing the insignia of the Communist party and brought them into the zone occupied by the White Army.

My nephew Grand Duke Dimitry would be dead today had it not been for the part taken by him in the assassination of Rasputin. Exiled by the Czar to Persia, he was able to join the British Expeditionary Corps operating in Mesopotamia. His sister, Grand Duchess Marie (the author of *The Education of a Princess*), had married a commoner, Prince Sergei Poutiatin, during the revolution, and the Bolshevik patrol, not versed in the social goings-on, failed to discover a grand duchess in the possessor of a passport issued in the name of Marie Poutiatin.

All other members of the Russian imperial family were shot by the orders of the Soviet Government during the summer of 1918 and the winter of 1918-1919.

My brothers, Grand Duke Nicholas Michailovich and Grand Duke George Michailovich, met their doom in St. Petersburg in the Fortress of Peter and Paul, where all the Russian Czars had been buried since the reign of Peter the Great. The Bolshevik writer Maxim Gorky pleaded with Lenin for the life of Nicholas Michailovich, who was highly respected even in Bolshevik circles for his valuable historical researches and for his well-known liberalism.

"The Revolution does not need historians," answered the head of the Soviet Government and signed the death warrant.

Grand Duke Paul—father of Grand Duchess Marie—and Grand Duke Dimitry Constantinovich were shot together with my two brothers on the morning of January 18, 1919. The warden of the jail, a certain Gordienko, who used to receive valuable presents from the Czar each Christmas, commanded the firing squad. According to the soviet newspapers, Nicholas Michailovich kept his favorite Persian cat in his lap till the very last moment. Dimitry Constantinovich, a fanatically religious man, prayed aloud for the salvation of the souls of his executioners.

My third brother, Grand Duke Sergei Michailovich, was killed several months later, together with Grand Duchess Elizabeth (elder sister of the Czarina), three young sons of Grand Duke Constantin, and Prince Paley, the morganatic son of Grand Duke Paul and a half-brother of Grand Duchess Marie. All six of them were thrown alive into the pit of a coal mine situated near the town of Alapaevsk in

Siberia. Their bodies, when found by the army of Admiral Kolchak, showed that they had died in excruciating pains. They were murdered on July 18, 1918, that is to say, two days after the assassination of the Czar, the Czarina, and their five children in the town of Ekaterinburg in Siberia.

The exact date of the execution of the Czar's younger brother, Grand Duke Michael Alexandrovich, was never established. Taken from his house in the city of Perm together with his English secretary, Mr. Johnson, on a July night of 1918 by five strangers, who pretended to be the rescuers sent by Admiral Kolchak, he probably was killed in the woods nearby. His morganatic wife, Countess Brassova, arrived in London in 1919 still refusing to believe that her husband was dead. But for that matter, neither did the Dowager-Empress Marie ever trust the soviet commiqué describing the burning of the bodies of the Czar and his family. She died expecting to receive, sooner or later, the news of the miraculous escape of her poor Nicky. My own wife and my sister-in-law seemed to share their mother's point of view. I respected their feelings, but I knew the Bolsheviks sufficiently well to realize the sheer impossibility of a "happy ending."

Years later, a strange unbalanced girl came to America introducing herself as Grand Duchess Anastasia, the youngest daughter of the Czar. She claimed to have been saved by a soldier of the firing squad. She said that the nervous shock made her lose the fluent command of English and French possessed by my late niece. It sounded plausible enough. I would have liked nothing better than to be capable of persuading myself that the favorite child of the Czar was here, in New York, alive. I was even willing to overlook the striking difference between the facial features of the real Anastasia and those of the excitable pretender. Unfortunately, the doctors tell us that the most strenuous nervous shock cannot make a Russian acquire a pronounced Polish accent.

I remember the endless visits paid to me in connection with

this story by the zealous New York reporters. They wanted a "statement": did I or did I not accept the claims of Miss Tchaikovsky? Was she or was she not Grand Duchess Anastasia? I felt hurt for my wife and my sister-in-law. "Now, gentlemen," I said to the news-gatherers, "let us forget for a while about myself. But do you think that Grand Duchess Xenia and Grand Duchess Olga would sit quietly in Europe ignoring the appeals of a daughter of their brother? Do you think that the King of England would let his cousin fight her case in the American newspapers?"

The gentlemen of the press were seemingly convinced, and the name of the New York pretender lost its hold on the front pages. I do not doubt, however, that better equipped impostors will appear in years to come, telling tales of miraculous escape and trying to profit by the grim saga of the family of the Romanoffs.

CHAPTER TWENTY

THE RELIGION OF LOVE

FOR thirteen years now I am leading the life of an exile. Some day I shall write another book dealing with revelations, both joyful and disappointing, that awaited me along the road which was not illuminated by the rays of the Ay-Todor lighthouse.

My natural restlessness coupled with a desire for spiritual betterment kept me from staying in Paris, in an atmosphere of senseless regrets and continuous sighs. When in Europe, I always experience a peculiar feeling of walking through the beautiful alleys of a mammoth cemetery where every stone reminds me of a civilization which committed suicide on August 1, 1914.

In 1927 I made a trip to Abyssinia. In December, 1928, I came for the third time to the United States to make my second start in life. My present work in America, my first ten years in the navy, and the time spent with my family—those are the only three periods of my career which gave me satisfaction. The rest caused a great deal of trouble, pain and suffering. Were I to begin life anew, I would commence by surrendering my imperial title and would preach the necessity of a spiritual revolution. I could not have pursued this work in Russia. Under the Czars I would have been persecuted in the name of God by the Greek Orthodox clergy; under the Bolsheviks I would have been shot in the name of Marx by the proletarian high priests of spiritual slavery.

I regret nothing. I am not discouraged. The hands of my grandchildren—I have four of them—shall stretch further and may reach a better world. I do not consider this present one civilized and I am certain it is not Christian. When I

337

hear of millions of people starving in Europe, Asia and America, while untold numbers of bushels of wheat are rotting in storage I recognize the inevitability of a radical change. The fate of the three European empires shook my belief in the idea of Great Powers. Thirteen years of the Communistic experiment killed my illusions of the great power of Ideas. There is no third way left for humanity so long as it remains in its present state of spiritual ignorance.

Official Christianity, insolvent since 1914, continues its efforts to make us slaves of God, thus leading us to a fatalism similar to that which was responsible for the tragic end of Russia and its Czar. The Religion of Love, based on the Law of Love, should be substituted for all creeds and denominations and today's slave of God given a chance of becoming His active collaborator. If we are not to benefit by our sufferings, then His sacrifice was useless, and then it is true that the last Christian was crucified nineteen hundred years ago.

There would be no sense in my writing this book at all, unless its moral lesson should prove of value to at least some of its readers. For me it is a lesson full of meaning and rich with warnings. Once more I think of the companions of my youth, trying to visualize them not as they were in the last days of the tragedy but as I knew them in the brighter days of our lives. In my dreams I often see Nicky, Georgie, Sergei and myself, lying in the tall dewy grass of the imperial park near Moscow and talking, lazily and cheerfully, of that mysterious, incredibly beautiful future which has a habit of lighting its signal fires across the horizon.

A little patience—and we shall reach it, all of us.

New York—Paris
  1931.

INDEX

INDEX

INDEX

INDEX

INDEX

❖❖❖

INDEX

INDEX

INDEX

INDEX

INDEX

Printed in the USA
CPSIA information can be obtained
at www.ICGtesting.com
LVHW090934061123
762866LV00004B/83